D1537248

A GUIDE TO

NEW RELIGIOUS
MOVEMENTS

EDITED BY

Ronald Enroth

InterVarsity Press
Downers Grove, Illinois

InterVarsity Press
P.O. Box 1400, Downers Grove, IL 60515-1426
World Wide Web: www.ivpress.com
E-mail: mail@ivpress.com

InterVarsity Press®, is the book-publishing division of InterVarsity Christian Fellowship/USA®, a student movement active on campus at hundreds of universities, colleges and schools of nursing in the United States of America, and a member movement of the International Fellowship of Evangelical Students. For information about local and regional activities, write Public Relations Dept., InterVarsity Christian Fellowship/USA, 6400 Schroeder Rd., P.O. Box 7895, Madison, WI 53707-7895, or visit the IVCF website at <www.intervarsity.org>.

Design: Cindy Kiple
Images: Todd Davidson PTY LTD/Getty Images

ISBN 0-8308-2381-6

Printed in the United States of America ∞

Library of Congress Cataloging-in-Publication Data

A guide to new religious movements / edited by Ronald Enroth.
 p. cm.
Includes bibliographical references.
ISBN 0-8308-2381-6 (pbk.: alk. paper)
1. Cults. 2. Christian sects. 3. Christianity and other religions.
I. Enroth, Ronald M.
BP603.G85 2005
209—dc22

                       2005000232

P	19	18	17	16	15	14	13	12	11	10	9	8	7	6	5	4	3	2	1
Y	21	20	19	18	17	16	15	14	13	12	11	10	09	08	07	06	05

To my daughters, Kara and Rebecca

CONTENTS

1

WHAT IS A NEW RELIGIOUS MOVEMENT?

Ronald Enroth

North American society has become a spiritual supermarket, offering something for everyone—the careful shopper as well as the impulse buyer. This has not always been the case. At one point in our history, our religious tendencies were fairly homogeneous. That is, despite our denominational differences, we could all identify with a common religious core, something we referred to as our "Judeo-Christian tradition." Even folks who did not often attend church knew something about the religious consensus that constituted the "moral fabric" of our society. We were a Christian nation.

The religious scene is now very different. We can no longer take for granted a Christian consensus or assume that spiritual seekers will turn to the church in their search. For those experiencing spiritual hunger, today's world offers a catalog of offerings including UFO cults, neopagan groups, New Age gurus, Eastern mystics, and self-improvement programs, along with a confusing array of Christian-sounding groups all claiming to have Jesus on their team.

In his 2003 presidential address to the Society for the Scientific Study of Religion, Princeton sociologist Robert Wuthnow noted that American religion is undergoing a profound transformation—the growing cultural presence of non-Western religions affects how ordinary citizens as well as scholars think about religion.[1] This new diversity, he argues, "holds potential for profoundly altering America's historic self-identity, especially its civil religion, which, from the start, has emphasized the Christian tradition."[2] In addition, increased religious diversity raises a number of practical considerations, including questions about clothing, food, holidays in public schools and chaplains in the military.[3]

Large numbers of North Americans, particularly young adults, have been attracted to unconventional religious movements and quasi-religious, high-intensity groups intent upon self discovery. At the same time, our society has been experiencing rapid technological and cultural change, the byproducts of which are often alienation, restlessness, uncertainty and what sociologists call *anomie*, or the absence of clear norms. Enter the new religious movements. During times of cultural upheaval, people find themselves dislocated from previously stable social structures and sometimes question the relevance of traditional institutions such as family, government and conventional religion. When a society is characterized by transition, tentativeness and marginality, its members are often drawn to new religious movements. Martin Marty links the rise of the new groups to "boredom or discontent with the existing tradition and to the search for identity."[4]

Many of the groups discussed in this book are especially attractive to young adults. What is their appeal? Why do affluent, well-educated, middle-class young people pursue vague and ill-defined spirituality? One reason is that young people are subject to the inherent vulnerabilities of that ambiguous social status known as adolescence. Their dilemmas are associated with a prolonged limbo between childhood and full adulthood, and they find in new religious movements a resolution to their problems. In a society that demands extended and highly specialized training in a context of continuous change and uncertainty, an all-encompassing religious movement provides a moratorium on growing up, a secure environment where decisions about careers, education and starting a family can be deferred or avoided.

For this reason, new religious movements tend to attract a dispropor-tionate number of young adults who lack self-direction and who need an external source of authority to provide a framework for their lives. In effect, they need someone to co-sign for their lives. They are looking for definite answers, clear moral and spiritual guidelines, and firm struc-tures. In new religious groups they find these needs met—simple black-and-white answers, a group structure to help them overcome insecurity and loneliness, and leaders who manifest conviction and certainty. Some observers have suggested that such groups can be viewed as escapist al-ternatives to the complexity of contemporary life, avoidance mecha-nisms for those unable to cope with their feelings of anxiety, insecurity and isolation.

It would be incorrect, however, to conclude that all spiritual seekers are youthful members of religious communes, living apart from the American mainstream. One of the contributors to this volume, Charles Strohmer, has written a book about the "New Spirituality" in which he describes the kind of people who make up the movement:

> Millions of fed-up materialists are asking, "Is that all there is?" And they are seeking to connect with the spirit. So they're not just dressed in saffron robes meandering along California beaches or chanting "Hare Krishna" in Central Park. They style your hair at Supercuts, sell real estate through Century 21, or work alongside you at Sears. . . . The people of the New Spirituality are disillu-sioned with the West's secular worldview and disenchanted with traditional, that is, patriarchal, religion. As a result, they have cho-sen not Christianity but a confusing swirl of beliefs and practices that form an alternate spirituality to Christianity. In this unpredict-able ebb and flow of otherworldliness they seek to resolve their cri-sis of hope and fill their spiritual hunger.[5]

New religious movements have been the focus of serious academic study, ridicule and amused disinterest. Television reporters representing CBS's *60 Minutes* and NBC's *Dateline* remind us regularly that religious cults and movements make for interesting copy. Academic scholars from a variety of disciplines dissect and analyze new religious movements, and concerned parents warn about their impact on families. Evangelical authors have produced an impressive list of books on new religious groups, ranging from countless critiques of the New Age movement to insider accounts of the Jehovah's Witnesses.

So why another book on new religious movements? First, a few comments about what this book is not. It is not an encyclopedic handbook on religious movements. It is not an exhaustive, in-depth survey of all the religious beliefs and practices that can be found in North America at the beginning of a new century. It is not aimed primarily at the Christian cult-watchers who are engaged in commendable apologetic and educational ministries. They are already familiar with most of the content of this book. And it should not be seen as an attempt to discredit new religious movements. Although an author might clearly disagree with the beliefs and practices of a certain group, the reader should not infer a lack of commitment to religious freedom and the right of any group to freely promote its beliefs. America has a rich history of religious diversity and all contributors to this book are committed to the preservation of pluralism.

All the contributors to this volume are evangelical Christians. They are not only knowledgeable about new religious movements, they are committed to helping average Christians understand the various manifestations of religiosity in today's world so they can effectively communicate the evangel—the gospel—to people they care about. Biblical Christians should want to share their faith not only with the unchurched and irreligious, but also with individuals involved in groups and movements outside the parameters of orthodox biblical faith. And although most secular academicians are not concerned with evaluative concepts such as truth and error, all of the authors here approach the topic of new or unconventional religious groups in the context of a Christian theology.

From our perspective, categories of truth and falsehood do not indicate a constricted fundamentalist mentality but are crucial to retaining a posture of orthodoxy. "We must affirm the proposition that God has revealed himself in the person of his Son, Jesus Christ, and that his Word, the Bible, serves as the only baseline for comparison when ascertaining truth and error. After all, what really matters is not a label of 'conventional' or 'unconventional' religion, but God's objective truth."[6] Belief in the existence of a firm framework by which to evaluate the claims of other groups may be seen as presumptuous by some, but it is vital to all those who write in these pages.

The purpose of this book, then, is to help serious, caring Christians compassionately understand several contemporary religious movements and equip them to introduce people in those groups to Jesus our Lord. While many secularists have ignored the theological aspects of new religious movements, evangelical Christians have focused almost exclusively on doctrinal concerns and neglected the psychosocial dimensions of these groups. This disdain for sociological analysis is illustrated in the writing of professor Alan Gomes of Talbot School of Theology—who prefers the word *cult* to "new religious movement." He argues that a meaningful sociological definition of the phenomenon is impossible. Therefore,

> cults must be defined theologically, not behaviorally; examining the group's doctrinal system is the only way to determine whether it is a cult. Sociology is useful, but cannot be the basis on which cults are defined. . . . Value judgments and religious truth claims fall in the realm of theology, philosophy, and ethics—areas in which sociologists have no particular expertise.[7]

This volume is intended to demonstrate a more holistic approach to new religious movements and includes the insights of the social and behavioral sciences. Whether we are theologians or sociologists (and I am a sociologist), philosophers or readers of the morning newspaper, we need to draw on various perspectives when examining new religious movements.

History is one such perspective we must consider in order to gain a more comprehensive understanding of religion and its role in contemporary life. In the mid-nineteenth century, for example, a time when the United States was undergoing considerable change, a number of novel, nontraditional religious groups emerged and flourished. Sects such as the Shakers, founded by Mother Ann Lee, and the Oneida Community of John Humphrey Noyes were attracting widespread attention and curiosity. The Mormons, the Spiritualists and the Theosophists gained adherents for many of the same reasons that people today join the Unification Church, the Hare Krishnas or the Church of Scientology. Then as now, people joined new religious movements more for personal and social reasons than theological and doctrinal considerations. In fact, some people are attracted to new religious movements for the same reasons that others are drawn to the Christian faith—they seek direction and authority in their lives. People everywhere need fellowship, community and a sense of commitment. New religious movements are successful because they meet basic human needs. Only after those needs are met do converts think seriously about theological matters.

The new religious movements we discuss in this book are all currently active throughout North America. Several are large and visible, such as the Mormons and Jehovah's Witnesses, which have been part of the American religious landscape for well over a hundred years. They are among the "older" new religious movements, whereas an organization such as the Unification Church of Rev. Moon has been around only since the 1960s. Whether new religious movements are recent arrivals on the cultural scene or established religious bodies, the terminology used to describe them deserves examination. The word *cult*, for example, means many things to many people. For many readers, it probably has derogatory or pejorative connotations.

Traditionally, most evangelicals have considered a cult to be a group of religious people whose belief system and practices deviate significantly from the Holy Scriptures as interpreted by orthodox biblical Christianity and expressed in such statements as the Apostles' Creed.[8] In short, this theological understanding focuses attention on the truth claims of any given group and compares them with the testimony of Scripture. More recently, some evangelical observers have moved away from using the word *cult* because of the imprecise nature of the term and the negative image it embodies: who can forget the extremist actions of the People's Temple of Jim Jones, the Branch Davidians of David Koresh and Heaven's Gate of Marshall Applewhite? "It can be argued that to speak of 'the cults' is to engage in an overgeneralization that ignores the great complexity and diversity found in a variety of groups and movements. Perhaps more importantly, adherents within new religions consider the term pejorative."[9]

Journalists and other popular writers usually describe cults in sensational, sometimes exotic, contexts, and most people develop an image of what cults are like from the news media. Reporters are frequently required to sacrifice in-depth research and careful analysis in favor of a story that sells, a story with human interest appeal. While some cults do engage in behavior that seems unusual or bizarre, it is not our purpose here to focus on the more sensational aspects of the new religions. Members of new religious movements are usually no different from our next-door neighbors or our colleagues at work, as Charles Strohmer observed earlier. Christians should be especially sensitive to the problem of contributing to unfair stereotypes.

Although they use the words *sect* and *cult* with more precision and technical nuance than lay people, academicians disagree on what these terms actually mean. In a footnote to a journal article, sociologist Thomas Robbins wrote that the term *cult* is increasingly applied to "a disparate collection of groups and movements, and consequently has become unsuitable as a precise legal or social scientific category. . . . In effect, a 'cult' is any group stigmatized as a 'cult.'"[10]

In addition to the terms *cult* and *sect*, various experts and academic commentators have used designations such as "unconventional religions," "emergent religions," "nonnormative religions," "marginal religious movements" and, most commonly, "new religious movements" to refer to new and nontraditional religious groups. Professor Robert Ellwood has written a book whose title conveys something of this classificatory diversity: *Alternative Altars*.[11]

Although most scholars have distanced themselves from the more popular usages of the *cult* label, including its association with what is called the "anti-cult movement," some have used it in the literature—with important qualifications. Professors Rodney Stark and William Bainbridge, for example, distinguish between sects and cults. Sects are schismatic groups; that is, they have a prior link with another religious body. Sects present themselves as the revitalized, authentic, restored version of the faith from which they split. Cults, on the other hand, do not have a prior organizational tie with a parent religious body. A cult may represent an alien or imported religion, or it may be a domestic, though totally new, form of religious expression.[12] Bainbridge and Stark describe a "religious movement" as a deviant religious organization that may take the form of a social movement. "In particular, it is an organized group that seeks to cause or prevent change in the religious life of members or of society at large."[13]

Other scholars cite important differences between churches, sects and cults. Churches are culture-accepting religious organizations; that is, they have accommodated, in varying degrees, the dominant cultural and social realities. Sects and cults, in contrast, are culture-rejecting. Not only are their belief systems typically outside the Judeo-Christian tradi-

tion, but these groups often exhibit alienation from other dominant social structures and the prevailing culture. In the words of sociologist
John Lofland, cults are "little groups" that break off from the "conventional consensus and espouse very different views of the real, the possible, and the moral."[14]

Some readers may question the appropriateness of including chapters
on Buddhism and Hinduism in a book such as this. After all, are they not
world religions, along with Christianity, Judaism and Islam? They are indeed, but our concern here is primarily with the Hindu and Buddhist
communities in North America whose influence has been considerable
especially since the mid-1960s. True, Eastern religious faiths have a long
tradition in the United States, but actual membership has always been
insignificant. That is beginning to change. In 1965 President Lyndon
Johnson rescinded the Oriental Exclusion Act, unleashing a massive
Asian immigration and setting the stage for the importation of many new
religions and gurus from the East. There are, for example, several dozen
Buddhist temples in the greater Los Angeles area alone. And as the chapter on New Age religion will demonstrate, the impact of Eastern mysticism on New Age thinking is enormous.

A recent study by sociologists Robert Wuthnow and Wendy Cadge
documents the growing influence of Buddhism in America. They point
out that scholarly interest in American Buddhism has emerged only in
recent years. "The reasons for this interest include the growing number
of immigrants in the United States who are from predominantly Buddhist countries, an evident rise in the number of Buddhist temples and
meditation centers, and a great deal of attention to Buddhist leaders and
practices in the mass media."[15] The data collected by Wuthnow and
Cadge show that "one American in seven claims to have had a fair
amount of contact with Buddhists and that one person in eight believes
Buddhist teachings or practices have had an important influence on his
or her religious spirituality."[16]

Since the mid-1960s, Asian religions have demonstrated a new missionary zeal as large numbers of gurus, swamis and other Eastern teachers have taken up residence in North America. From the earliest times, gurus have played a unique role in the religious life of Hindus. However, according to C. V. Mathew, the twentieth century witnessed an explosion of what he terms "missionary Hinduism." Disenchanted with the traditional religious structures of the West and disillusioned by its pervasive materialism, many people are looking to charismatic gurus from the East to provide purpose, discipline and satisfaction in life. The guru is more than a teacher, however. He is a doorway to the divine, a representative of a new society.

Some of the best-known Hindu gurus who have brought an Eastern worldview to the West in recent decades include Maharishi Mahesh Yogi of Transcendental Meditation fame; A. C. Bhaktivedanta, founder of the International Society for Krishna Consciousness or Hare Krishnas; Guru Maharaj Ji of the Divine Light Mission; Rajneesh; and Swami Muktananda. The Dalai Lama is perhaps the best known Buddhist leader and has made numerous appearances throughout the West. But as Wuthnow and Cadge point out, "Buddhism is not always an exclusive religion like Christianity, Judaism, or Islam, meaning that people who do not consider themselves Buddhist may nevertheless be influenced by some of its teachings and practices. The number of 'nightstand Buddhists,' as they have been called (those who keep a book of Buddhist sayings on their nightstand or who practice a little Zen meditation when they get out of bed in the morning), is often thought to be larger than the number of people who actually call themselves Buddhists."[17]

Let's now return to further consideration of the concept of new religious movements. In a seminal article appearing in *Nova Religio: The Journal of Alternative and Emergent Religions*, sociologist of religion Eileen Barker of the London School of Economics encourages students of religion to retain an awareness of the "newness" of new religious movements.[18] Barker reminds us that there is a sense in which nothing under the sun is new, and yet it can be argued on the other hand that everything is new; "social reality is an on-going process that is mediated through individuals who bring new perspectives and understandings as they continually recreate even the oldest of traditions."[19]

Barker notes that new religious movements share a cluster of distinguishing features by the very fact that they are new. What follows is a brief summary of those characteristics, modified here to complement our perspective. The reader is urged to examine her more complete discussion of the basic question, "In what ways are [new religious movements] new and in what ways are they traditional?"[20]

NEW COMBINATIONS

Some of the new religious movements attempt to distill elements from several spiritual or mystical traditions and reformulate those differing components into a single religious system. By putting together new formulations of "truth" (syncretism) selected from various sources (eclecticism), they can achieve, from their perspective, the best of all spiritual worlds. Such syncretistic combinations of religious traditions—both old and new—can result in what Barker calls "unique, emergent properties."[21]

An example of this kind of syncretism can be found in the theology of the Unification Church of Sun Myung Moon. The beliefs and practices of the Unificationists reflect elements of Eastern philosophy and mysticism mixed with novel interpretations of traditional Christianity. Devout disciples believe that Moon is the "Lord of the Second Advent," the messiah figure promised in the group's revelatory scripture, Divine Principle.

NEW LOCATIONS

A religious system that has been recognized in another culture for centuries may establish a new locus of activity and institutional structure in our society and be considered a new religious movement.[22] Many new religious movements seem strange, curious and unconventional to the average Westerner but are simply Eastern imports with unfamiliar spiritual technology such as chanting, meditation and various forms of yoga. Such practices, despite their growing acceptance in the West, still represent nonnormative behavior vis-à-vis traditional religion.

The Judeo-Christian mainstream denominations have persisted for generations and are accepted, respectable and traditional parts of the religious landscape of America. Many of the "new" religious movements are not new at all; some, in fact, antedate Christianity. However, they are strangers to these shores. The larger society views them with suspicion and anxiety in much the same way that the American mainstream population received newly arrived ethnic groups during the era of mass immigration. They generate an aura of unfamiliarity.

A DICHOTOMOUS WORLDVIEW

A "them and us" mentality characterizes many new religious movements. Clear black-and-white distinctions separate right from wrong, truth from falsehood, acceptable behavior from unacceptable behavior. "An individual's identity is defined primarily according to whether s/he is or is not a member of the [new religious movement], with any other role or status being of secondary importance. The sharp division between 'them' and 'us' is not easily permeated, and to cross the boundary can be seen as both treason and heresy."[23]

In his well-researched book about the Watchtower Society, Andrew Holden describes a movement that stands in antithesis to modern society. He tells how the Jehovah's Witnesses "draw clear boundaries between themselves and non-members, establish strict entry criteria and keep their involvement with the wider society to a minimum. . . . In addition to a strong condemnation of the outside world, the Witnesses' millenarian orientation involves the rejection of all other faiths as errant."[24]

"Them versus us" thinking can, according to Barker, engender an atmosphere that discourages dissent and questioning as well as manifest clear divisions between the "now" and "then"—the time before conversion and the time after conversion.[25]

ATYPICAL MEMBERSHIP

Converts to new religious movements are not representative of all segments of the population. During the past few decades new members have been disproportionately young, middle-class, well-educated and white.[26] Recruiters have largely targeted eighteen- to twenty-five-year-olds for membership. As a result, members tend to be healthy, lacking dependents and, as Barker notes, "enthusiastic but inexperienced."[27] These distinguishing traits carry implications for both the movements themselves and for their interaction with larger society.

Young adults join new religious movements because they hope such groups will fulfill their perceived needs. These needs are generated in large part by the changing and confusing society that is America today, and they reflect a spiritual vacuum in what many believe is rapidly becoming a post-Christian culture. New religious movements promise simplistic solutions to the discontinuities of that culture.

CHARISMATIC LEADERSHIP

A crucial dimension of a new religious movement is the presence and strong influence of a charismatic (in the Weberian sense) leader who commands total loyalty and allegiance. "The authority may be accorded to the leader by the followers as much as it is a characteristic of the leader, but, for whatever reason, the end result is that the leader is seen to embody what the followers consider to be a legitimate right to tell them how to live all aspects of their lives, and to change this at a moment's notice."[28]

The leader exercises authority over both doctrine and practice, and members accept his or her interpretation of the "truth" without question.

Members redefine their self-identity and life goals as having meaning only in relation to the leader and the group. For Eastern-oriented new religious movements, the veneration of the guru is a primary feature. He is believed to have accumulated a tremendous wealth of spiritual power and knowledge over many years and many lifetimes. Tangible evidence of the leaders' significance can be seen in their titles: "Perfect Master" (Guru Maharaj Ji) of the Divine Light Mission, "Father David" or "Moses" (David Brandt Berg) of The Family, "Mother of the Universe" (Elizabeth Clare Prophet) of the Church Universal and Triumphant, and "True Parent" (Sun Myung Moon) of the Unification Church.

New religious movements and their authority structures reflect important transitions in people's lives. "Becoming a member of an alternative religion is not merely a relatively minor change from one Christian denomination to another. It means that the convert is embarking on a new venture that implies the acceptance of a radically different lifestyle and belief system. The convert is charting for himself or herself a new religious map."[29]

EXTERNAL CONTROVERSY

Many new religious movements engender controversy and are met with hostility and antagonism. Professor Robert Ellwood in his book *Alternative Altars* speaks of the "oppositional stance, style and substance" of new religious movements.[30] Their beliefs, practices and values are often counter to those of the dominant culture. Allegations of fraudulent fundraising techniques, charges of gender discrimination, and purported incidents of child abuse and medical neglect have resulted in serious public relations problems for some new religious movements. In April 2004, for example, ISKCON (International Society for Krishna Consciousness) was facing a $400 million lawsuit over charges of emotional, physical and sexual abuse brought by one hundred individuals who were part of the organization's school system in the 1970s and 1980s.[31]

While it is true that new religious movements often place themselves in an adversarial role against major social institutions, the fear and suspicion associated with their activities is not always warranted. As Professor Barker notes, converts are perceived as "adopting 'incredible' beliefs, indulging in unusual 'abnormal'/'unnatural' practices and lifestyles, cutting themselves off socially if not geographically from the rest of the world (apart from procuring new members and money), unquestioningly following a leader who ignores and/or denounces the rules and traditions of 'normal' society—and so on."[32]

It follows that perceived (or actual) persecution is one of the defining traits of many new religious movements, especially for first-generation converts. The literature, public statements and in-house discussion of new religious movements all convey the theme that in one form or another their group is being singled out for persecution—by traditional religions, the press, parents or the government.

CHANGE

Another distinguishing characteristic of new religious movements, according to sociologist Eileen Barker, "is that they undergo transformations and modifications far more radically and rapidly than the vast majority of older religions under normal circumstances."[33] She contends that if a first-generation new religious movement is going to survive, it must of necessity experience a number of changes "due to the fact that its newness becomes less new than it was."[34] Internal changes such as the death of the founder and the arrival of children, as well as external factors such as changes in the larger society and the advent of the Internet all have the potential for significant impact.[35]

A prime example of an evolving new religious movement composed largely of twentysomethings is the International Churches of Christ (not to be confused with the mainline Churches of Christ denomination). The movement, earlier known as the Boston Church of Christ, is often associated with that city because it was founded there by Kip McKean in 1979. It spread rapidly throughout the United States, taking root primarily in metropolitan areas and recruiting many converts from university campuses. Wherever the church has expanded, controversy has followed. In November 2002, founder McKean announced his resignation in a letter spelling out his own arrogance and family difficulties.[36] He was forced to step down because of his own rule that leaders must resign if their children leave the church. What was once one of the fastest-growing churches in North America began to collapse. Dozens of local church leaders resigned or were fired. In the June 2003 issue of *Christianity Today*, Al Baird, one of the movement's remaining leaders, is quoted as saying, "We've been too narrow in saying we've got a corner on the truth and we're the only way." The future of the movement is uncertain as membership drops and suggestions of reform are met with skepticism.

Some new religious movements will undoubtedly end up being no more than a footnote in the history of religion. Others, like the Mormons and the Jehovah's Witnesses, have demonstrated that they have staying power. The viability of second and subsequent generations is a crucial indicator of whether these groups will be viewed with increased legitimacy by the host society. "Practices and lifestyles may become more negotiable and beliefs may become more flexible as [new religious movements] accommodate to successive generations and wider pools of potential converts, especially if they have had to deal with the passing of end-time dates."[37]

To conclude this essay, we return to a theme discussed earlier, namely, the primacy of identifying and preserving the truth claims of the Christian gospel. Whatever label we apply to those who worship at "alternative altars," we need to respect the beliefs of others while at the same time recognizing the fundamental differences between all the major faiths. That understanding will cause us to penetrate the core beliefs of our Christian faith and lead us into conversation, rather than confrontation, with members of new religious movements. The primary task of the

Christian church is to proclaim the gospel, not to fight the so-called cults. Too often evangelical zeal to convert "cultists" takes on the appearance of a crusade. We want to stamp out Satan in the next three weeks! But we are not cult-busters; we are agents of reconciliation, bearers of good news to those who do not know Jesus our Lord.

The word *gospel* means "good news." This presupposes that there is also some "bad news," or at least some unsatisfactory situation that the good news addresses. The bad news, of course, is the human condition—our fallenness, our sinfulness. Many new religious movements do not acknowledge human sinfulness, or they redefine and reinterpret the concept of sin. I am reminded of an ad I once saw for the Vedanta Press and Bookshop in Hollywood, California: "It is a sin to call anyone a sinner. It is a standing libel on human nature. Vedanta does not believe in sin, only error, and the greatest error is to think you are weak."

New religious movements offer their own prescriptions for alleviating or rectifying human brokenness. The Unificationists speak of restoration, the TM devotees offer enlightenment, and the Hare Krishnas chant their way back to godhead. It is at this very point of striving that the Christian gospel separates itself from all other religious endeavors. For the good news of the New Testament is the proclamation that God has taken the initiative to disclose himself through the sacrifice of his Son on the cross. The gospel thus originates with God and is a uniquely divine message. It is not a product of philosophy and clever argumentation but a forthright statement about human nature spoken from God's perspective, and it embodies the final solution to the problems of evil, suffering and death. It is not a mystical message of secret wisdom for an initiated few. The secret is out: Jesus Christ is Lord!

■ ■ ■

"Always be prepared to make a defense to any one who calls you to account for the hope that is in you, yet do it with gentleness and reverence" (1 Pet 3:15 RSV).

JEHOVAH'S WITNESSES

Ron Rhodes

The Jehovah's Witnesses published their ten billionth piece of literature during the late 1980s, representing about one hundred years of publishing. The next ten billion pieces took only about a decade. The Jehovah's Witnesses presently devote over 1.1 billion hours per year distributing Watchtower literature and spreading Watchtower doctrines.

With a twice-monthly printing of twenty-five million copies per issue, *The Watchtower* magazine presently approaches the circulation of *Reader's Digest* and *TV Guide* and easily surpasses the combined total of *Time*, *Newsweek* and *U.S. News & World Report*. *The Watchtower* is now simultaneously published in 121 languages.[1]

With such impressive literature distribution, it is no wonder that some fifty new Jehovah's Witness congregations emerge each week worldwide, and nearly six million Bible studies are conducted each month with prospective converts.[2] It all started with a man named Charles Taze Russell.

CHARLES TAZE RUSSELL (1852-1916)

Charles Taze Russell was born in Pittsburgh, Pennsylvania, on February 16, 1852. His parents were committed Presbyterians, and young Charles received a religious upbringing. His mother, who died when Charles was only nine, encouraged him to consider ministry as a vocation. As it happened, however, Charles got involved in his father's clothing business at age eleven, working part-time while attending school.

In his teenage years, Russell abandoned the Presbyterian church because he disliked its doctrines of predestination and eternal punishment. Eventually he came into contact with some Adventists and became impressed with their prophetic views. He also appreciated their rejection of eternal punishment. The Adventists taught that "hell" was just another word for the grave and that death involved annihilation.

One Adventist who greatly influenced twenty-three-year-old Russell was Nelson Barbour of Rochester, New York, who published a magazine called *The Herald of the Morning*. Barbour held that the Lord had been spiritually present on earth since 1874 and that 1914 would mark the year when Christ's kingdom would be fully established on earth.

Convinced that Barbour was correct, Russell curtailed his business interests and dedicated his time and money toward spreading these doctrines. He sent Barbour back to his home with money and instructions on preparing a book. It wasn't long, however, before Russell split with Barbour over differences regarding the nature of the atonement.[3]

In 1879, Russell founded a new magazine, *Zion's Watch Tower and Herald of Christ's Presence*, which would eventually become today's *Watchtower* magazine. In this periodical, Russell promoted the idea that Christ returned invisibly to earth in 1874 and that God's kingdom would be established on earth in 1914.

Headquartered in Pittsburgh, Russell in 1881 established Zion's Watch Tower Tract Society, known today as the Watch Tower Bible and Tract Society of Pennsylvania. Realizing that 1914 was rapidly approaching, Russell recruited hundreds of evangelists to go door-to-door distributing the magazines, books and tracts that he and his associates had published.

By 1904 Russell had written the six-volume *Studies in the Scriptures,* which would be foundational to all future Watchtower theology. Russell proclaimed that if someone read these volumes alone, even without consulting the Bible, that person would have "the light of the Scriptures."[4]

Toward the end of Russell's ministry, the society decided to move to a city more suitable for shipping and communication. They selected New York City as the most suitable center for the "harvest work" that would take place during the few remaining years before 1914.[5] That year, however, passed uneventfully.

JUDGE JOSEPH FRANKLIN RUTHERFORD (1869-1942)

After Russell's death in 1916, Judge Joseph Franklin Rutherford became the second president of the Watchtower Society. He turned the Watchtower into an organized hierarchy and took an authoritarian approach in running it.

During the 1920s and 1930s, the society began to emphasize house-to-house witnessing even more heavily. Rutherford wrote relentlessly during this time, penning about a hundred books and pamphlets. He also tried his hand at Bible prophecy, focusing attention on the year 1925. Not only was the old order of things to pass away that year, but the Old Testament patriarchs were to be resurrected and usher in the righteous government of Jehovah. In expectation of this event, the organization constructed a magnificent residence called Beth Sarim in San Diego.[6]

The patriarchs never showed up in 1925, which led to bitter disappointment for many Witnesses. Rutherford himself ended up spending winters at Beth Sarim with a staff of servants until his death in 1942.[7]

Under Rutherford's leadership, the name of the society's magazine changed to *The Watchtower Announcing Jehovah's Kingdom*. This change reflected the Watchtower's abandonment of Russell's chronology (which taught that Christ's presence had become a reality in 1874) and its shift to the teaching that Christ's presence began, rather than ended, in 1914.

A distinctive of the Rutherford presidency was the use of portable phonographs by Jehovah's Witnesses in door-to-door witnessing. The Witness on the doorstep would play a recording from Rutherford that concluded with an appeal to buy a Watchtower book. In addition, cars with loudspeakers on top would cruise through neighborhoods blaring out Rutherford's messages.

Rutherford died of bowel cancer in 1942 at Beth Sarim.

NATHAN KNORR (1905-1977)

Nathan Knorr became the next president of the Watchtower Society. Knorr did not have the charisma of his predecessors, nor was he a prolific writer, but he was an energetic businessman and good administrator. Knorr's greatest distinctive was that he instituted a program to train Jehovah's Witnesses in giving presentations on the doorstep—including how to answer common objections. Witnesses no longer played phonograph records but articulated Watchtower beliefs on their own.

The organization also produced a new Bible translation under Knorr's leadership. The New World Translation allegedly "restored" the divine name *Jehovah* two hundred thirty-seven times in the text from Matthew to Revelation.

Unfortunately, the society still had not learned any lessons from its past prophetic failures. It told its followers that six thousand years of human history would come to an end in 1975. Armageddon was to occur that year and Christ was to set up an earthly paradise. Many Witnesses were again disillusioned when 1975 passed quietly.

A change in leadership protocol took place in 1975. Until that time the organization had been run by a president, with the Watchtower governing body playing only a supportive role. In 1975, the governing body sought more authority in day-to-day operations. The 71-year-old Knorr reluctantly accepted this change and died eighteen months later from an inoperable brain tumor.

FREDERICK FRANZ (1893-1992)

On June 22, 1977, two weeks after Knorr's death, eighty-three-year-old Frederick Franz was elected president of the society. Though not professionally trained in biblical studies, he was undisputably more knowledgeable than the previous Watchtower presidents. He became the premier theologian of the movement.

Toward the end of Franz's reign, a crisis developed when many Witnesses began to examine Watchtower history independently. Some of those raising questions were prominent leaders—including Raymond Franz, nephew of the president and a former member of the governing body. After being disfellowshiped, Raymond wrote *Crisis of Conscience*, a shattering book that revealed the unbiblical nature of the society and documented how it had uttered false prophecies, altered key teachings and policies, and participated in lying and cover-ups.

MILTON HENSCHEL (1920-2003)

After Frederick Franz's death in 1992, Milton Henschel was elected the Watchtower's next president. Henschel's most significant contribution was to solve a major dilemma relating to an earlier Watchtower prophecy. The prophecy stated that some of the generation alive in 1914 would still be alive when Jehovah's kingdom was finally established (see Mt 24:34). The problem was, almost everyone alive in 1914 had died by 1992. Through the years the Watchtower had continually revised its teaching, saying in 1968 that the 1914/Matthew 24 "generation" referred to Witnesses fifteen years old in 1914,[8] then in 1980 saying it referred to Witnesses ten years old in 1914,[9] then in 1984 saying it referred to babies alive in 1914.[10] All these efforts failed to solve the problem.

Enter Milton Henschel. In 1995 Henschel redefined the generation of Matthew 24 as wicked mankind in general—more specifically, people anywhere and in any generation who "see the sign of Christ's appearance but fail to mend their ways."[11] This "generation" could be people today, or a hundred years from now, or thereafter. Problem solved.

In late 2000 a radical restructuring of leadership took place at the Watchtower Society when Milton Henschel resigned and Don Adams, a fifty-year veteran of the organization, became the new president. Six other directors resigned along with Henschel, although they all remained in the governing body, which until this time had exercised unchallenged control over the society.

In the organizational shakeup, religious and administrative duties passed from the governing body to three new nonprofit corporations. Kingdom Support Services Inc. focuses on everyday needs in individual congregations. The Religious Order of Jehovah's Witnesses works with Witnesses involved in full-time ministry. The Christian Congregation of Jehovah's Witnesses oversees religious matters. The governing body, relieved of administrative tasks, now focuses on the "ministry of the word."

WATCHTOWER BELIEFS

Jehovah's Witnesses believe it is through the Watchtower alone that God teaches the Bible to humankind today. One issue of *The Watchtower* refers to the society as "an organization to direct the minds of God's people."[12] Watchtower literature urges, "Avoid independent thinking . . . questioning the counsel that is provided by God's visible organization."[13] And, "We should seek for dependent Bible study, rather than for independent Bible study."[14] Following are some of the doctrines Jehovah's Witnesses are expected not to question.

Jehovah is the one true God. Jehovah's Witnesses believe that superstitious Jewish scribes long ago removed the sacred name of Jehovah from the Bible. Their New World Translation "restores" the name in the Old Testament where the Hebrew consonants YHWH appear and inserts the name in the New Testament where the text refers to the Father (though no original New Testament manuscripts support this). Witnesses believe it is crucial to refer to God by this name.[15]

The folly of the Watchtower position is evident in the fact that the word *Jehovah* is a manmade term. Out of fear of violating the Third Commandment, which deals with taking God's name in vain (Ex 20:7), ancient Hebrew scribes decided to combine the vowels from the word *Adonai* (a-o-a), meaning "Lord," with the consonants YHWH, the result being *Yahowah*, or *Jehovah*.[16] The more proper designation of God is Yahweh, not Jehovah. Furthermore, Yahweh is not the only name by which God is known in the Bible. He is called "Elohim" (meaning "mighty God," Gen 1:1), "the Lord of Hosts" (Ps 89:6, 8) and "the God of Abraham, God of Isaac, and God of Jacob" (Ex 3:6), among many other designations. Jesus never referred to the Father as "Jehovah" in the New Testament, not even in the Lord's Prayer (Mt 6:9). Believers are uniquely privileged to call God "Father" (Rom 8:15; Gal 4:6).

The Trinity is a pagan lie. Jehovah's Witnesses believe that if people were to read the Bible without any preconceived ideas, they would never arrive at a belief in the Trinity. The word *Trinity* is not even in the Bible. In addition, they claim that this doctrine is rooted in paganism, for there were trinities of gods in ancient Babylonia and Assyria. Hence God cannot be the author of this doctrine.[17]

Though the word *Trinity* is not in the Bible, the concept is clearly derived from the Bible. Scripture indicates that there is only one true God (Deut 6:4) but that three distinct persons exist within the Godhead. Each of the three is called "God" in Scripture: the Father (1 Pet 1:2), the Son (Jn 20:28) and the Holy Spirit (Acts 5:3-4). Moreover, each of the three Persons possesses attributes of deity, including omnipresence (Ps 139:7; Mt 19:26; Mt 28:18), omniscience (Mt 9:4; Rom 11:33; 1 Cor 2:10) and omnipotence (Mt 28:18; Rom 15:19; 1 Pet 1:5). Finally, there is three-in-oneness within the Godhead. Jesus told his disciples to "go and make disciples of all nations, baptizing them in the name of the Father and of the Son and of the Holy Spirit" (Mt 28:19). The word *name* is singular in the Greek, indicating one God, but there are three distinct persons therein.

As for the claim that the Trinity is a pagan concept, the Babylonians and Assyrians believed in triads of three separate gods who headed up a pantheon of many other gods. This polytheism is in contrast to the monotheistic doctrine of the Trinity, which maintains that there is only one God consisting of three persons. There is no pagan connection.

Jesus is a lesser god. Jehovah's Witnesses say Jesus was created as the Archangel Michael billions of years ago. He was allegedly created first and then used by Jehovah to create all other things (see Col 1:16). Witnesses concede that Jesus is a "mighty god" but deny he is God Almighty like Jehovah. To support this claim, they point to passages that seem to indicate Jesus' inferiority to the Father. For example, Jesus said, "The Father is greater than I" (Jn 14:28). First Corinthians 11:3 says, "The head of Christ is God." Jesus is called the "firstborn over all creation" (Col 1:15). Witnesses also argue that Jesus was never worshiped.[18]

Numerous scriptural facts prove Jesus was not the Archangel Michael. In Daniel 10:13, Michael is called "one of the chief princes" and is hence not totally unique. Jesus, by contrast, is God's unique (Greek: *monogenes,* or "one of a kind") Son (Jn 3:16), the Creator of the angels (Col 1:16) and the King of kings and Lord of lords (Rev 19:16). Jesus is not an angel but is worshiped by the angels (Heb 1:6). Scripture affirms that the world is not ruled by an angel nor will it ever be (Heb 2:5), but Christ is consistently said to be the ruler of God's kingdom (Mt 2:1-2; Lk 1:32-33; Rev 19:16).

Jesus is not a "lesser god." When Jesus said the Father was greater than he (Jn 14:28), he was referring to his lowly position in the incarnation. He was soon to be nailed to a criminal's cross, during which time the Father would be seated on the throne of highest majesty in heaven. While 1 Corinthians 11:3 says "the head of Christ is God," Paul says in this same verse that the man is the head of the woman, even though men and women are equal in their essential human nature (Gen 1:26-28). This indicates that equality of being and functional subordination are not mutually exclusive. Christ and the Father are equal in their divine nature (Jn 10:30), though Jesus is functionally under the Father's headship (1 Cor 11:3). While Jesus is called "firstborn" in Colossians 1:15, this word (Greek: *prototokos*) does not mean "first-created" but rather "first in rank, preeminent one, heir."[19] Christ is positionally preeminent over creation.

The Watchtower New World Translation renders John 1:1 to say that Jesus was "a god," noting that the Greek does not include a definite article before the word *God* in reference to Jesus. However, it is not necessary to translate Greek nouns without definite articles as nouns with indefinite articles. *Theos* ("God") without the definite article *ho* ("the") does not need to be translated as "a god." The presence or absence of the definite article does not alter the fundamental meaning. Properly understood, John 1:1 indicates that in the beginning the second person of the Trinity (Jesus) was "with" the first person of the Trinity (the Father), and that the second person (Jesus) "was" God by nature, just as the Father is God by nature.

Scripture consistently upholds the absolute deity of Christ. He is called "God" (Jn 20:28; Heb 1:8). The divine names *Yahweh* and *Elohim* are ascribed to him (Is 9:6; 40:3). He possesses the attributes of deity—including omnipresence (Mt 18:20; Jn 1:47-49), omniscience (Jn 2:25; 16:30) and omnipotence—evidenced by his creation of the universe (Jn 1:3; Col 1:16-17; Heb 1:2-3). Furthermore, a comparison of the Old and New Testaments proves his deity. While Yahweh in Isaiah 43:11 says he is the only Savior, Jesus is called the Savior in the New Testament (Lk 2:11; Jn 4:42; Tit 2:13-14). While Yahweh in Isaiah 44:24 says he is the only Creator, Jesus is portrayed as the agent of creation in the New Testament (Jn 1:3; Col 1:16).

Moreover, Christ was worshiped as God many times, according to the Gospel accounts (Mt 2:11; 8:2; 9:18; 28:9; 28:17; Jn 9:38; 20:28; Heb 1:6). That Jesus willingly received worship on various occasions says much about his true identity, for Scripture says only God can be worshiped (Ex 34:14).

Jesus was born and died as a mere man. Jehovah's Witnesses claim that to "ransom" humankind from sin, Michael gave up his existence as an angel when his life force was transferred into Mary's womb by Jehovah. This was not an incarnation, or manifestation of God in the flesh. Rather, Jesus was born and died as a mere human. The human life he laid down in sacrifice was exactly equal to the human life Adam fell with. If Jesus had been God, we are told, the ransom payment would have been way too much.[20]

Biblically, the incarnate Christ was God in human flesh. Jesus in the incarnation was 100 percent human and 100 percent God. Scripture says, "For in Christ all the fullness of the Deity lives in bodily form" (Col 2:9). That is why Jesus in the incarnation is called "Immanuel," meaning "God with us" (Mt 1:23).

Jesus was a perfect mediator between God and man precisely because he was both God and man. If Christ had been only God, he could not have died, since God by nature cannot die. It was only as a man that Christ could represent humanity and die as a man. As God, however, Christ's death had infinite value sufficient to provide redemption for all humankind (see 1 Tim 2:5; Heb 2:14-16; 9:11-28).

Jesus was spiritually resurrected from the dead. Jehovah's Witnesses say that three days after Jesus' death, he was raised, or "recreated," as an archangel—a spirit creature. Jesus proved his resurrection to the disciples by materializing in a temporary body, as angels do on occasion.[21]

The resurrected Jesus, however, flatly denied that he was a spirit but asserted that he had a real flesh-and-bones body (Lk 24:39; Jn 2:19-21). Furthermore, the resurrected Christ ate food on four occasions, proving his physicality (Lk 24:30, 42-43; Jn 21:12-13; Acts 1:4). Several people also touched his resurrected body (Mt 28:9; Jn 20:17).

The Holy Spirit is God's active force. In Watchtower theology, the Holy Spirit is neither a person nor God but rather God's impersonal "active force" for accomplishing his will in the world.[22] In defense of this view, Jehovah's Witnesses argue that Scripture portrays people as being "filled" by the Holy Spirit, an expression that could be true only if the Spirit were a force. After all, how can a person "fill" thousands of believers at the same time? And if the Holy Spirit were a person, they say, it would have a name like the Father and Son do.[23]

Such a view fails to recognize that spiritual beings are not always named in Scripture. For example, evil spirits are rarely named but are identified by a particular characteristic—"unclean," "wicked" and so forth. In the same way the Holy Spirit is identified by his primary characteristic—holiness. Besides, the Holy Spirit is related to the "name" of the other persons of the Trinity (Mt 28:19).

The argument that the Spirit cannot be a person because he fills many people at the same time cannot be correct because Ephesians 3:19 speaks of God filling all believers. Likewise, Ephesians 4:10 speaks of Christ filling all things.

The three primary attributes of personality are mind, emotions and will. Scripture indicates that the Holy Spirit has a mind (Rom 8:27), emotions (Eph 4:30) and a will (1 Cor 12:11). Moreover, the Spirit does things only a person can do, including teaching (Jn 14:26), testifying (Jn 15:26), guiding (Rom 8:14), commissioning (Acts 13:4), issuing commands (Acts 8:29), interceding (Rom 8:26) and speaking (Jn 15:26; 2 Pet 1:21).

People do not consciously survive death. Jehovah's Witnesses do not believe human beings possess a spirit that goes on living as an intelligent personality after death. They say that a person's "spirit" or "soul" is a life force, and at death that life force wanes. Because people have no surviving immaterial nature, they are not conscious of anything after death. Even the righteous remain unconscious in the grave until the future resurrection. Nor do wicked people consciously suffer in hell, for hell is defined as the common grave of all humankind.[24]

Scripture teaches, by contrast, that the believer's spirit survives death (Lk 12:4) and is consciously present with the Lord (2 Cor 5:8) in a better place (Phil 1:23) where other souls are talking (Mt 17:3) and even praying (Rev 6:9-10). Likewise, the unbeliever's soul is in a place of conscious torment (Mt 25:41; Lk 16:22-26; Rev 19:20—20:15). Furthermore, Scripture assures us that hell is a real place of eternal suffering (Mt 5:22; 18:8; 25:41; Jude 7; Rev 20:14).

Salvation must be earned. Though Jehovah's Witnesses give lip service to salvation by grace through faith in Christ, in reality they believe in a works-oriented salvation. Salvation is impossible apart from total obedience to the Watchtower and vigorous participation in its various programs (Phil 2:12).[25]

Scripture, on the other hand, indicates that salvation is based entirely on God's grace and not on human works. The word *grace* literally means "unmerited favor"—favor that is undeserved and cannot be earned. Indeed, if grace is not free, it is not truly grace (Rom 11:6). Romans 5:1-11 asserts that God freely gives grace to those who deserve the opposite—that is, condemnation. "The *free gift of God* is eternal life in Christ Jesus our Lord" (Rom 6:23, italics added).

Close to two hundred times the New Testament says the grace-gift of salvation is by faith alone. John 3:15 states that "everyone who believes in him [Jesus] may have eternal life." In John 11:25 Jesus says, "I am the resurrection and the life. He who believes in me will live, even though he dies." John wrote his Gospel "that you may believe that Jesus is the Christ, the Son of God, and that by believing you may have life in his name" (Jn 20:31).

Jehovah has two peoples: the "anointed class" and the "other sheep." In Watchtower theology there are two classes of saved people—with very different destinies and sets of privileges. Only 144,000 Witnesses go to heaven, and these are the "anointed class" (Rev 7:4; 14:1-3).[26] This "little flock" of true believers (Lk 12:32) allegedly began with the twelve apostles and other Christians of the first century, and it was complete by 1935 (Rutherford received a "revelation" to this effect). The primary activity of the anointed class in heaven will be to rule with Christ.

Witnesses who are not members of the anointed class (all Witnesses since 1935) look forward not to a heavenly destiny but to living eternally in an earthly paradise. These individuals make up what Revelation 7:9 calls the "great multitude," or what John 10:16 calls the "other sheep."

Biblically, Jesus never restricted the kingdom of heaven to 144,000 people as Jehovah's Witnesses do. He taught that all people should seek the kingdom, and that whoever sought it would find it (Mt 9:35-38; Mk 1:14-15; Lk 12:22-34). A heavenly destiny awaits all who believe in Christ (Eph 2:19; Phil 3:20; Col 3:1; Heb 3:1; 12:22; 2 Pet 1:10-11). The righteousness of God that leads to life in heaven is available "through faith in Jesus Christ for all those who believe; for there is no distinction" (Rom 3:21). Jesus affirmed that all believers will be together in "one flock" under "one shepherd" (Jn 10:16).

WATCHTOWER APPEAL

What is the appeal of the Watchtower Society? Why do some people choose to become Jehovah's Witnesses? Following are a few contributing factors:

The failure of traditional churches. Many churches fail to give people a sense of belonging. By contrast, a new convert visiting a Kingdom Hall (where Jehovah's Witnesses meet) for the first time is typically embraced by everyone and made to feel like part of a family.

A convincing doorstep sermon. A trained Jehovah's Witness can win converts by delivering a well-rehearsed mini-sermon that points to the failure of traditional churches, emphasizes prophecies of the end of the world and explains Jehovah's promises of a coming paradise on earth. One survey showed that 46 percent of Witness respondents first made contact with the Witnesses through a doorstep sermon, while only 3 percent sought out the Witnesses on their own initiative.[27]

Every objection answered. Witnesses are trained how to anticipate common questions and objections to what they say.

Invitation to a Bible study. In this weekly Bible study, a knowledgeable Witness leads a potential convert through a Watchtower publication. The teacher asks the newcomer questions about the reading assignment and then gives him or her high praise for correct answers. Such continual praise is a powerful motivational incentive for the recruit to continue the Bible study.

An appearance of true spirituality. Jehovah's Witnesses read their Bibles a lot, attend several religious services each week, share their faith with others, dress modestly, use decent language and avoid worldly activities. From all outward appearances, Jehovah's Witnesses may seem to resemble true Christianity.

The need for security. We live in a hostile and often unpredictable world. Belonging to the "one true people of Jehovah" can provide a sense of security and acceptance.

WATCHTOWER IMPACT ON THE FAMILY

The Watchtower Society can have a profound effect on family relationships. For example, the Watchtower warns new converts that Satan may use family members to dissuade them from remaining Jehovah's Witnesses.[28] When family members do try to convince them to leave, the Watchtower appears to be prophetic. This in turn encourages further loyalty.

An individual within a family of Jehovah's Witnesses faces crushing opposition should he or she decide to leave the society. Witnesses are warned that if they leave the Watchtower organization or are disfellowshiped (a consequence of questioning doctrine or practices), they will be shunned by family members who remain.[29] Fear of such a split makes it very difficult for Witnesses to leave, for the sacrifice is heavy.

Many divorces have resulted from one spouse joining the Jehovah's Witnesses and the other not, or one spouse leaving when both had previously belonged. These situations often lead to painful child custody cases with both the Witness parent and the non-Witness parent seeking to rescue their child from what they see as religious deception.[30]

Children in Jehovah's Witness families are deprived of many opportunities that most people consider normal and acceptable. For example, Watchtower children are forbidden to celebrate birthdays and other holidays. Birthdays are considered evil because the Egyptian Pharaoh, on his birthday, executed the chief baker (Gen 40:20-22), just as Herod, on his birthday, executed John the Baptist (Mt 14:6-10). They are also forbidden to salute the flag, which has obvious social implications.

Watchtower indoctrination can have a negative effect on how children view the world. Former Jehovah's Witness Randall Watters says children are taught that everything outside of the Watchtower is controlled by the devil and that all non-Jehovah's Witnesses are misled by Satan. Children of Witnesses are instructed to avoid "worldly" (i.e., all) magazines, movies, TV shows and music.[31]

Some Jehovah's Witness couples have decided not even to have children because of the teaching that only a short time remains before the end. Without a family they can spend more time serving Jehovah by distributing Watchtower literature door to door.

REACHING JEHOVAH'S WITNESSES

Despite the strong pull Witnesses feel toward the Watchtower belief system and way of life, many have left the organization when their eyes have been opened to the truth of the biblical gospel. It is possible to reach them with compassion and a firm but gentle adherence to Scripture. Here are a few guidelines to keep in mind.

Be loving. Someone once said, "People don't care how much you know until they know how much you care." Let the Witnesses with whom you speak know that you care about them.

Encourage an examination of beliefs. The Watchtower magazine "invites careful and critical examination of its contents in the light of the Scriptures."[32] Take them up on this invitation.

Emphasize context in interpreting Scripture. If the interpretation of a specific passage contradicts the rest of what Scripture teaches about that subject, the interpretation is erroneous. Individual verses do not exist as isolated fragments but as parts of a whole. Therefore we must figure out their proper relationship to each other and to the entire Word of God.

Ask questions. Jesus often asked questions to get people thinking about the truth (Mt 16:13; 22:33; Mk 3:33). Follow his lead.

Be ready to answer objections. The apostle Peter said, "Always be prepared to give an answer to everyone who asks you to give the reason for the hope that you have" (1 Pet 3:15).

Demonstrate that the Watchtower is a false prophet. The Watchtower Society, which claims to be a prophetic organization, has a long track record of inaccurate predictions. It foretold that 1914 would mark the overthrow of human governments and the full establishment of God's kingdom on earth.[33] Didn't happen. The Watchtower predicted that in 1925 certain Old Testament saints would rise from the grave and live in San Diego.[34] Didn't happen. The Watchtower predicted that in 1975 human history would end and the thousand-year reign of Christ would begin.[35] Didn't happen. Biblical prophets, by contrast, were 100 percent accurate (Deut 18:22).

Pray consistently. Only God in his mighty power can lift the veil of deception and darkness from the human heart (Jn 8:32; 2 Cor 3:17; 4:4). Pray fervently for those to whom you witness, and pray for them often (Mt 7:7-12; Lk 18:1-8; Jas 5:16).

YOGA AND HINDUISM

Vishal Mangalwadi with Ronald Enroth

In recent years yoga has invaded Western popular culture. It has inspired a cover story for *Time* magazine, provided "strength and empowerment" for people dealing with health issues, and fueled the sale of yoga apparel—to name just a few examples. An estimated fifteen million Americans participated in some form of yoga in 2003. According to a survey conducted by *Yoga Journal*, that number represents a 28 percent increase over 2002. Yoga has moved from the fringes to the mainstream.

For people who view yoga as a "sacred path to divine realization," these consumer-driven trends—yoga for pets, yoga for improving your golf game—demean the spirituality of this ancient Eastern practice. Critics see the commercialization of yoga as the antithesis of the Indian principles that true yoga is based on.

Despite its trendy trappings, the current yoga blitz prompts deeper questions: Is yoga just deep breathing and gentle stretching, or is there more involved? Is yoga a science? Are its touted benefits medically verifiable? Can it really produce peace of mind? Does yoga always involve spiritual practice, or can it be "just exercise"? The January 7, 2001, *New York Times* offers a partial answer: "After mastering the physical discipline, many students are eager to embrace yoga's underlying philosophy.

. . . Yoga isn't just a stretch class; it's supposed to be a place where the physical and the spiritual meet."

The pursuit of physical fitness and mental well-being is an appropriate goal for Christians. So should yoga be part of a Christian's health program? The answer depends on which Christian you talk to. Some believe that classical physical yoga cannot be separated from its Eastern religious roots. Others view yoga as a harmless cultural artifact of ancient India that has been transposed into yet another lifestyle toy for affluent Westerners. Most exercises are good for us, though my physician says that walking is better for me than yoga.

In our view, yoga cannot be dismissed as simply another aid to physical fitness. Someone has said that there is no Hinduism without yoga and no yoga without Hinduism. Yoga's connections to Eastern religious metaphysics are clear. The philosophy of yoga certainly undermines physical fitness as a value. To view yoga as a spiritually neutral practice is to ignore 5,000 years of teaching that the physical body is a virtual gateway to spiritual perfection and enlightenment.

In ancient Indian philosophy yoga was not meant to be a fitness regime. Rather, it was a means to salvation or liberation (*moksha*) through the isolation of the soul from the body. Out-of-body experiences are still the goal of some popular forms of yoga. Later, after other schools of Indian philosophy had adopted yoga, its goal was reinterpreted as the union of the human self with the cosmic self, or God. Physical yoga (that is, hatha yoga) is only one form of yoga. Hindu gurus have taught many different forms of yoga, or ways to obtain salvation. Indian yogis have in fact observed that Western advocates abuse the practice when they use it primarily for physical fitness.

The average Westerner, however, finds it easier to conceptualize yoga as a stress management technique than as a way of salvation. It's difficult for Jews, Christians and Muslims to accept that physical exercise could contribute to spiritual salvation. Our purpose here is to explain the religious (Hindu) worldview behind yoga. Let us begin with a question: Is the basic human problem biological, moral or metaphysical?

THE BASIC HUMAN PROBLEM

Materialists believe that evolution has made us bad and that our problem therefore is biological or genetic. Perhaps one day, they say, genetic engineers will make us good—loving, caring, just and upright. The Jews popularized the idea that the human problem is moral, that human beings are sinners, guilty of having broken God's law. Christianity and Islam share this perspective. Yoga's worldview assumes that the basic human problem is neither biological nor moral but metaphysical.

Some ancient Hindu traditions did take moral weakness and failure seriously. There are teachings that recommend ritual sacrifices for the propitiation of sins similar to those taught in the Old Testament. Some Hindu rites even foreshadow the New Testament teaching that Jesus sacrificed himself for sin as a substitute. Nevertheless, more recent Hinduism abandons morality as the key to the human condition.

Originally yoga techniques were a part of *Samkhya* philosophy, a dualistic approach that postulates two ultimate realities: *purusha* (soul) and *prakruti* (physical nature). *Samkhya* teaches that soul is pure but physical nature is evil. Somehow the soul has become entangled with the physical body, and our liberation, or *moksha*, lies in separating the two. Yoga developed as the technique by which to achieve isolation of the soul. Today, yoga generally is defined not as isolation of soul from body but union of soul (*atma*) with God (*Brahma*). This change occurred gradually as other schools of Indian philosophy that rejected *Samkhya* philosophy adopted yoga.

A prominent version of Upanishadic Hinduism teaches that the human soul is not distinct from God: *Brahma*, or the universal self, is the same as *atma*, or the inner self. This nondualistic teaching is called *adwaita*, meaning that the human self and the divine self are not distinct entities. It is also called monism, from *mono* or "one," emphasizing the oneness of everything, especially God and humankind. The monistic gurus teach that humans have forgotten their true nature as they have become entangled in finite, personal consciousness. So long as they remain in this ignorant state, they are repeatedly born into this world of suffering. Salvation lies in transcending personal consciousness and merging into the infinite impersonal consciousness, thereby escaping the cycle of birth and death. In this school of thought, yoga is considered a technique of uniting, or "yoking," the human soul with the divine soul.

Although the monists rejected *Samkhya* philosophy, they still saw the central human problem as metaphysical rather than moral. We are God; we cannot therefore break any divine moral law. Our problem is not sin but ignorance—the fact that we have forgotten our divinity. We need to experience, realize or perceive that divinity, not repent of anything or seek moral transformation. Salvation lies in attaining the original state of consciousness that has been lost. If we are God, we cannot expect a god to come and save us. We have to realize our own divinity, and yoga is the path by which to experience God-consciousness.

Salvation, in other words, is a matter of perception or realization. In this context, perceiving is not a cognitive activity. It is not a matter of intellectually knowing or logically deducing our divinity, but rather transcending our cognitive, rational consciousness and experiencing a higher state of expanded consciousness, which is believed to be God, or our true self.

Of course, not all gurus teach monism or nondualism. Some sects, such as Hare Krishna, do not believe that humans are God or ever become God. According to Hare Krishna, God is a personal being—Krishna. Humanity's original state is "Krishna-consciousness" and our true nature is to be a loving servant of Krishna. Our problem is that we have forgotten our Krishna-consciousness and become entangled in this material world. We have to re-establish our link with Krishna, and only then will we escape the cycle of birth and death and live forever in *Goloka*, or heaven. (A note on the sexes: Traditional Hinduism does not accept the equality of male and female. While some contemporary gurus affirm equality, the traditional view is that a woman needs to be reborn as a male before she can find salvation, or *moksha*.)

To sum up, then, salvation in Hinduism is found in the realization, perception or experience of our so-called true nature, which takes place when we attain a "higher" state of consciousness. We attempt to reach this state of consciousness through manipulation of the nervous system, and the techniques that help us do this—techniques developed over several millennia—are found in yoga. What follows is a discussion of a few types of yoga that have been popularized by modern gurus.

HATHA YOGA: SALVATION THROUGH PHYSICAL EXERCISES

Some chemicals make us sleepy while others excite us, intoxicate us or cause hallucinations or psychedelic experiences. Chemicals can change our mood and make us imagine things that appear real. By using certain substances to manipulate our brain chemistry, we can experience altered states of consciousness. And just as we can manipulate our central nervous system chemically, we can also affect it physiologically. The brain relies on oxygen and blood to function normally, so we can modify its chemistry by regulating our breathing and deliberately reducing oxygen intake, or by standing on our heads and altering blood flow.

Hatha yoga, which consists of physical and breathing exercises, is an ancient method of liberation. "Going within" oneself and experiencing inner consciousness depends on the state of one's nervous system, which depends in turn on physical condition. By manipulating our bodies, hatha gurus say, we can affect our nervous system and alter our consciousness.

One of hatha yoga's attractions is its stretching exercises, which make the body extremely flexible. It also trains adherents to consciously regulate their breathing and blood circulation, which changes mood. The problem, however, is that real mastery is a long and tedious process requiring much discipline and a competent teacher.

Hatha yoga is often advertised as nonreligious. It is promoted for fitness and stress management, as well as for its therapeutic value. Health and wellness-oriented institutions, for example, call yoga "the practice of unifying body, mind and spirit." Obviously, taking one's attention off the pressures of life and focusing for a while on one's breathing can be beneficial, but does it help more than a session in the swimming pool or meditating on a tank of goldfish? We do not yet have sufficient comparative studies to make a judgment.

Some gurus promote hatha yoga in secular, even misleading, terms in the hope that people interested in physical well-being will try it and experience altered states of consciousness. This experience will make them want to explore more of the spiritual aspects of yoga—and eventually accept the philosophy on which yoga rests. Other teachers of hatha yoga, of course, are not interested in propagating its spiritual teachings but merely want to impart health or make money.

No thinking person would deny hatha yoga's potential contribution to health. However, practicing yoga strictly for its therapeutic benefits raises a question: is nonspiritual yoga even yoga? The physical exercises of yoga are intended to alter consciousness or to cause loss of individual consciousness in an experience called "merging into God." In fact, Indian schools of hatha yoga emphasize the regulation of breathing (*pranayam*) much more than physical postures (*asanas*).

Someone may ask, "What's wrong with artificially altering consciousness?" In itself, nothing. Sleepwalking, hypnosis, hallucination and even madness are all altered states of consciousness. There is nothing morally wrong with these conditions, even if some of them are undesirable. The problem is philosophical. Does an altered state of consciousness mean you are God? If not, does it matter if you consider yourself to be God in that altered state of consciousness? If your inner self is not God, then you could be looking for God in the wrong place. You may wonder, what does it matter? Consider this: Would you want a map to the most important destination of your life to be drawn by someone who mistook east for west or north for south?

JAPA YOGA: THE "MECHANICAL PATH" TO SALVATION

Japa is the repetition or chanting of a mantra, usually a name of a god or demon. (This may sound strange to dualists, but it is not strange if you believe in the oneness of everything. Then god and demon are not distinct, nor is good different from evil.) The Hare Krishna movement is a good example of japa or *bhakti* (devotional) yoga. Its devotees chant the names of Krishna and Rama:

> Hare Krishna, Hare Krishna ·
> Krishna Krishna, Hare Hare
> Hare Rama, Hare Rama
> Rama Rama, Hare Hare.

To give a name to something is to distinguish it from others. The monistic gurus believe there is only one soul, God, and it permeates everyone and everything. Therefore they prefer not to use a specific name for God. They use a symbolic name, such as *om*, or a mantra with an unknown meaning so that the name or mantra will not create any thoughts or images in the mind by association.

The brain is constantly bombarded with stimuli it receives from the eyes, ears, nose, tongue and skin. The five senses make us aware of the external world—the world of *maya*, or deception, according to Hindu philosophy. How can we forget the world and become aware of the inner self, or God? One way is to constantly repeat a sound, which concentrates the mind and blocks the awareness of other stimuli. If we keep repeating the mantra, eventually it too becomes a nonstimulus. Our mind goes blank. We are conscious but unaware of anything or any thought—you could say we are conscious only of consciousness. This state of mind is what gurus call "pure consciousness" or "transcendental consciousness."

In order for this technique to be effective in "God-realization," it must be practiced for three or four hours a day. Maharishi Mahesh Yogi, who popularized a type of japa yoga called transcendental meditation (TM), prescribes the technique for only forty minutes a day to new initiates. This is meant to give them a taste for the practice and help them gain a "vision of possibilities."

During the initiation ceremony into TM (known as the *puja*), the instructor invokes the blessings of various gods and goddesses and then gives a mantra to the initiate. Usually the mantra is a short, meaningless word, such as *om, hrim, sring* or *aing*, or the name of a Hindu deity, such as Ram. The initiate is not to bother with the meaning of these words. The objective is to enable the seeker to go beyond rational thinking, to empty his or her mind. Eventually, the disciple will transcend all thoughts and feelings and will enter the transcendental state of consciousness.

Mahesh Yogi calls this process the "mechanical path to God-realization." He says realizing God is a matter of perception, and "the process of perception is both mechanical and automatic." In order to perceive external objects, we just "open our eyes and the sight of the object comes automatically without the use of intellect or emotions." Likewise, in order to experience the inner consciousness, we just turn our attention inward and automatically come to perceive it.

Maharishi Mahesh Yogi developed a very effective marketing campaign for his brand of japa yoga. He insisted that TM was not a religious practice but a scientific technique to reduce stress, induce relaxation, lower blood pressure, increase concentration and productivity, and enhance creativity. He also emphasized the social benefits of TM—better relationships, lower crime, higher economic growth and a better world.

As a result, TM gained acceptance in many spheres, including academia, politics and the corporate world.

SURAT-SHABD YOGA: THE PATH OF SOUND AND LIGHT

"God is light," many gurus declare, and add that this light is within us. "In the beginning was the Word, and the Word was with God, and the Word was God," Christians declare, quoting John 1. Then there are groups that combine these two ideas. These groups say that the "word" is within us, and when a soul establishes contact with it internally, the word takes the soul back to the godhead, the soul's original home.

The Divine Light Mission and religious movements such as Radha Soami Satsang Beas, have been chiefly responsible for popularizing su-rat-shabd yoga in our day. *Surat* in this tradition means "soul" and *shabd* means "word" or "sound," so surat-shabd yoga is union of the soul and the word. The movement practices what is called Nam Bhakti, which means "meditation on the sound."

The Divine Light Mission and groups like it try to keep their techniques secret. They call their practices by words such as *nam* ("name") and *updesh* ("knowledge") to deliberately mislead outsiders. Their focus is on physiological manipulation of the senses. They meditate on what they call the "primeval sound" or "logos" and breath control.

Unlike transcendental meditation groups, the sects that teach the path of sound and light do not initiate everyone who asks for it. An individual must be spiritually "ready" for initiation. There are no objective criteria for determining this readiness; it simply depends on the judgment of the initiator, who claims to have reasons but does not reveal them. Some sects set a few objective conditions, such as giving up alcohol and drugs and switching to a vegetarian diet.

After a person has been chosen for initiation, he or she is taken into a closed room, where the initiator explains the importance of the *updesh* (gnostic "knowledge"), the *satsang* (a weekly gathering for fellowship and teaching) and the *satguru* (the "true teacher"). In most sects the would-be initiate takes a vow of secrecy and promises to follow no other guru. In the course of initiation, a new disciple of the Divine Light Mission learns four major techniques:

Seeing the divine light. In order to see the "divine light," devotees close their eyes and place the middle finger and thumb on the eyelids. Starting from the corner of the eyes, they press their eyeballs upward from the bottom so that if their eyes were open, they would be looking at a point between the eyebrows and just above the nose, which is supposed to be the location of the "third eye." If initiates concentrate on this point, they can usually see a light. Some people see only a small point, others see a blinding light, some see a psychedelic "movie" of pulsating patterns and brilliant colors, and still others see nothing at all.

Hearing the divine music. In order to hear the "divine music" or "the sound," novices are asked to block their ears with their thumbs so they cannot hear any external noises. If they listen long enough to their inner silence in this way, they can often hear something or imagine they hear something. Some initiates hear what sounds like celestial music, while others think their favorite tune is being played on a heavenly instrument.

Tasting the divine nectar. The third technique in the Divine Light Mission is a difficult yogic exercise: tasting the "divine nectar." Usually initiates experience the nectar only after much practice. To do this, they curl the tongue up the back of the throat, then swallow the tongue in such a way that it points upward. Here the tongue is supposed to hit a point and make contact with the "divine nectar" that is constantly flowing through the body. Gurus claim that this nectar is the living water of which Jesus spoke, and it is indescribably delicious.

Contacting the word. The main meditation is a breathing exercise called hearing or contacting "the word." Devotees are asked to sit in the lotus position with both hands on their knees. They concentrate on breath: inhaling and exhaling. This technique is supposed to connect them to the "primordial vibration," the word or logos that created the universe and sustains it. By constant meditation disciples reach *samadhi*, or the expanded state of consciousness in which, according to their gurus, they become full of the divine light. At initiation the light may appear as a small dot, but in *samadhi* it overtakes the devotee, who feels (or perceives) that he or she has become a part of it.

There can be no doubt that these experiences are real in the sense that they are vivid psychological experiences within the minds of Divine Light disciples. But are they real in an objective sense? Does the soul (*surat*) actually leave the body with the word (*shabd*) and visit other worlds? One yogi said to me, "These Americans have gone to the moon only now. We have been traveling to other galaxies for centuries." I replied, "The difference is that the yogis never bring back rocks from other planets, so there is no way to know if they ever left this earth."

KUNDALINI YOGA: SALVATION THROUGH THE "SERPENT POWER"

Hindu psychology teaches that in the human body at the base of the spine is a beautiful triangle in which lies the *kundalini*, also called the *shakti*, or "serpent power." The kundalini, which is defined only vaguely in Hindu writings, is supposed to be red and white in color and is described as "coiled power" or the "creative sex energy." It is taught that the kundalini normally lies coiled and dormant, but when awakened it arises and begins to travel upward. In its journey from the base of the spine to the top of the head it passes through six psychic centers called *chakras*, imparting various psychic experiences and powers at each one. When it reaches the top chakra, called the *sahasrara* (or "crown") chakra, the kundalini supposedly empowers the individual to perform miracles and achieve liberation.

Yoga uses many means to awaken the kundalini. Techniques range from breathing exercises such as *pranayam* to homosexual handling of the genitals. The most influential kundalini guru in the last few decades was Swami Muktananda of Ganeshpuri, near Bombay. He described kundalini yoga as *mahayoga* ("great yoga") or *siddhayoga* ("perfect yoga"), for he said it was the only yoga in which the aspirant need do nothing. The individual simply surrenders to the guru, whose grace does everything.

Thousands of people have testified that Muktananda awakened their kundalini through the use of an occultic (hidden or secret) method. Some stories suggest that the guru was using demonic power. Kundalini yoga has not been popular in India because many of its experiences involve what William James, the nineteenth-century psychologist and comparative religion expert, called "diabolical mysticism."[1] It produces pain, makes people depressed, and even leads to madness in some cases.

Muktananda's own initiation into kundalini yoga illustrates what William James meant:

> On reaching my destination I sat . . . for meditation. Soon I started feeling restless and uneasy. Within moments things were happening to me. I could not understand it. I was perturbed mentally and emotionally. My mind seemed deluded. By the time evening came this delusion became worse. Generally I am a man of great courage but that day I was overcome by fear. I felt I would soon become insane. My mind was terribly agitated.[2]

That evening, at about nine o'clock, Muktananda sat again for meditation:

> I felt there was great commotion around. My entire body started aching and I automatically assumed *padmasana,* the lotus posture. The tongue began to move down the throat, and all attempts to pull it out failed, as I could not insert my fingers into the mouth. My fear grew; I tried to get up, but I could not, as my legs were tightly locked in padmasana. I felt severe pain in the knot (*manipur chakra*)

below the navel. I tried to shout but could not even articulate. It seemed as if something was stuck in my throat. Next I saw ugly and dreadful demon-like figures. I thought them to be evil spirits. I then saw blazes of fire on all sides and felt that I too was burning. After a while I felt a little better. Suddenly I saw a large ball of light approaching me from the front; as it approached, its light grew brighter and brighter. It then entered unobstructed through the closed doors of my *kutir* [hut] and merged into my head. My eyes were forcibly closed and I felt a fainting sensation. I was terrified by that powerfully dazzling light, and it put me out of gear.[3]

Kunkalini yoga continues to draw devotees, but Muktananda's sect has split into multiple factions due to charges of sex abuse, rape, murder and financial scandals.

TANTRA: SALVATION THROUGH SEX

Tantra is sometimes portrayed as the opposite of yoga because it is a path of indulgence, whereas hatha yoga is a path of discipline, effort and self-denial. Both, however, aim at the same end—unity with the divine, which is found within oneself. The tantrics claim that their form of yoga is the original and easiest way of salvation. *Samadhi*, or "unity-consciousness," is possible during sexual intercourse, they say, for in orgasm rational consciousness is transcended in a pleasurable experience of oneness. Tantra is in part a system of techniques for prolonging orgasm in order to experience "God."

Tantra may have originated in India's prehistoric fertility cults. It started to come into prominence in India around A.D. 600, and three centuries later at least sixty-four tantric texts were in circulation. By the year 1000 tantric art dominated the cultural scene in India. By the nineteenth century, however, tantricism had sunk to such levels of crudity, cruelty, witchcraft and superstition that it became unacceptable in sophisticated society. In its crudest forms it included worship of sex organs, orgies that involved the drinking of blood and human semen, black magic, human sacrifice, and contact with evil spirits through rotting bodies in cremation grounds. The tantrics were feared for their occult powers and hated because they kidnapped children and sacrificed them to demons. Self-respecting Brahmins, Muslims and Christian missionaries all opposed tantra. Consequently it went underground in India.

Tantra's history confirms the apostle Paul's profound observation. He noted that when men suppress the truth in unrighteousness and begin to worship creation instead of the Creator, God gives them over "in the sinful desires of their hearts to sexual impurity for the degrading of their bodies with one another" (Rom 1:24). And their base minds and lusts lead them to unbelievable depths of filth and foolishness.

It was the counterculture movement of the 1960s in the West that revived tantra and gave it fresh respectability. It fused sexual permissiveness and the occult with spirituality. Although still suspect and despised in India, tantra, or sacred sex, is now at the root of virtually all *religious* forms of yoga adopted by the West—that is, yoga practiced for religious reasons rather than physical fitness.

Tantra uses duality as the surest path to cosmic unity. Tantrics believe that human beings are microcosmic versions of the universe, because in them the finer consciousness and grosser body coexist. Polarity is the key to existence, they say, and the division of male and female is the basic polarity in the human race. Therefore the reunification of male and female in sexual intercourse is humanity's point of contact with the cosmic powers and its own divine reality. In tantra, humans reach reality by embracing illusion—their own bodies.

Tantra, like other schools of Hindu thought, admits that the world is *maya*—unreal in a fundamental sense. However, unlike other Hindus, tantrics do not scorn the world as a source of temptation. They embrace it as the raw material of enlightenment. For tantra, the realm of *maya* is the only available context of liberation.

Although Swami Vivekananda introduced tantra to the West in 1893 and the hippies of the 1960s revived it, it was not until the 1970s that Westerners embraced tantricism with enthusiastic abandon. This was when the flamboyant personage of Bhagwan (later Osho) Rajneesh came on the scene. Rajneesh was as famous for the Rolls Royce fleet at his Oregon ranch as he was for his book *From Sex to Superconsciousness*,[4] which summed up his tantric creed. Rajneesh was no simpleton. He had taught philosophy in an Indian university before becoming a guru. He knew that the Age of Reason was dead and that human rationality alone was incapable of knowing truth. Boldly Rajneesh described the human mind as our "chief villain." Intellect, he said, acted like a prism. It divided one ray into many. The mind held us in bondage and ignorance because it could see an object only by separating it from others, by labeling or categorizing it. Therefore, he concluded, the aim of the religious quest was to "kill the mind"—to choose insanity.

Tantra uses mantras as one of the weapons to kill the mind. Words are sounds with meaning, but the mindless repetition of words aims to sever sense from sound. Mircea Eliade says, "All indefinite repetition leads to destruction of language; in some mystical traditions, this destruction appears to be the condition for further experiences."[5]

Once an adherent of tantric yoga has learned to reach *samadhi*, or superconsciousness, through sex, says Rajneesh, he does not even need a woman. He can have sex with the whole universe, "with a tree, with the moon, with anything."[6] He can simply shut himself in a room and reach superconsciousness using the female kundalini within him.

As Rajneesh has admitted, tantric sex is not about making love or achieving mutual satisfaction. Tantrics use sex as a means to their own enlightenment, which usually leaves their partner sexually frustrated. Shirley MacLaine, Hollywood actress and a popularizer of tantra, admits that sex in tantra is not meant to fulfill two people by uniting them in one bond. It is used by one or both partners to discover their own completeness as androgynous beings so that each may become complete without the other.[7]

Tantra unabashedly embraces human sexuality in its spirituality. But by using sex for personal gain rather than for human bonding in love, it frustrates sex. It does not cause sexual fulfillment, nor does it celebrate life. It seeks to deny the plan of creation by transcending the essence of what we are as male and female.

MANY WAYS TO SALVATION?

There are many forms of yoga because there are many ways to alter personal consciousness and many types of mystical experience. The question is whether salvation is obtained by human effort or God's grace. If it is by human effort, then there can be as many ways to find it as there are ways to exert human effort. If salvation is a gift of God's grace, then no effort on our part can qualify us to merit it. Grace by definition is unmerited favor.

Whether yoga is considered an attempt to isolate the soul (*purusha*) from the physical nature (*prakriti*), or as an attempt to unite the human self with the divine self, the result is a low view of physical reality and the human body. In a yogic worldview there is no motivation to study science or consider the human body an awe-inspiring creation. In addition, the monistic view that the human self is the same as the divine self and that everything is one undermines individuality, which destroys the basis for affirming the unique value of every individual.

In light of this, it should not surprise us that the Indian philosophical tradition, despite its brilliance, could not produce a culture that recognized human rights and the intrinsic worth of the individual. Nor could yogic monism give to Indian society a framework for moral absolutes, a strong sense of right and wrong. Yogic exercises indeed give flexibility to our bodies, but unfortunately the philosophy of yoga gives too much flexibility to our morals.

The apostle Paul wrote, "Physical training is of some value, but godliness has value for all things, holding promise for both the present life and the life to come" (1 Tim 4:8). The pursuit of physical fitness is desirable because our bodies are a part of God's good creation. God made our bodies his temple. Furthermore, there is a certain logic in the yogic tradition of making spirituality the real goal of physical training. The spirituality of yoga, however, is errant, even if the exercises are beneficial.

The Bible teaches that the human problem is moral rather than biological or metaphysical. God is holy—morally pure. We are sinful, not merely ignorant, as yoga would have us believe. We have done what we know to be wrong and failed to do what we know to be right. A holy God must judge and punish our sin. God and sin cannot coexist any more than light and darkness. To remedy this situation, we need not altered consciousness but transformation of the core of our being and character.

God created human beings good. Our first parents, according to Genesis, chose to disobey God and thereby became sinners, passing down that trait to us all. Although we are still God's image-bearers and capable of goodness, none of us is perfect. From childhood our tendency is toward evil. We need teaching and training to live moral lives. Yet even if we receive the best training, we fail morally. We are sinners. We need a divine Savior who will forgive our sins and transform our inner self. That Savior is Jesus Christ.

Yoga and Hindu philosophy seek union with God. The problem is that they seek it in the wrong place. Jesus offers true salvation as a free gift, and this salvation does bring about genuine reunion with God. Our union with him fulfills our individuality. It does not obliterate it. It makes our bodies precious—temples of the living God.

GLOSSARY

adwaita. nondualism; the belief that God and the human self are not distinct

aing. mantra with an unknown meaning

atma. soul; the human self

Brahma. God; the universal self that permeates everything and everyone

chakras. the psychic centers of the body

devas. nature spirits

hrim. mantra with an unknown meaning

Jainism. non-Brahminical Indian religion of strict asceticism, founded around 600 B.C.; from a word meaning "saint" or "victor"

karma. good or bad deeds or destiny; past lives dictating present and future lives

kutir. hut

lila. the play of cosmic consciousness

maha. great

maithuna. sexual ritual in tantra

mantra. chant; a sacred sound or name of God to be repeated as meditation

maya. illusion; unreality, as in a dream

om. sound representing ultimate reality or God

padmasana. the lotus position

prakriti. physical nature

pranayam. breathing exercises

purusha. soul

sadhu. holy man; ascetic

samadhi. expanded state of consciousness

samsara. world or life as a wheel of suffering

Samkhya. Indian dualistic philosophy concerned with the pure soul and the impure body

sandha-bhasha. symbolic language of tantra

satsang. sacred gathering for fellowship and teaching

surat. soul; beauty

shabd. word; sound

siddha. perfect

sring. mantra with an unknown meaning

4

UNIFICATION CHURCH

James Beverley

In the summer of 2002 full-page ads in major newspapers across the world drew attention to a religious document titled "A Cloud of Witnesses: The Saints' Testimonies to the True Parents." The editors of an organization known as the Family Federation for World Peace and Unification introduced the text, which drew particular attention to a "proclamation ceremony" held the previous year in the eternal spiritual world in honor of Sun Myung Moon, the controversial and dynamic leader of the Unification Church.

According to "A Cloud of Witnesses," Jesus, Peter, Paul, Martin Luther and Karl Barth, among others, led the Christian confession of Moon as messiah, savior and lord. Confucian, Hindu, Buddhist and Muslim leaders joined in the proclamation, and Communist leaders Marx, Lenin, Stalin and Deng Xiao Ping added ringing endorsements as well. The ceremony is alleged to have taken place at noon on December 25, 2001, and God the Father sent a letter to earth as final vindication of the famous Korean leader.

The Unification Church continues to be one of the most interesting of the new religious movements, due largely to the provocative and fascinating founder Sun Myung Moon. Though he turned eighty-four at the beginning of 2004, Moon continues to exercise a vital and powerful hold on the church and the many organizations and movements he started in the last fifty years.

A BRIEF HISTORY

The Reverend Sun Myung Moon was born January 6, 1920, in what is now North Korea. His parents joined the Presbyterian Church in 1930. Moon claims to have received a direct revelation from Jesus at Easter in 1936 that called him to complete the mission of Christ. Moon began his ministry in 1946, was imprisoned by Communist authorities in 1948 and was liberated by United Nations forces on October 14, 1950.[1]

Moon developed his ministry in Pusan, South Korea, in the early 1950s and moved to Seoul in 1953. That same year his first marriage ended, and in 1954 he officially started the Holy Spirit Association for the Unification of World Christianity.[2] In 1960 Rev. Moon married seventeen-year-old Hak Ja Han, who has since given birth to thirteen children. Moon has one son from his first marriage.

The early years of the Unification Church were difficult. Moon was jailed briefly in 1955, and mainline denominational leaders brought charges of heresy and sexual immorality against him. The latter accusations were never proven. And then in 1959 Young Oon Kim, who became one of the most important Unification theologians, was sent by Rev. Moon to the United States.

Moon visited the United States in 1965 and toured the country. The "Korean prophet" made much of his visit with the famous medium Arthur Ford, who used his spirit guide Fletcher to comment on Moon's significance. Moon moved permanently to the States in December 1971, making New York his home. The Unification Church received incredible media attention in late 1973 through Moon's support of Richard Nixon at the height of the Watergate crisis.

The church also received scrutiny in the seventies for its giant rallies at Madison Square Garden, Yankee Stadium and the Washington Monument. Moon was becoming the target of criticism as a leader, with accusations of brainwashing, arms manufacturing and anti-Semitism. Unification members were often subject to kidnapping and deprogramming.[3]

In 1981 the United States government charged Moon with income tax evasion. The trial began on April 1, 1982, and Moon was found guilty and sentenced to eighteen months in prison. He began his term in a prison in Danbury, Connecticut, in the summer of 1984 and was released from a Brooklyn halfway house on August 20, 1985. Moon received significant sympathy in his portrayal as a victim of religious persecution.[4]

In late 1983, Rev. and Mrs. Moon's son Heung Jin was in a car accident near Poughkeepsie, New York. The crash, his subsequent death and his alleged postmortem ministry represent one of the most significant developments in Unification theology and ritual. On February 20, 1984, Sun Myung Moon married his deceased son to Hoon Sook Pak, the daughter of one of Moon's top aides, Colonel Bo Hi Pak.

Since then various Unificationists have claimed to channel the spirit of Heung Jin. In 1987 a church member from Zimbabwe named Cleopus Kundiona suggested that Heung Jin was using his body as a medium. Kundiona traveled to the United States, met the Moon family and led the Unificationists in revival meetings that included physical beatings. Kundiona was also accused of beating up Colonel Bo Hi Pak.[5]

Unificationists were elated with Moon's meetings with Mikhail Gorbachev in 1990 and North Korean leader Kim Il Sung the following year. Both meetings were interpreted as proof of Moon's triumph over Communism. He took credit for the fall of the Berlin Wall in 1989 and claimed a significant part in ending the Persian Gulf War in 1991.

Since the mid-1990s Rev. Moon has invested heavily in land purchase and development of Unification projects in South America. New Hope East Garden is located in western Brazil and provides a vast site for educational and ecological work. The church has also bought thousands of acres of land in Uruguay, and Unificationists regularly visit both countries for spiritual exercises.[6]

Church members also take part in repentance exercises at the Chung Pyung Center in South Korea. Unificationists receive messages from the deceased mother of Mrs. Moon at workshops led by Hyo Nam Kim. Members also look for guidance from the deceased Heung Jin. A temple was built at Chung Pyung for Moon's eightieth birthday celebration in 2002.[7]

Two major events rocked the Unification Church in the late 1990s. In 1998 Nansook Hong, Moon's former daughter-in-law, published *In the Shadow of the Moons*, her devastating memoir about life inside the church. In the book Hong accused her ex-husband, Hyo Jin Moon, of drug abuse, physical violence, verbal abuse and adultery. She also charged Sun Myung Moon with adultery and claimed he had had an illegitimate child who was raised by another Unification family.[8]

Second, Young Jin (Phillip) Moon, another son, fell to his death from the seventeenth floor of a hotel in Reno, Nevada, in October 1999. Young Jin's death, ruled a suicide in preliminary police reports, created a new round of turmoil for church members. Some Unification members speculated that Young Jin died from demonic attacks, but church leaders dismissed these reports as baseless rumor. Rev. Moon proclaimed that the death was providential and that Young Jin died as a "sacrifice" so that Satan could not directly attack the True Parents.[9]

In the spring of 2001 the Unification Church ran afoul of Catholic orthodoxy when Archbishop Emmanuel Milingo and Maria Sung, a Unification member, were married in a mass ceremony led by Rev. Moon at the New York Hilton. Several months after the wedding Milingo wrote a letter to Pope John Paul II defending his marriage and asking the pope to release him from his vows of celibacy. A week later the Congregation for the Doctrine of the Faith, led by Cardinal Joseph Ratzinger, issued a judgment against Milingo. It ordered him to separate from his wife, sever all links with the Unification Church and affirm his commitment to celibacy and obedience to the supreme pontiff. The document stated, "Should Archbishop Milingo not formally act by 20 August 2001 to fulfill what is hereby required of him, excommunication reserved to the Holy See will be imposed."

Milingo met with the pope at his summer residence, and shortly afterward announced that he would return to the Roman fold. The Vatican lifted its threat of excommunication. Milingo's wife announced a hunger strike and accused the Vatican of kidnapping her husband. Milingo agreed to meet her in Rome, where he told her that his vow of celibacy took precedence over his marriage. Milingo has since written a book about the scandal and accused the Unification Church of brainwashing him.[10]

UNIFICATION THEOLOGY

The Unification movement retains the outline though not the substance of classical Christian doctrine. While the themes of Christian orthodoxy form the framework for Moon's ideology, he is not hesitant to abandon many of the central doctrines that have grounded Christianity for two millennia. In the main, however, Moon operates from a Christian background, influenced by specific Korean religious and cultural realities.

Sources of authority. Divine Principle, the famous Unification "Bible," is the centerpiece in Unification evangelism and in-house teaching. Video series have been built around its contents, and academics have often been invited to seminars to hear extensive defenses of its theological integrity. It serves as the standard one-volume guide to Unification doctrine. Rev. Moon told his followers in 1978, "Theologians at Harvard Divinity School are studying Divine Principle more than you are, and soon they will come forward and say that it is the most refreshing, logical and revolutionary theology they have ever seen."[11]

Despite this rhetoric, academics have often overstated the importance of Divine Principle, suggesting that it is the final source of authority for

Unificationists. Rev. Moon has made it clear that his teachings and sermons constitute the ultimate source of modern revelation, beyond both the Christian Bible and Divine Principle. He views these texts as lesser guides to divine truth. Moon never hesitates to ignore clear biblical teaching or advance new revelation that shows virtual disregard for the Bible's testimony.

Doctrine of God. The Unification Church is committed to monotheism but does not adopt a trinitarian understanding of God. Though Moon adopts the use of "Father, Son and Holy Spirit" in his language, he shows no interest in following the model of Nicea or Chalcedon in his understanding of the Godhead. Divine Principle explicitly distances Unification doctrine from a classical understanding of the Son and the Spirit.

Moon's sermons are replete with references to his unparalleled obedience to God but also hint constantly that God is fortunate to have Moon on his side. "I know I am the only person on earth who truly knows God and can comfort him," he once said. "God has now said I have done enough and he told me to relax because he has been comforted by me, but that is the one command from God that I am defying."[12] He stated in 1992 that his goal and mission is "to liberate God, to save God."[13]

Doctrine of salvation. Unification understanding of salvation begins with a realization of the significance of the fall of humanity in the Garden of Eden. In 1978 Moon stated, "The bombshell news that resounded most fearfully to God was the news of the fall of man. God practically passed out in that moment. He lost his composure, his reason, his emotion. The history of God after the fall is that of trying to recover and recompose himself."[14]

Moon teaches that Satan seduced Eve sexually. The Korean leader believes that eating of the tree of the knowledge of good and evil is a reference to Eve's sexual transgression with Satan. Eve also sinned by engaging in sex with Adam before the proper time allowed by God. A ransom motif dominates Moon's interpretation of the relationship between God and Satan. Satan holds humans in captivity and God has to work within the boundaries of the protocol that exists between himself, Satan and humanity. In other words, God is limited by his contractual obligations to Satan. For Moon, the sins of the first couple extend to their blood lineage. Ever since the fall God has been looking for a Messiah who would be the new Adam and find a new Eve.[15]

During the first two decades of Unification life in America, Moon was somewhat ambiguous about his role and spiritual identity. However, after his release from prison in 1985 he increasingly claimed to be the Lord of the Second Advent, or Messiah. Unificationists believe that Moon is the new Adam and his wife is the new Eve. He also became more explicit about the spiritual, political and intellectual failures of other leaders.

Moon's understanding of salvation involves the redemption of humanity through the restoration of the family, which is why he puts such great emphasis on the marriage ceremony ("the Blessing") as a central component in Unification ritual. Before Unificationists are married— usually in the famous mass weddings—they engage in the Holy Wine ceremony, wherein they partake of wine derived from the wine created by Moon for his wedding day in 1960.

Couples also participate in what is known as the Indemnity Stick ceremony. With roots in Korean shamanism, this tradition involves the prospective bride and groom beating each other on the posterior. The rite is intended to teach both the need for human involvement in the salvific process and the pain and humiliation connected with physical abuse. After the Blessing and a period of waiting, married couples follow a special Three-Day ceremony in which they engage in specific sexual patterns and positions in order to reverse the impact of the distorted sexuality that brought humanity's fall.[16]

Unification soteriology has virtually no place for the biblical doctrine of justification by faith alone. The concept of grace emerges only in Moon's frequent comments that his followers and the world are not worthy of him. Unificationists are constantly told that salvation hinges on their obedience to the specific instructions of their leader. In 1974 Moon told his followers, "The destiny of three billion people of the world hinges upon our shoulders and on what you do in the next couple of weeks."[17]

View of Jesus. Moon's teachings about Jesus build on explicit views given in Divine Principle that (a) Jesus was not sent to die on the cross, (b) Calvary was a secondary option that resulted largely from the disobedience of John the Baptist, and (c) the ideal plan for Jesus was to have found a true Eve to restore humanity. Because God's perfect will was not achieved, the death of Jesus did not accomplish full salvation.

What is implicit in Divine Principle becomes explicit in Moon's sermons: Jesus failed in several key ways and as a result God has had to look to Sun Myung Moon as the new Adam, as Messiah, as Lord of the Second Advent. There is no longer any vagueness about Moon's stature and identity. He teaches explicitly that he is the second coming promised in the New Testament. Moreover, according to Unification thought, Jesus is subservient to Moon and recognizes him as the true savior of humanity.

Moon denies the classical Christian affirmation of the Virgin Birth. Instead, he contends that Jesus is the product of a sexual relationship between Mary and Zechariah, the father of John the Baptist. According to Moon, Mary never told Joseph who Jesus' real father was. Moon states, "Day and night, Joseph said, 'Whose son is this?' and fought with Mary. Because of this, everybody heard about Jesus' birth. Who wants to become one with a bastard who was born by the blood of another person?"[18]

According to Unification teaching, Jesus paid a deep emotional price for this uncertainty about his earthly father. Moon even states that Mary and Joseph purposefully left Jesus behind in Jerusalem at age twelve. Jesus was actually at the temple "because he was forsaken by his mother and father!" Moon adds, "The fact that Jesus could not get married was directly due to the failure of responsibility on Mary's part. How can Mary be a great woman?"[19]

Unificationists have often objected to the allegation that they believe Jesus failed. At an early scholarly conference on Unification theology, Lynn Kim contended, "We never ever say Jesus failed. That's put on us from outside. We don't ever talk of Jesus as a failure."[20] George Chryssides has also made this point in his work *The Advent of Sun Myung Moon*: "Unification Church members often find themselves foisted with the belief that Jesus' mission was a failure. Divine Principle does not say this at any point, and UC members feel justifiably indignant when their critics persistently ignore their attempts to explain what they really believe about Jesus."[21]

The chief problem with these indignant statements is the explicit teaching of the Unification leader himself. Though Moon said in 1977 that the lack of fulfillment in the first advent "does not mean that Jesus failed,"[22] he has overtly stated the opposite on other occasions. In 1971 Moon told his followers that Jesus "failed in fulfilling his mission on the earth."[23] He stated in 1974 that he had to "go beyond the failure of Adam, the failure of Abraham, the failure of Moses, the failures of Jacob, Moses and John the Baptist, and Jesus."[24]

Moon also objects to the prayer of Jesus in Gethsemane and his lament at Calvary that he felt forsaken by God. "Father [Moon] does not accept Jesus' Gethsemane prayer, and the prayer of Jesus Christ on the Cross. . . . He does not buy that kind of terrible statement."[25] Moon even suggests that Jesus had a selfish streak, unlike himself: "Jesus was a little insensitive. Whenever anyone puts 'I' in front, then he definitely perishes."[26]

Eschatology. The Unification understanding of eschatology is derived both from Divine Principle and from Moon's sermons. Divine Principle provides an extensive though tedious argument that the biblical narrative is being retraced in the stages of history from Jesus to the advent of the second Messiah. Thus, the events of the four centuries between Malachi and the New Testament are duplicated by divine providence in the period between Luther and the new Lord of the Second Advent.

Though Divine Principle does not explicitly claim that Moon is the Messiah, it is clear from the bulk of Moon's sermons that he is the fulfillment of the eschatological vision of the Unification sacred text. His teachings leave no doubt that Moon believes himself to be the center and apex of history and that eschatology finds its focus in him. In a 1971 message Moon argued that his 1960 marriage was the turning point of history.[27] He made the same claim for his rally at the Washington Monument in 1976.

For years Moon argued that Unificationists would create heaven on earth during the twenty-one year period from 1960 to 1981. In 1978 he announced, "The next two and a half years will be the grand finale. After that the third seven-year course will be over. Then I would like to ride down Fifth Avenue on a white horse. In two and a half years the word 'Moonie' shall become an honorable name and we will have demonstrations and victory celebrations from coast to coast."[28]

Moon placed enormous responsibility on his members for bringing paradise by 1981. Moon simply declared that the twenty-one year timetable was ahead of schedule and proclaimed the end of the three periods of seven years on April 15, 1980.[29] Though it was a "momentous day," he immediately announced the beginning of another twenty-one year dispensation. In 1981 a grand jury indicted Moon on charges of income tax evasion, putting to doubt his claim that after 1981 "the whole world will be manipulated at our will."[30]

Prison didn't stop Moon from continuing to interpret his life as the centerpiece of human history. He referred to his 1985 release as his resurrection. Unificationists viewed his 1990 meetings with Gorbachev as the end of World War III.[31] At the time Moon said, "Right now Gorbachev is in a very difficult position. He really listens to Father. When Father writes him a letter, he says, 'Hurry, hurry, translate this into Russian.' He reads it with a red pencil and underlines the important parts.

It is a recognized fact that the entire world is now looking on Father as the world's spiritual leader. The world leader. Period."[32]

Moon also claimed that the 1988 Olympic Games in Seoul were focused on him and his wife. Then he took credit for both the fall of Communism and the success of Allied forces during the Persian Gulf War. In his God's Day sermon of 1992 Moon proclaimed, "True Parents have been crowned at the pinnacle of the mountain. President Bush is not leading this country; actually True Parents are leading the entire world and the United States is part of the world."[33]

Moon attaches cosmic significance to major events in Unification life and also proclaims that the supernatural realm is in tune with his wishes. In a mass wedding at Madison Square Garden in June 1998, Moon married not only human couples but also thirty-four spirits, including representatives of good (Jesus, Confucius, Buddha, Muhammad and Socrates) and evil (Hitler and Stalin).

The freedom gained from this Blessing ceremony for the spirit world led to the August 2000 announcement of the "Ceremony for the General Liberation of the Spirit World." The Unification Church then announced the "Coronation of God's Kingship" on January 13, 2001. Twelve months later, on Christmas Day, the heavenly leaders of five great religions recognized Moon as the Savior, Messiah and second coming of Jesus, as reported the following summer in "Cloud of Witnesses."

On February 6, 2003, more than eight thousand Unificationists gathered in Korea to witness the marriage of Moon and his wife before God and the coronation of Sun Myung Moon as king of all humanity. Their earlier marriage in 1960 was marred by the failure of Christians in Korea to accept the Unification movement. That blot on history's most important wedding has been erased by the success of this recent "Marriage Supper of the Lamb," which fulfills the wedding scene described in the book of Revelation.

Moon teaches that eventually all humans will be saved. But this teaching seems to contradict the frequent references to hell in his sermons and his claims that certain sins cannot be forgiven. Moon repeatedly exhorts his followers to learn Korean, an instruction rooted in the belief that Korean will be the language of heaven. Members will be ashamed on judgment day if they have not learned their own savior's native tongue. Furthermore, a member's proximity to the center of heaven will correspond directly with his or her ability to speak the Korean language.

THE MIND OF A MESSIAH

The core of Unification theology in its doctrinal expression and ritual observance is the person of Sun Myung Moon. The Unification Church represents a radically Moon-centered ideology. Just as Christianity rises or falls on the person of Jesus, the credibility of Unificationism is linked to the person of Sun Myung Moon.

And when it comes to credibility, Moon is his own worst enemy. His sermons reveal an ego of unlimited size matched only by his dogmatism on almost any topic, all set in the context of obvious adoration by his followers and repeated claims of humility on the part of their messiah. That the Unification Church has survived Moon's teaching is proof that anything is possible in the world of religion.

He is not shy about his intellectual prowess. For example, he has stated that "in the world of literature, I can grasp the concepts of the great masterpieces and great writers so quickly."[34] He has bragged about his head being "an extraordinary size" and stated in another sermon, "I do not have an ordinary brain. You can see that I have a large head! I have a big brain and I know things that you don't know."[35]

In 1977 he contended, "I'm not just a philosopher. There is nowhere else under the sun that you can find someone who is like me." Moon has argued that he has "a good enough brain" to win "dozens of different doctorates in different fields."[36] He states often that he is a man of mystery and contends that there is no scale "big enough" to measure him.[37]

Moon gave one of his more explicit claims about his brilliance in 1982, when he stated, "Even if the greatest computer companies wanted to run all the data about me through their sophisticated equipment, they wouldn't be able to enter everything into their computers. I wouldn't register on the screen, because I just don't compute![38] Moon also argued at one point that "one hundred professors together could never equal what I have in the way of knowledge."[39]

In 1979 he asked his followers a rhetorical question: "Am I near the bottom of the list of great modern thinkers, or at the top? I am a man of complicated thought who has considered things that no one ever imagined."[40] Like many populists, Moon uses a biblical sense of calling to counteract a relative lack of secular credentials. In 1983 he commented, "This kind of knowledge is not rivaled by anything at Harvard University. No library contains fragments of this kind of knowledge. You have studied from Rev. Moon's 'heart library' and there is no other source like that."[41]

Moon's self-perception is reflected in other assertions. He asked rhetorically at one point, "What if I did not exist? It would be as if all the world were here but were empty."[42] Moon also brags, often somewhat crudely, that he is able to resist all sorts of sexual temptation. He claims that women have written him love letters in their own blood but that he has ignored them.[43] In 1979 he said, "If the most beautiful woman who thought she could seduce any man crept into my bedroom to tempt me, I would know how to make a Moonie out of her."[44]

In his own view, he is the most persecuted person in the world and yet he "fears nothing."[45] His comments about the president in 1986 are quite revealing: "If President Reagan came here trying to take the place of Rev. Moon, he could not lead the Unification Church for even one day, that's for sure. But if Father were to move to the White House, I could guide the country with no problem."[46]

Moon claims that he is good in all sports, "a handsome man" and "a dramatic person, tasty and irresistible."[47] In a 1990 message Moon even stated that God had finally learned the true meaning of love because of him. "God has to be educated. People will say that I am a heretic, but it is true. God doesn't know about love—he hasn't experienced it before. God has no sexual organs, so until a man becomes one with God, [God] cannot experience making love to a woman. Through me, God has done this."[48]

In 1976 he told his followers, "I really keep the FBI busy trying to keep track of me. After the Washington Monument rally their biggest question was what in the world I would do next. Even Satan is saying, 'What is Rev. Moon's next move? Where should I take my big guns?' But most important is that even God is asking, 'Where are you going next?' My plan is simple and clear; I am inexorably moving toward the absolute center of the universe."[49]

Moon's descriptions of his self-denial can take some crude and bizarre forms. In a 1989 sermon he told his followers, "Every time I sit on the toilet I fall asleep, but do you think God will ridicule me for that? No, God will be sympathetic and encourage me to rest a few minutes right there. Sometimes for enjoyment God treats me to a tour of spirit world during those moments, showing what he is going to give to me, and then sends me back to work."[50] In another message he stated, "When I stay at East Garden, I want to wear the same underwear, T-shirt and pants several days or more. Sometimes I don't change underwear for a whole week but Mother complains. I keep saying I can wear them another day. Sometimes things become soiled and I turn them inside out and wear them again. Do you think I do this because there is no washing machine at East Garden or because I have no extra clothes? No, I do it because I am thinking of you. When I take a bath at night, Mother very sweetly takes away all the soiled underwear and puts it in the laundry bin. Then, when she is looking at something else, I come out, take the underwear out of the bin, and wear them again! I do this because my mind is always on you."[51]

There is little indication that Moon exercises any restraint whatsoever in his speeches to his followers. Rather, it seems as if every observation he makes—no matter how coarse—serves as proof of his self-understanding and calling. He stated in one speech, "When I was young I thought that bodily waste should be an object of love. I looked down the toilet and saw the different bits of waste and touched them, thinking, 'This is my mother's, this is my brother's, and so on.' I thought, 'What if I died and never touched this?' The world is beginning now to realize Father's value."[52]

Most Unificationists accept everything their leader teaches, while only a few acknowledge his crude language and egocentric statements.[53] Most outsiders who have attended Unification-sponsored conferences or joined Moon in social and political projects have never heard such comments or paid serious attention to their significance. Likewise, most academics who study Moon ignore the off-the-wall sermon material that raises questions about Moon's integrity and the consistency between his private teachings and public ecumenical vision.

People who do hear about Moon's more eccentric statements often reply that they are taken out of context. It is true that comments to his followers need to be considered alongside Moon's public speeches. However, it cannot be denied that Moon's sermons repeatedly and consistently show evidence of narcissism and grandiosity. If anything, later sermons show less restraint and greater indication of his self-idolization.[54]

APPEAL OF THE UNIFICATION CHURCH

At the height of what Bromley and Shupe call "the great American cult scare" of the 1970s, many people attributed the appeal of Sun Myung Moon and his church to brainwashing.[55] And there are still many who believe that certain religious "cults" recruit members by programming their brains.[56] But Eileen Barker shows in her study *The Making of a*

Moonie that there is nothing to suggest brainwashing as a plausible theory for why people join the Unification Church or stay in it.[57]

Better explanations lie in the more mundane realities of religious and social life. First, other religious movements in Korea were teaching in the 1960s that the Messiah would come from Korea, and some of Moon's original followers would have come out of these organizations. Other early members would have been attracted to Moon as a dynamic and dedicated Korean prophet willing to endure persecution and jail for his beliefs. In addition, many current members have been raised in the Unification Church and were instructed from an early age that Moon is the Lord of the Second Advent. It's as natural for them to believe in him as for someone raised in a Southern Baptist home to trust in Jesus as Savior.

Converts to the Unification Church are often introduced to Moon through an extensive and somewhat mind-numbing series of lectures about the Divine Principle. This exercise usually leaves a deep impression that the Unification Church message is rooted in a pervasive understanding of Christianity. Moreover, the convert often comes away with a strong sense that the mission of Sun Myung Moon closely parallels that of Jesus Christ.

The Unification Church excels at public relations and image, and as a result it attracts new converts and reinforces the loyalty of current followers. Members have welcomed many of the world's leading academics to Unification-sponsored events. Moon continually attracts distinguished politicians, clergy and media figures to his public forums, including Jerry Falwell and former President George H. W. Bush. Former Polish leader Lech Walesa attended the Unification-sponsored World Summit on Leadership and Governance in Seoul in February 2003.[58]

Moon has also gained credibility through his many educational, media, political and religious organizations. He drew significant attention when he founded *The Washington Times* in 1982 as he was facing income tax charges by the United States government. He also owns the *Segye*

Times (Korea) and the *Middle East Times* (Cairo) and has taken over United Press International (UPI). He is the founder of the International Conference on the Unity of the Sciences, the Professors World Peace Academy, the Summit Council for World Peace and the World Media Conference, among other enterprises.

He also started the Sun Moon University in Korea and runs Bridgeport University in Connecticut. He has initiated the International Highway Project, attempting to unite China, Korea and Japan, and is credited with founding several ballet and dance schools, most notably the "Little Angels" program. He is also involved in the World Culture and Sports Festival and created the Women's Federation for Peace in Asia.

It would be a mistake to dismiss all of these organizations as Moon's "front groups."[59] His involvement in them is so visible and his financial backing so significant that they should be viewed instead as part of a genuine attempt to address all aspects of life in terms of a Unification worldview. Unificationists receive strong affirmation for their faith from Moon's wide-ranging vision and from the incredible endorsements of leaders who participate in his multifaceted projects and conferences.

The 176-page volume *The Hope of All Ages* illustrates the apologetic power of Moon's projects. Released on the occasion of his eighty-second birthday, the book contains elaborate commendations of Moon from political, academic and religious leaders, including Timothy Boyd, vice president of the Theosophical Society of America, Cromwell Crawford of the University of Hawaii, and Khamba Lama Choijiljav Dambajav, vice president of the World Fellowship of Buddhists. Moon also receives tributes from E. V. Hill of Mt. Zion Baptist Church, Kessai Note, president of the Marshall Islands, Dan Quayle, former vice president of the United States, and Dae Wood, Korean Buddhist priest and poet, among many others. Several of these writers argue that Sun Myung Moon should be nominated for the Nobel Peace Prize. Much of the praise is directed toward Moon's vision as expressed in the conferences, organizations, newspapers and educational institutions that he finances.[60]

Of course, the most direct appeal of the Unification Church lies in the power of a utopian vision fostered by a dedicated and committed following. The movement's public message is one of radical love for God, professed allegiance to Jesus Christ, openness to all religions and deep commitment to solving the world's problems. In spite of his egocentrism and his anti-Christian teachings, Moon has inspired a generation of highly moral and loving disciples. Moon's followers are his best advertisement as they work tirelessly to obey their messiah's call to love and to serve.

LATTER-DAY SAINTS

Robert M. Bowman Jr.

The Church of Jesus Christ of Latter-day Saints is as American as apple pie. Its members, commonly called Mormons, include the Osmond family, Gladys Knight (who converted in 1997), golfer Johnny Miller, author Stephen Covey and Senator Orrin Hatch.[1] Ezra Taft Benson, Eisenhower's secretary of agriculture, went on to become the president of the LDS Church from 1985 to 1994.

Some of the institutions closely associated with the Latter-day Saints are also ingrained into American culture. The Mormon Tabernacle Choir is probably the best-known choir in the United States, perhaps even the world. In February 2002, they performed in the opening ceremonies of the 2002 Winter Olympics, hosted in Salt Lake City where the church is headquartered. Brigham Young University, a respected academic institution, has highly ranked schools of law and business. And speaking of business, Mormons are very much part of the American economy. In 1999 Mormons held the top executive positions in many major U.S. businesses, including Marriott, Albertsons, Black & Decker, Times Mirror, Madison Square Garden, Iomega and Hollywood Video.

The cultural success of Mormons in America is part of the story of the church's impressive numerical growth. Founded in 1830 with six original members, the LDS Church took nearly 120 years to reach a million members worldwide. Since 1950 it has been doubling in size every fifteen years, exceeding eleven million members in the year 2000. There are now more Mormons in America than Presbyterians or Episcopalians. And toward the end of the century the Mormon population outside the United States began to exceed the U.S. Mormon population.

The growth of Mormonism may be explained by a variety of factors, but two stand out. The first is its missionary program. Most Mormon men, after graduating from high school, take two years away from any other plans to work full-time (at family expense) as missionaries. For several years now this missionary force of about sixty thousand young men has been converting roughly three hundred thousand people a year to the LDS Church. This hard work accounts for the bulk of the church's growth during the last thirty or forty years.

A second factor is the value the church places on families. Most religious bodies express esteem for the family, but in Mormonism "family values" are the core of the religion, dominating its rituals and theology. The LDS Church vigorously encourages its members to marry and have children—large families are quite common—so that the birth rate among Mormons is higher than that in America generally. The emphasis on family life is also without a doubt the number one element of the appeal of the missionaries' message. This emphasis is not mere talk: the church's programs and rituals cultivate family life in concrete and, at least in some respects, positive ways.

Whatever one may wish to say about the Mormons' religious beliefs and rituals, it is clear that the Latter-day Saints are not on the sociological fringe of society. Mormons are very much part of the cultural mainstream in America—and if they continue to grow as they have been, by the middle of the twenty-first century they may be the mainstream in many places even outside Utah.

JOSEPH SMITH

The Mormon Church has not always played such a comfortable role in American culture. Its story begins with Joseph Smith Jr. (1805-1844), who founded the Church of Latter-day Saints in either Fayette or Manchester, New York, on April 6, 1830.[2] About two weeks earlier, Smith had begun selling copies of the Book of Mormon, which years later he would call "the keystone of our religion."[3] We will have more to say about the Book of Mormon later.

Smith did not see himself as starting a new denomination, nor was he trying to start a movement that transcended denominational lines. Rather, Smith claimed to be the prophet of the one and only true, restored church. Before founding the church, Smith had already issued several messages as revelations from the Lord, most but not all of them pertaining to the work of translating the Book of Mormon. These and later revelations are collected in a book called Doctrine and Covenants (commonly abbreviated as D&C), which Mormons also view as scripture.

The most startling and controversial revelation Smith ever published concerned an experience he claimed to have had in the spring of 1820. According to the official account, written about 1838 and first published in 1842, the teenager Joseph, confused by the competing claims of different denominations during a revival, went into the woods to ask God which church to join. He was answered with a vision of God the Father and Jesus Christ. The account—part of the Mormon scripture known as Pearl of Great Price—reports that Jesus told Smith to join none of the churches.

In the earliest known, handwritten version of the story, dated to 1832, Smith reported that he went into the woods seeking forgiveness of sins because he had *already concluded* that all churches were wrong. He was answered with a vision of the Lord assuring him of his salvation. The major contradictions between these two accounts (both originating with Smith himself), the historical evidence that no revival took place in that region during the period in question and the fact that no one seems to have heard an account of this "First Vision" story before 1832, all give skeptics solid grounds for questioning whether Smith ever had such an experience.[4]

Almost immediately after founding the new church, Smith began leading his followers westward, first to Kirtland, Ohio, where the first Mormon temple was built, and later to Far West, Missouri. Under his leadership there the Mormons began expanding into other counties. Tensions rose, skirmishes of violence erupted between Mormons and non-Mormons, and the governor ordered the Mormons driven out or exterminated. Smith and other Mormon leaders were jailed and charged with murder, treason and other crimes. Most Mormons fled and settled in Commerce, Illinois, which they quickly dominated and renamed Nauvoo (which Smith said was Hebrew for "Beautiful Place").

In 1839 Smith escaped his imprisonment and joined the Mormon settlers in Nauvoo. He formed a militia with himself as general and in 1844 announced his candidacy for the presidency of the United States. Meanwhile he had secretly begun practicing polygamy, marrying at least thirty and perhaps more than forty women—many of whom remained married to other men—between 1841 and 1843. During this same period Smith produced new scriptures and began teaching that many gods existed and that the Mormons could themselves become gods. These and other actions on Smith's part stirred more and more dissent and brought the movement to its most serious crisis. On June 10, 1844, Smith had a dissident newspaper, the *Nauvoo Expositor*, destroyed. The legality of this action and some of Smith's other decisions was a matter of strenuous debate at the time and remains so today. In any case, on June 25 he was arrested in Carthage, Illinois, and on June 27 a mob stormed the jail. Joseph and his brother Hyrum were killed. Although they died in a gun battle with Joseph managing to wound one of the attackers, Mormons regard the two men as martyrs.

FROM BRIGHAM YOUNG TO THE PRESENT

A small contingent of the Latter-day Saints, including Smith's first (and only legal) wife Emma, remained in the Midwest after Smith's death and accepted his son, Joseph Smith III, as his successor and the new prophet. The church thus formed was organized in 1860 as the Reorganized Church of Jesus Christ of Latter-day Saints. Since 1920 this branch of the church has been headquartered in Independence, Missouri, and has increasingly distanced itself from the Latter-day Saints tradition. In 2001 it adopted the name Community of Christ.

The larger body of Mormons declared Smith's right-hand man, Brigham Young, who was also head of the church's "twelve apostles," as the new president of the church. In 1846 most of the group literally followed Young in a famous trek west, arriving in 1847 at the Salt Lake Valley in Utah, where the Mormon pioneers built Salt Lake City. Brigham Young became governor when the territory of Utah was formed in 1850, which gave him a firm grip on political as well as religious power. His defiance of the federal government led to violence against many non-Mormons, or "gentiles," as the church called them. The most notorious event of this type was the Mountain Meadows massacre in 1857, when a wagon train of people headed for California was murdered.[5]

Meanwhile, in 1852 Young publicly announced the church's adherence to the practice of polygamy. The official basis for this practice was a revelation that Joseph Smith had issued privately in 1843 to suppress criticism of his polygamous unions. Young himself had fifty-five wives, and under his leadership polygamy became more and more prevalent throughout Utah. In 1876 Smith's revelation concerning polygamy was added to the LDS scriptures in Doctrine and Covenants (chapter 132).

When Young died the following year, a legal battle was heating up over polygamy that would radically change Mormonism. For a while many leaders, including Young's successor John Taylor, went into hiding to avoid arrest. Even after Taylor's successor, Wilford Woodruff, issued a manifesto in 1890 advising Mormons not to contract plural marriages (a document included as an appendix to Doctrine and Covenants), polygamy continued among the Latter-day Saints, including its leaders, for decades. In 1904 the Mormon Church's sixth president, Joseph F. Smith, ruled that new polygamous unions would be punished by excommunication. It took another generation for the practice to disappear from the church—and then it simply continued in a dissident movement of "fundamentalist" Mormons. Thousands of people in Utah and the surrounding states continue to practice polygamy to this day.

Meanwhile, in gradually abandoning polygamy the Mormon Church became increasingly integrated into American culture. Its growth in such countries as Brazil and the pressures of the civil rights movement of the 1960s eventually led to another change. The church, which teaches that all human beings are spirits in heaven before coming to earth, for most of its history also taught that black skin was a curse on people whose lives as spirits had been less honorable. On that basis the church did not allow blacks to hold its priesthood, an honor that all worthy Mormon males must take to be full-fledged members of the church. In 1978 president Spencer W. Kimball announced the lifting of this ban.

During the next quarter-century the church's membership tripled from four million to about twelve million worldwide, with particularly impressive growth in Africa. Mormonism's international appeal was on display in 2002 when Salt Lake City hosted the Winter Olympic Games. The Mormon Church has successfully transformed itself from a lawless, marginal sect to a culturally mainstream international religion.

THE BOOK OF MORMON

The main story line of the Book of Mormon tells of an Israelite family that migrated from Jerusalem shortly before the Babylonian Exile (about 600 B.C.) to a land somewhere in the Americas. It also tells of the history of two warring peoples, the Nephites and the Lamanites, who were descended from that family. The most famous part of this story is an account of Jesus Christ appearing after his resurrection to preach to the Nephites. Some four hundred years later, a prophet named Mormon is said to have produced an abridged edition of all of the Nephite scriptures on metal plates and to have given them to his son Moroni, who added a short book bearing his name and then buried the plates in a metal box on the hill Cumorah, in what is now upstate New York, about A.D. 421. There the plates remained until Moroni, after becoming a glorified being, showed them to Joseph Smith in 1823 and in 1827 allowed him to remove them. Smith then translated the plates from their "reformed Egyptian" into English by a supernatural gift from God and had them published in 1830. According to Smith, after he had completed his translation, the metal plates were taken by Moroni into heaven.

Because the plates are said to be in heaven, any Christian inquiring into the authenticity of the Book of Mormon faces certain difficulties. On the one hand, there is no evidence for the Book of Mormon; on the other hand, there is no simple way of disproving its claims. We have no copies of any portion of the text in its supposed original language. Indeed, we don't even know what that language was, other than the text's claim that it was a form of Egyptian altered by the Israelites who populate the book. We have no independent confirmation that the individuals and nations described in the Book of Mormon ever lived in the Americas. Moreover, it isn't even clear that the Book of Mormon refers to real geographical locations in the Western Hemisphere. Most Mormon scholars today believe that the lands described in the Book of Mormon correlate with a region of Central America consisting of southern Mexico and Guatemala, but this theory has some significant difficulties and no proof. Again, though, it's difficult to prove the negative claim that the Book of Mormon is not referring to real people and places.

For some time now, a significant body of scholarship defending the authenticity of the Book of Mormon has been growing. The contemporary era of this apologetic scholarship dates from 1979, when Mormon scholars established the Foundation for Ancient Research and Mormon Studies (FARMS). For a long time most evangelical critics of Mormonism gave this scholarship little attention, but toward the end of the 1990s their attitude began to change.[6]

The most glaring problem for defenders of the Book of Mormon is its apparent dependence on other sources, most obviously the King James Version of the Bible. A whopping sixteen out of fifty-five chapters in the first two books of the Book of Mormon (1 Nephi 20—21; 2 Nephi 12—24; 27) are acknowledged duplications of twenty chapters from Isaiah (Isaiah 48—52; 2—14; 29; 53). In the remainder of the Book of Mormon a full seven chapters are repeated from the Bible (Mosiah 14 = Isaiah 53; 3 Nephi 12—14 = Matthew 5—7; 3 Nephi 22 = Isaiah 54; 3 Nephi 24—25 = Malachi 3—4). In all, more than a tenth of the chapters in the Book of Mormon are repetitions of chapters in the Bible.

Of these duplicated chapters, the most difficult to explain satisfactorily are the chapters that repeat the Sermon on the Mount. It is highly improbable on a number of levels that Jesus would deliver virtually the exact same sermon to the Nephites as he had to the Jews. For one thing, Jesus was criticizing the Pharisees, a religious group that originated in Palestine some four centuries after the Nephites supposedly left Palestine. It looks as if Jesus may have pulled out some old sermon notes when he arrived in the land of the Nephites because he forgot to prepare a new message!

When all is said and done, Latter-day Saints' confidence in the authenticity and inspiration of the Book of Mormon is grounded in their "testimony," a spiritual experience in which they believe the Holy Spirit assures them that it is the word of God. The last chapter of the Book of Mormon instructs its readers to "ask God, the Eternal Father, in the name of Christ, if these things are not true; and if ye shall ask with a sincere heart, with real intent, having faith in Christ, he will manifest the truth of it unto you, by the power of the Holy Ghost" (Moroni 10:4). Mormons routinely cite this passage and urge prospective converts to read the Book of Mormon and ask God if it is true. They "bear their testimony" to having done so themselves and claim to be convinced that the Book of Mormon is true.

There are some serious problems with this approach. First of all, some people have read the Book of Mormon and have asked God to show them whether it is true or not. Instead of receiving a testimony of its truth, they have become convinced that it is false. All a Mormon can really say to such people is that they must not have prayed "with a sincere heart" or "real intent." But such a judgment can be made only on the assumption that the Book of Mormon is true—that is, only by assuming the very thing in question.

Second, the Moroni 10:4 prescription is not supported by the Bible and in fact contradicts it. Sometimes Mormons cite James 1:5 in support, but James is directing believers to ask God for wisdom to overcome temptation (Jas 1:2-18), not to reveal to them whether he inspired a particular book. The Bible tells us to apply objective tests to alleged revelations (Deut 13:1-5; Mt 7:15-23; 1 Jn 4:1-6), not to seek a purely subjective confirmation of a written revelation.

MORMON DOCTRINE

The exposition of Mormon doctrine I will present here is based on the LDS manual called *Gospel Principles*. This manual, which is not attributed to any author, is published by the church's curriculum department for use in teaching doctrine to Latter-day Saints throughout the world. It has been used continuously since 1978 and is currently in its eighth edition. Although it is not regarded as inspired scripture, *Gospel Principles* may fairly be considered a reliable source for defining the official doctrine of the LDS Church.

God the Father. According to Mormonism, "God is the one supreme and absolute being in whom we believe and whom we worship. . . . He has all power. He knows all things" (9).[7] However, this was not always so. As Joseph Smith once said, God "was once a man like us. . . . God himself, the Father of us all, dwelt on an earth, the same as Jesus Christ himself did" (305).[8] Through a process of exaltation, "our Heavenly Father became God" (305). Even now, "God has a body that looks like ours . . . a tangible body of flesh and bones (see D&C 130:22)," though it is different in that it "is perfected and glorified" (9).

The heavenly family. All human beings who will ever live on earth were first "spiritual children of our heavenly parents" before coming here to live as physical beings (11). The term "heavenly parents" refers to the Latter-day Saints' belief that humans were procreated in heaven as spirits by a heavenly Father and also a heavenly Mother. Their heavenly offspring included their firstborn spirit child, Jesus Christ (11), all of the spirits who would go on to live as humans on earth (11), and Lucifer (Satan), along with the spirits who followed him in rebellion against Heavenly Father's plan. These rebellious spirits will never receive mortal bodies (18-19). Angels are spirits that did not rebel but have not yet received a mortal body. Adam, for example, was Michael the Archangel before becoming the first man (31).

Jesus Christ. The LDS Church teaches that Jesus lived a perfect, sinless life, performed miracles, died on the cross, and rose physically from the grave (64-68, 73). On these points Mormon beliefs agree with the Bible. It is what the church teaches about Jesus' divine identity and his relationship to the Father that is strikingly different from the biblical view.

As has already been mentioned, Mormons believe that Jesus was the first spirit child born to our heavenly parents and is the literal spirit brother of all humans and angels. Before his human life, he was "known as Jehovah in the premortal existence" (60, 17). Jesus "created this world and everything in it" as well as "many other worlds" through "the power of the priesthood, under the direction of our Heavenly Father" (27).

"Heavenly Father, Jesus Christ, and the Holy Ghost are called the Godhead. They are unified in purpose" (37). Jesus Christ, however, though a member of the Godhead, is not properly the object of our prayers, which must always be addressed to the Father (41). In order to bring about God's purpose for his spirit children, Jesus became a human being with a unique parentage. "Jesus is the only person on earth to be born of a mortal mother and an immortal father. That is why he is called the Only Begotten Son" (64). That is, God the Father, the literal father of all human spirits, including Jesus, was "the literal father of Jesus Christ" in the flesh (64).

Human sin and Christ's atonement. Our heavenly parents "wanted us to develop the godlike qualities that they have," but they knew that for this to happen "we needed to leave our celestial home to be tested and to gain experience" in choosing good over evil (13). In a "Grand Council" in heaven, the Father revealed his plan for this test away from home. We would be given physical bodies on this planet, have our memories of heaven removed so that we would have to choose good over evil freely, experience weakness and death, and in the Resurrection "receive immortal bodies like those of our heavenly parents" (14).

In order to die, though, we would have to become mortal, and in order for that to happen, we would have to become sinners. Furthermore, had our first human parents not fallen, they would not have been able to procreate physical bodies for our preexistent spirits to inhabit. Thus, in what was actually a noble act, Adam and Eve transgressed God's commandment in the Garden in order to set in motion the Father's plan. As the Mormon scripture called the Book of Moses (5:11) puts it, "Adam fell, that men might be" (32-34).

As a result of this noble fall, mankind universally became subject to both physical death (separation of spirit from body) and spiritual death (separation from God). In order for us to live forever back in heaven with our heavenly parents, both kinds of death needed to be overcome. In

God's plan this need was met through Christ's atonement, which he accomplished "by suffering in Gethsemane and by giving his life on the
cross" (73). As a result, all human beings will be resurrected to immortality and thus freed from physical death regardless of their faith or conduct (74). "Although all people will be resurrected with a body of flesh
and bone, only those who accept the Atonement will be saved from spiritual death" (74-75). To do so, we place our faith in Christ, "repent of
our sins, are baptized, receive the Holy Ghost, and obey his commandments" (75). Only people who do these things "may return to live with
our Heavenly Father" (78).

   The church. From what has been said so far, it might seem that Mormons believe all Christians, whether Latter-day Saints or not, will be
saved from spiritual death. This is not the case. In order to be "baptized,
receive the Holy Ghost, and obey his commandments," one must be a
member of the Church of Jesus Christ of Latter-day Saints. Only Mormon men can hold "the priesthood," which is required to administer
baptism and to lay hands on others to receive the Holy Ghost (81, 83,
104, 138). The authority to do these things was lost in the Great Apostasy, "the period of time when the true Church no longer existed on
earth" (105), and that period came to an end with the restoration of the
priesthood in 1829 and the establishment of the LDS Church in 1830
(111). In order to repent, then, one must accept the Mormon Church:
"We are not repentant if we do not sustain the authorities of the Church"
(125). The commandments include such matters as paying tithes to the
church, keeping the church's health rules (called the Word of Wisdom),
and participating in certain rituals in the Mormon temples, of which two
rituals deserve special mention.

   The first ritual is eternal marriage, a ceremony in which a man and
a woman are "sealed" to be husband and wife when they return to the
Father's celestial heaven. "The temple is the only place this holy ordi-
nance can be performed. . . . If we are married by any authority other

than by the priesthood in a temple, the marriage is for this life only"
(242, 243).

The second temple ritual of note is baptism for the dead. Most people
throughout history have had no chance to be baptized or sealed in an
eternal marriage. To solve this problem, Mormons undergo these ceremonies by proxy for their departed ancestors who never heard the LDS
gospel (256-57). In the spirit world, these ancestors have the gospel
taught to them and, if they accept it, "are waiting for the temple ordinances to be performed for them" (257).

Death, resurrection and exaltation to godhood. After human beings
die, they go to the spirit world, where they are either admitted to paradise with the righteous who have accepted the LDS gospel or assigned
to the spirit prison with the wicked and those who have not yet accepted
that gospel. Those in spirit prison who never heard the LDS gospel during their mortal lifetimes can accept it there and, after living Mormons
have performed the temple ceremonies for them, go to live in paradise
(291-92).

At the final judgment spirits "will be sent to one of four places" (297).
The highest, *celestial kingdom* will be inhabited by those who accepted
the LDS gospel, either in this mortal life or in the spirit world if they
heard it there for the first time. "All who inherit the celestial kingdom
will live with Heavenly Father and Jesus Christ forever" (297). The *terrestrial kingdom* is for those decent people who heard and rejected the
Mormon gospel in their mortal life but accepted it in the spirit world, as
well as for those Latter-day Saints who "were not valiant," meaning that
they did not follow the church's teachings and requirements faithfully
(297). "They will be visited by Jesus Christ but not by our Heavenly Father" (298). The *telestial kingdom* will be the home of the "numerous"
people who reject the LDS gospel both as mortals and in the spirit world.
"They will be visited by the Holy Ghost but not by the Father or the Son"
(298). The *outer darkness* will be inhabited by Satan and his angels and

by people who were members of the Mormon Church with spiritual "testimonies" of its truth but who nevertheless ended up abandoning the church or recanting their profession. In other words, ex-Mormons are the one group of humans with the prospect of suffering eternal punishment (298).

Where our heavenly parents and Jesus Christ live, "there are three heavens or degrees within the celestial kingdom" (301). Only those who "prove faithful to the Lord . . . will live in the highest degree of the celestial kingdom of heaven" (302). In addition to undergoing all of the temple rituals mentioned earlier, and beyond such generic expectations as living honest, chaste and loving lives, those who wish to attain this highest degree must attend meetings regularly, study the Mormon scriptures and obey the church's prophets (303-4). Those who endure to the end in these things will "become exalted, just like our Heavenly Father." This exaltation involves becoming perfect, possessing all knowledge and wisdom, and becoming a creator (302). "They will become gods . . . and will be able to have spirit children also. These spirit children will have the same relationship to them as we do to our Heavenly Father" (302). "This is the way our Heavenly Father became God. . . . He wants us to succeed even as he did" (304).

A BIBLICAL RESPONSE

Mormons do not accept the evangelical approach of basing all church doctrine on the Bible alone. However, they appeal heavily to the Bible, along with their uniquely LDS scriptures and modern revelation, to support many of their distinctive beliefs. For that reason, it is both helpful and important to contrast the teachings of Mormonism with those of the Bible.

God is not an exalted man. The linchpin of LDS theology is its view of the divine. Mormons believe that God was a man who attained exaltation to godhood and whose spirit offspring can potentially become gods with similar powers and glory. They can even become the creators and gods of their own offspring, starting the cycle all over again, ad infinitum. In sharp contrast to this view, the Bible speaks of the Lord, the God of Israel, as the only God for all ages: "Before me there was no God formed, and there will be none after me" (Is 43:10).

According to the Bible, the Lord did not become God by a process of exaltation but has always been God (Ps 90:2; Is 43:13; Rom 16:25-26; 1 Tim 1:17). He is by nature not flesh but transcendent spirit, not limited to any location (Is 31:3; Jn 4:20-24). The universe cannot contain God (1 Kings 8:27; Is 66:1; Acts 7:48-49). At the same time, God is present everywhere (Ps 139:7-10; Acts 17:28) and fills all things (Jer 23:23-24). Whenever the Bible does describe God in physical language, it is clear that the language is figurative. For example, the Bible says that heaven is God's throne and the earth his footstool (Is 66:1; Mt 5:34-35; Acts 7:49), but no one (I hope) thinks that God is literally tens of thousands of miles tall. Joseph Smith wouldn't have been able to see more than his big toe!

In defending their belief that Heavenly Father was originally a man, Mormons often point out that Jesus was a man, and this didn't prevent him from having divine characteristics. But this comparison overlooks a crucial difference. In Mormonism, the Father was a man who became God. In the Bible, the Son, Jesus Christ, was God and yet became a man (Jn 1:1, 14; Phil 2:6-7). Orthodox Christians do not object to the idea of God having a physical body as an abstract possibility removed from context. They object to the idea of God as a physical being who became exalted to Godhood.

God has no heavenly wife and kids. The Bible, of course, does not speak of a Heavenly Mother. (For that matter, neither do any of the LDS scriptures.) And the idea that human beings preexisted in heaven as God's spirit children is clearly unbiblical. First, not all human beings are God's children (Jn 8:44). Christians are called "sons of God," but this sonship is an adoptive status granted only to believers in Christ through the new birth effected by the Spirit (Jn 1:12-13; Rom 8:14-17; Gal 3:26—4:7; 1 Jn 3:1-2; 5:1-2). Jesus became our "brother" and "the firstborn among many brethren" by becoming a man and redeeming us to become adopted, Spirit-indwelled children of God (Rom 8:29; Heb 2:10-13).

Second, according to the New Testament, Jesus Christ is the only human being who preexisted in heaven. Christ came down from heaven (Jn 13:3; 16:28) and thus originates "from above," unlike John the Baptist, who originated from the earth (Jn 3:31). This earthly origin is true of all human beings besides Christ, including Adam (1 Cor 15:47).

According to the Bible, God created (not procreated) the angels just as he did the physical universe (Ps 148:2-6). All spiritual, heavenly creatures were created through and for the Son (Col 1:16). Thus, Jesus is not the elder brother of the heavenly spirits but their Creator.

Jesus is God. The Bible emphatically teaches that Jehovah ("the LORD" in most English Bibles) is God—indeed, that he is the only God (Gen 2:4; Ex 3:15; Deut 4:35, 39; 1 Kings 18:36-39; Ps 100:3; Is 44:6) and the one to whom prayer is properly addressed (Deut 9:26; 1 Kings 8:22-30; Ps 5:1-3; Dan 9:4; Jon 2:1). Mormons, who correctly identify Jesus as Jehovah, are therefore in error in teaching that Jesus is not the God to whom we should pray. The Bible clearly identifies Jesus Christ as God (Is 9:6; Jn 1:1; 20:28; Tit 2:13; Heb 1:8; 2 Pet 1:1) and indicates that he may properly be addressed in prayer (Jn 14:14; Acts 1:24-25; 7:59-60; Rom 10:12-13; 1 Cor 1:2; 2 Cor 12:8-10; 2 Thess 2:16-17).

It will come as no surprise that Mormons reject the doctrine of the Trinity taught in the creeds of the early church and accepted by the vast majority of denominations calling themselves Christians. Admittedly, the Bible offers no formal, systematized doctrine of the Trinity. However, the trinitarian doctrine is the only systematic position that accurately upholds the Bible's teaching that the Father is the Lord God (Mt 11:25; Jn 17:3), the Son is the Lord God (Jn 20:28; Rom 10:9-13; Phil 2:9-11; Heb 1:8-12), and the Holy Spirit is the Lord God (Acts 5:3-4; 2 Cor 3:17-18), and yet there is only one Lord, one God (Deut 4:35; 2 Sam 22:32; Is 43:10; 44:6-8; Jn 5:44; Rom 3:30; 1 Cor 8:4-6; 1 Tim 2:5; Jas 2:19).

God the Father was not Jesus' literal father. The Latter-day Saints teach that Jesus Christ is the "Only Begotten Son" because God the Father is his literal father in the flesh. However, the term "only begotten" (Greek *monogenēs,* an only or unique child) in the Bible refers to Christ before he became a man. For example, it speaks of God sending the *monogenēs* Son into the world, and of him becoming "manifested" when he came into the world in the flesh (Jn 1:14, 18; 3:16-17; 1 Jn 3:8; 4:9). These statements cohere with the point made earlier about Jesus being the only human who preexisted in heaven as God's Son and then came down to live on earth (Jn 3:31; 13:3; 16:28; 1 Cor 15:47).

Adam and Eve did a bad thing. Mormon doctrine regards mankind's fall into mortality as a necessary step downward in order to reach the platform from which they could ascend to deity. Such an idea is foreign to the Bible, which never has anything positive to say about Adam and Eve's actions—in fact, it plainly says they sinned (Rom 5:12, 14). The Fall did not, as Mormonism teaches, make it possible for people to have children. Rather, it made childbearing more painful for women than it would otherwise have been, implying that childbearing would have occurred, and been less painful, had they never sinned (Gen 3:16).

Christ's atonement saves only Christ's followers. Mormons are correct in believing that both the righteous and the wicked will be resurrected at the final judgment. However, the wicked will be resurrected in order to face the Lord "whole" before being consigned body and soul to everlasting punishment (Dan 12:2; Mt 10:28; Jn 5:28-29; Acts 24:15). They derive no benefit from Christ's atoning death. Only the righteous "in Christ"—those who belong to Christ—will be made alive and given immortality (1 Cor 15:22-23, 53-54).

The church consists of all Christ's true followers. The LDS claim that the church ceased to exist in a "Great Apostasy" lasting perhaps seventeen centuries cannot be sustained biblically. The Bible does speak of a falling away, or apostasy (Mt 24:10-11, 23-24; 1 Tim 4:1; 2 Thess 2:3). However, none of these texts speak of a complete or total apostasy; most of them explicitly say that some or even many will fall away—but not all. On the contrary, the Bible makes it clear that the church will continue to exist on earth until Christ's return (Mt 16:18; 28:20; Eph 5:25-27; Jude 3). The church's existence is based not on the authority of an institutional priesthood held by men on earth but on the authority of Christ's supreme ministry as high priest in heaven (Heb 1:3; 4:14; 6:19-20; 7:23—8:6). Rather than stating that the church will be taken over by apostates, the New Testament indicates that apostates will arise within the church but then leave it (Acts 20:29-30; 1 Jn 2:19).

There will be two kingdoms in eternity, not four. The Bible does speak of differing degrees of punishment (Lk 12:47-48) but not of three levels of eternal life or of three spiritual heavens. In 1 Corinthians 15:40, the "celestial bodies" are the bodies in the physical heavens—the sun, moon and stars (v. 41)—while the "terrestrial bodies" are the bodies on the earth, namely, those of humans and animals (v. 39). These verses are giving an analogy to illustrate the difference between the mortal, weak, humble body we have now and the immortal, powerful, glorious body believers will have in the resurrection (vv. 42-54).

The Bible repeatedly divides the resurrected into those condemned to eternal punishment and those welcomed to eternal life. The default standing of all human beings other than Christ is membership in Satan's domain of darkness; the only alternative is to be delivered from that doom into the kingdom of God ruled by his Son (Acts 26:18; Col 1:13). All human beings stand already condemned and under God's wrath unless they believe in Jesus Christ (Jn 3:16-18; Rom 3:9-26; 5:1-11).

We cannot become gods. We have already looked at the Lord's emphatic statement that there will be no gods formed after him (Is 43:10). Even he does not know of any gods beside himself (Is 44:8). The Mormon doctrine that human beings can become gods is predicated on the notion, which we have already critiqued biblically, that the Father was a man who became God. Christians do believe that in some respects we will become "like God." Through our union with Christ we will be made immortal and morally perfect (Mt 5:44-48; 1 Cor 15:49; Eph 4:24; Phil 3:21; Col 3:10; 2 Pet 1:4; 1 Jn 3:2-3). But the Bible does not teach that we can become all-knowing or all-powerful like God. Nor does it teach that we will become creators and procreate new heavenly families with ourselves as their gods. In the resurrection, the time for procreating new families will be over (Lk 19:34-36); we will instead be one family of God's adopted, perfected human children (Rom 8:23; Rev 21:3-7).

WITNESSING TO LATTER-DAY SAINTS

Perhaps the best point of entry for evangelizing Mormons is to talk about the conditions for living in the presence of God the Father forever. As we have seen, in LDS theology those conditions are extremely rigorous. In addition to living a morally exemplary life (a fine goal, but one that few people can claim to achieve), one must be baptized into the Church of Latter-day Saints, participate regularly in church meetings and temple work, and observe all of the church's rules governing sabbath observance, fasting, tithing and even diet. Most Mormons cannot honestly claim to have reached these goals and are probably unsure if they ever will. Our message to them is the good news that an eternal, blessed relationship with God the Father can be theirs as a free gift of his grace through the redeeming work of Jesus Christ. They need not, and should not, submit to all of these man-made ritual obligations, but should instead find their secured place in God's presence through Christ, who satisfied the Law's obligations on our behalf (Col 2:8—3:4).

ASTRAL RELIGION AND THE NEW AGE

Charles Strohmer

In the conference room of a pricey hotel in suburban Detroit, a retired Marine named Tom McKaye led thirty paying customers through a weekend seminar advertised simply as "Mind Development." Participants such as Kelly Maples, a head-turning, intelligent seventeen-year-old high school senior, and Art and Mary Tyler, a middle-aged blue collar couple from Saginaw, listened attentively as Tom gently guided them through meditative exercises he promised would open them to "untapped powers of the mind." During the Friday evening session Tom deftly addressed participants' worldview biases in order to prep them for the open-mindedness that would help them benefit from the spiritual potential of the seminar. During the Saturday morning talkback time, skeptics such as Randy the guitar player and Chuck the philosopher-astrologer voiced concerns. They got answers and talked them over during the lunch break. Randy decided it wasn't his cup of tea. He left me to finish the weekend without him. During the afternoon and evening sessions, my skepticism vanished and I believed.

Through many different visualization techniques, Tom and his assistants taught us how to contact the world of nonphysical entities, spirit beings who we were told lived as teachers and guides in an invisible belt surrounding the earth. We could learn how to contact these entities, request their esoteric wisdom and guidance, and apply the enlightenment to our own paths of spiritual evolution. The goal was to lead many others into this Aquarian spirituality and usher in a glorious new age of human potential.

It was 1971, years before people were talking openly about anything like this. Yet it seemed that weekend that some of us were being prepared to enter the mainstream as a vanguard of a new spirituality that would take the place of traditional religion. By Sunday afternoon we were asking excited questions about how to convince others about what we had learned. "Don't bother," came Tom's unexpected reply. "Best keep this to yourselves for now. Most people aren't ready for this. Just practice the meditations privately and get to know your guides, their names, their functions, their wisdom. The time will come when you can tell others, but for now the time is not right."[1]

CHANGING THE NOUNS OF THE GAME

That time came a decade later with the immediate popularity of Marilyn Ferguson's bible of "New Age" idealism. Ironically titled *The Aquarian Conspiracy*, it arrived in 1980 with great fanfare, preaching a new age of personal and social transformation. Within a couple of years the label "New Age movement" had become the shorthand for Aquarian spirituality, though most people didn't recognize those roots. Mainstream publishing houses, especially Bantam, created imprints to handle the flood of New Age titles pouring in. New Age magazines and radio programs sprang up.[2] The old bell-bottomed and tie-dyed Aquarians, now tidied up in suits and graduated from Ivy League schools, appeared in public discourse as "New Agers," although they usually pooh-poohed the label themselves.

In the mid- to late 1980s, Shirley MacLaine's books—well-thought-out autobiographies about her reluctant conversion to reincarnation, spirit guides and New Age thinking—sold in the multimillions. Sociologically the nation was turning a metaphysical corner. An American worldview that had for two centuries been dominated by Enlightenment rationalism and philosophical materialism was being spiritualized by the non-Christian religious philosophies of the New Age movement.[3]

American culture and the Christians within it were blindsided. Backstairs admonitions such as Tom's had been typical of the 1970s, and the public assumed that 1960s Aquarian spirituality had become passé. This profound mistake left both Christians and non-Christians unprepared for the New Age ideas and practices that burst on the scene in the early 1980s. The Aquarians hadn't disappeared, they had simply gone underground to rethink ways to garner mainstream acceptance of their religious beliefs and alternative practices. The key for more widespread accommodation was to change the nouns of the game: to present Aquarian ideals, practices and social goals in language that didn't carry the stigma of Eastern mystical, pagan and occult associations.

Generally unaware of the language revisioning, Christian response was initially stymied.[4] But a number of insightful and well-reasoned Christian books eventually were published in the 1980s, and these apologetics resources remain essential today.[5] The authors articulated New Age assumptions, beliefs and ideals even more systematically than New Agers did themselves. They explained the link between the New Age movement and 1960s Aquarianism, and they documented its historical-religious roots in Buddhism, Hinduism, Taoism, paganism, gnosticism, occultism, spiritism and so on. They explained the faith assumptions that New Agers could pick and choose from, such as reincarnation, karma and enlightenment, and the movement's leading practices, such as astrology, channeling, Wicca, yoga, psychic healing methods and occult visualization techniques. They also documented the slow but steady influence of New Age thought in science, the arts, family life, education, the business world and entertainment. Perhaps these authors' most notable contribution was to create the shorthand "pantheistic monism" (all is one, one is all, all is God) to highlight the disparity between fundamental New Age belief and Christian theism.

SECULAR ACCEPTANCE OF NEW AGE SPIRITUALITY

But history then repeated itself. Beginning in the early 1990s, both the secular and the Christian media decreasingly reported on "the New Age," and by the late 1990s, Christian books and seminars on the subject had dwindled considerably.[6] Today, the Christian community seems largely unaware of sophisticated New Age thinking, perhaps because as it increasingly adapts itself to American life, it becomes less recognizable. Some scholars, notably Wouter Hanegraff, speak of this trend as a "secularization" process.[7]

Generally, however, as in the 1970s, the Christian community seems either unaware of or uninterested in the ongoing expression and normalization of New Age thinking, which is following two parallel sociological tracks. One, a largely pragmatic and nonanalytical American public has become fascinated with the endless cascades of emotional, "New Agey" testimonials available on TV, in print and online. Two, with little public criticism from the Christian community, the secular media have shifted from a perspective of mild critique of New Age thought to one of cautious acceptance and then to wide-eyed optimism. This is new, and it is highly significant.

Television journalism in particular seems to have lost its ability to analyze New Age practices objectively. Producers air emotionally charged anecdotal programs under the tagline of "emerging science," adding a dash of soft criticism at most—a quick admonition about the placebo effect, a brief warning against unscrupulous practitioners, a reminder that alternative practices aren't meant to replace regular visits to the doctor. The positive tone of these pieces, however, far outweighs any quick cautions.

OPRAH AND GARY

Oprah Winfrey's once spirited advocacy of New Age writer and speaker Gary Zukav is typical of the widespread media acceptance of non-Christian religious beliefs. Zukav, who promotes a cosmopolitan spirituality, averaged one appearance a month on Oprah's show between the fall of 1998 and the summer of 2001. He originally gained notoriety with his 1979 book *The Dancing Wu Li Masters*. Like Fritjof Capra's more popular *Tao of Physics* (1976), *Dancing* explains subatomic particle physics from a point of view organized around Buddhist, Hindu and Taoist principles. Zukav's subsequent bestsellers *Seat of the Soul* (1989) and *Soul Stories* (2000), both glowingly touted on Oprah, contain elements of quasi science, pop psychology and New Age thought. Zukav weaves these principles into a kind of psychological-sociological East-West metaphysics of the soul.

Using deeply emotive language reminiscent of Ferguson's *Aquarian Conspiracy*, Zukav maintains that the human race is experiencing a world-shaking spiritual transformation, an evolution to a new age beyond power based on the five senses ("external power") to power based on perceptions of the soul ("authentic power"). In Zukav's worldview we are immortal souls first and physical beings second, and once we align our personalities to our souls we will evolve spiritually. His books contain "the outlines of a general New Age worldview, presented in a rather extreme ex cathedra mode: there are no notes, no arguments, just statement after statement. The whole book makes the impression of a channeled text."[8]

Soul Stories and *Seat of the Soul* explain Zukav's religious and social attitudes, which are in part codified in his concepts of multisensory perception, nonphysical beings and earth school. His impact on mainstream society is due largely to the fact that he keeps his television instruction simple, brief and anecdotal. That his religious philosophy runs counter to Christian theism is a topic left largely untouched in his books or on Oprah.

"Multisensory perception" (MSP) is Zukav's label for what traditionally has been called extrasensory perception, or ESP. "Taste, touch, smell, hearing, and sight," Zukav writes, "are different ways of sensing, but they are all part of a single system. That system is designed to detect one thing—the world as it appears to be outside of you. If you have only five senses by which to navigate, you are limited to this system."[9] MSP, he says, is a second system providing information that "allows us to see what is nonphysical as well as what is physical."[10] Zukav uses the word *intuition* synonymously with MSP and believes everyone is in the process of becoming multisensory.

In a chapter in *Soul Stories* titled "Nonphysical Beings," Zukav, who says he was once skeptical of channeling, gives his "reluctant convert" testimony (very similar to Shirley MacLaine's), describing how an entity named Ambrose became a trusted "friend and teacher" and led him to contact other spirit guides. "Becoming multisensory," Zukav writes, "allows you to become aware of nonphysical Teachers."[11] "Nonphysical teachers do not tell you what to do. They help you see your options. They help you think through choices. They help you understand what you are feeling, and why. They help you become more loving. They guide you to the fullest use of your life. . . . Nonphysical teachers . . . are Friends who share with you. Then you decide what to do."[12]

"Earth school" is Zukav's elementary presentation of classic karma and reincarnation theory. One's earth school is one's full-color, 3-D life today—merely an "episode" of many lives on the way to enlightenment. "The five-sensory personality is not aware of the many other incarnations of its soul."[13] Becoming multisensory and listening to nonphysical teachers helps one see his or her past lives.[14] Each earth school is a "physical arena" where the soul learns how to evolve.[15] Although Zukav may speak occasionally on television about overt spiritual themes, much of his religious philosophy was kept in deep background on Oprah's show and on her website, where people used to "chat with Gary" about addiction, temptation, forgiveness, judging others, falling in love and other perennial personal concerns.

Like many New Age views, Zukav's perspective on karma is self-contradictory. "Karma is not a moral dynamic," he writes. "Moral ability is a human creation. The Universe does not judge. The law of karma . . . serves humanity as an impersonal and universal teacher of responsibility."[16] Likewise, we should not judge either: "When we judge, we create negative karma."[17] If Zukav is correct, however, and there are no moral judgments, then we can never know if our decisions are right or wrong; we can never know whether we are accruing good or bad karma, whether we are evolving. We might be going backward.

In *Seat of the Soul*, for instance, Zukav illustrates that his followers should show compassion to a man sleeping in a gutter on a winter's day.[18] Fair enough. But if there is no moral judgment (no "bible") anywhere in the universe by which to determine what love and compassion are, then people cannot know if an action is compassionate, or selfish and greedy. Perhaps a person's act of compassion will be seen by the laws of karma as being motivated by selfish pride, a deed done merely to gain good karma. Would that action not then be more worthy of *bad* karma? Furthermore, by assisting the man in the gutter, the "helper" might prevent him from learning a life-lesson in his own earth school and hinder his own spiritual evolution. The man might have to return to the gutter or an equivalent setting in the future to learn the interrupted life-lesson. More bad karma for our rescuer. It's a lose-lose situation. One can never know which action will produce which karmic result.

These juridical problems extend to the very heart of the theory. For if karma is based on law, as Zukav claims, then karmic action and result must involve some kind of discriminating or judging function taking place somewhere in the universe. So it cannot be impersonal, as Zukav also contends. In short, without moral judgment there is no law. The theory of the law of karma ultimately outwits itself.

At its root, the philosophy of karma and reincarnation is a doctrine of self-salvation: the person who offends pays. This is incompatible with the Christian doctrine of divine saving grace, which acknowledges moral judgments and human offenses and which states that the person who offends cannot pay. Instead, God has paid the price of human sin in the death and resurrection (not reincarnation) of his son Jesus Christ, and God provides that payment substitutionally to those who believe in Jesus. In their private and social lives, believers read Scripture to know the good from the bad and learn how to live the good. Whenever they fail morally, they ask God to forgive them and to change in them what produced the failure. And when it is required, they ask others to forgive them. Their acts of mercy (helping others) and repentance (moral change) are not means by which they evolve spiritually. They are simply obediences along the path of following Jesus Christ, who did good for others. Christian theism removes the pressure of spiritual performance implicit in karma theory.

YOGA AND NEUROTHEOLOGY

Another indication of the sociological shift to less criticism and more acceptance of New Age philosophy is the language used by yoga instructors and the emerging discipline of neurotheology. At the time of the Beatles, who spent several weeks in India with the yogi Maharishi (the transcendental meditation guru), yoga was seen as a path to spiritual rebirth, and its Eastern religious connotations were no secret to its Western practitioners. These people understood full well that yoga positions, or postures, represented various spiritual stages of mystical, or even occult, enlightenment. It never occurred to anyone to explore yoga for physical reasons. One practiced yoga and meditated to be spiritually cleansed and enlightened.

Yoga has come a long way socially since the 1960s, when scientific studies chiefly focused on how yogis in deep meditation slowed their heart rates. During the 1980s, yoga language shifted to a vocabulary sans spirituality and the practice gained notoriety as a way to relax, reduce stress or simply work out. By the early 1990s, testimonials abounded from overworked executives bound to leather chairs and muscle-kinked business travelers cramped from airline seating and a different motel bed every night. These people took yoga classes for physical relief. Although leery of what colleagues might think, they enjoyed their one or two hours a week relaxing, stretching, bending, breathing deeply, balancing and posing. The much-needed physical ministrations became a luxury. Religious and spiritual considerations went out the window along with the stress, even though instructors often wandered among practitioners murmuring New Agey bromides and mantras straight from Buddha or the Maharishi.

By the mid-nineties, anecdotal "evidence" had piled up from quasi-scientific medical studies and word of mouth that yoga helped with weight loss, insomnia, addictions, acrophobia and asthma. Although people claimed symptomatic relief in such areas, no empirical double-blind tests confirmed that the mechanism for relief was yoga. Yet research has now broadened to discover whether yoga can help cure cancer, fend off heart attacks, improve the lymph system and rejuvenate postmenopausal women. In other words, is yoga more science than spirituality? In a major story for *Time*, Richard Corliss reported that although most Western doctors are not prescribing yoga carte blanche, an increasing number of mainstream hospitals offer yoga classes for people recovering from surgery or undergoing drug treatment.[19] Corliss suggests that the widespread scientific study of yoga, whether justified or not, accounts for the huge surge of interest today. Should any Eastern mystical connotations haunt the discussion, as they do in Corliss's article, they are not critiqued. Rather, commentators usually set up a simple polemic— Indian culture versus Western science, the mystical against the medical—and readers are left to sort the implications on their own.[20]

The increasing interest in physical yoga sits comfortably within recent studies of the mind-body connection, research that has evolved far beyond the brain wave investigations, left brain-right brain studies, and consciousness theorizing of the seventies and eighties. Researchers today are fascinated by people's transcendental experiences. How are the brain's neural networks involved? Is the brain receiving and interpreting something from a dimension outside time and space, or does it all begin and end with the brain?

Neurotheology is the study of the neurobiology of spirituality and religion (or "searching for the God within," as some only half-jokingly call it), and it uses brain imaging to help scientists identify the neural circuits that are active when, for instance, Buddhists meditate and nuns pray. In a *Newsweek* cover story, Sharon Begley reported that in neurotheology "psychologists and neurologists try to pinpoint which regions [of the brain] turn on, and which turn off, during experiences that seem to exist outside time and space. . . . [The] studies try to identify the brain circuits that surge with activity when we think we have encountered the divine, and when we feel transported by intense prayer, an uplifting feeling or sacred music."[21]

These studies, however, do not answer questions about whether scientists should be speculating about theology; neither do they explain whether our brains created the idea of God or whether God created the brain. Nor do they consider "God within" religious assumptions. If the scientific community concludes that the power of religious belief and spiritual experience (feeling closeness to God, meditative tranquility, states of enlightenment, or epiphanies) boils down to the way our brains are wired, that notion may further convince spiritual seekers that God exists within them rather than as an independent, external reality.

UFOS AND NEW AGE RELIGION

Another example of social accommodation of New Age beliefs is today's mainstream acceptability of UFO phenomena and related literature. The shift in public attitude during the last fifty to sixty years toward UFO phenomena is truly remarkable. Once controversial, belief in UFOs and extraterrestrial beings is now widespread and even glamorized. The trend may even have surpassed the increasing public acceptance of other Aquarian-New Age beliefs and practices.[22]

Broadly speaking, during the 1930s and 1940s, people who admitted seeing UFOs were considered kooks—people thought twice about associating with such individuals. But after the alleged UFO sighting at Roswell, New Mexico, in 1947, a small group of tentative believers emerged to give some sightings the benefit of the doubt. The world's oldest organization for the study of UFOs, the British Flying Saucer Bureau, was founded in 1953. Most people, however, still relegated UFO phenomena to the social far fringe.[23]

By the 1980s and 1990s, a new generation of believers was arising as millions of viewers seemed unable to keep the fantasy worlds created by Hollywood films and sci-fi television separate from reality. The social mindset was such that people began to view these movies and TV shows beyond mere entertainment. A growing constituency let itself become educated by the fiction. Organizations founded to privately fund UFO research, such as the Center for UFO Studies, and the advent and growth of Internet UFO sites have also helped shift public attitude. If audience response to guests who discuss UFOs on Letterman or Leno is any indication, people who don't believe in UFOs are narrow-minded and stuck in the Stone Age.

In the mythological relativism of astrology, the "Age of Aquarius" refers to a new era of great human potential that is dawning on earth to produce peace and harmony for the next two thousand years.[24] Although that terminology is now dated, the hope of a glorious new age to come still captures and drives much of the social imagination. Long-standing Aquarian-New Age expectations of unprecedented social transformation have set the stage for the central UFO message: prepare for impending apocalyptic events that will usher in a glorious new age. Allegedly, some people have even been willing to die for the belief.[25] Over the course of a few days in late March 1997, thirty-nine members of Heaven's Gate and their leader Marshall Applegate committed suicide on their Southern Californian compound, the press alleging that the members thought they would be joining a spaceship hidden in the tail of the passing Hale-Bopp comet. Between October 5, 1994, and March 1997, dozens of people linked to the Order of the Solar Temple, including leaders Luc Jouret and Joseph Di Mambro, participated in what appeared to be a murder-suicide pact in Canada, France and Switzerland. This UFO group was said to be steeped in occult philosophy and claimed contact with alien spirit beings in the Sirius star system.

Other groups are not thanatotic but nevertheless exhibit behavior emerging from fantastic beliefs. Members of the Unarius Foundation have maintained a huge UFO landing pad near San Diego, complete with a large sign reading "Welcome Space Brothers!" Some UFO groups employ biblical names and motifs, but biblical meanings are replaced with the organization's body of myths. The Raelian Movement claims that its leader, Claude Vorilhon, was born of a virgin, renamed Rael by aliens, and sent to be the messiah of a new world order for this generation. Aliens are said to have taken Vorilhon to the planet Elohim, where he met the aliens Yahweh and Satan, the latter a scientist who helped create humanity in a laboratory. In Raelian mythology, Christ was crucified but scientifically revived by aliens, who took him back home to the planet Elohim.

UFO ESCHATOLOGY

Like many religions, UFO organizations espouse views about ultimate destinies. Three eschatologies, broadly speaking, emerge from the lore: 1) UFO evacuation of chosen human beings from the planet before its destruction; 2) UFO salvation of the planet; 3) UFO evacuation and later recolonization of the planet. Heaven's Gate typified the first belief system. Humans were refusing to evolve and so the world was soon to be "spaded under" and "recycled." Salvation would come only to those select humans evacuated before the apocalypse began. When committing suicide, its members did not think they were dying but shedding their physical bodies ("containers" for the soul) and being metaphysically transported to the Hale-Bopp UFO, which would spirit them away to a better life. The Solar Temple suicides seem also to have believed they should withdraw from this world to the "Kingdom of Spirit." Their bodies consumed in flames, they themselves would wake up in the Sirius star system in paradise.

The Aetherius Society, the Unarius Foundation, and author and alleged UFO abductee Whitley Strieber[26] represent a planetary salvation eschatology. The Aetherius Society, which has branches throughout the United States, was founded in 1955 by George King, a London taxi driver and yoga practitioner. The foundation has evolved a mystical system of worship in which Jesus is said to be living on Venus. Unlike numerous other founders of UFO groups, King, who died in 1997, never claimed to be Christ. He did, however, profess to be in touch with Christ telepathically and is said to have wowed audiences by channeling beings from other worlds. Among his channeled revelations: a New Age messiah is coming to earth, but it won't be Jesus Christ; those who won't cooperate in the coming age will be removed and reborn on a less evolved planet; and those left will unite and transform earth.

A UFO group calling itself Ashtar Command espouses an eschatology that combines evacuation and planet salvation. The "space brother Ashtar," a supernatural angel-like alien, commands numerous spaceships that are circling the earth and ready to beam people up, Star Trek transporter-style, to prepare them for the coming age. Jesus, Lucifer and other aliens aboard these ships are anxious to transform the evacuated humans and eventually return them to earth in youthful immortality, to rebuild the planet, and to guide it into a new age after apocalyptic events.

Other groups are difficult to pin down eschatologically. Vorilhon's Raelian Movement, which made headlines in late December 2002 when it claimed to have cloned the first human being, promises immortality through cloning. "Four percent of the human species will clone themselves and travel through universe, populating virgin planets 'in our own image' in the future."[27] If not in outer space, then here—cloning will usher in a new age on earth. The Raelian Movement for $50,000 offers to clone your child if he or she dies of an incurable disease or as the result of an accident.[28] Vorilhon, a former French sports journalist and race car driver, claims 55,000 members worldwide, with the largest following in Japan at 5,500 members. Vorilhon once vowed to challenge in the Supreme Court any U.S. laws that ban cloning.[29] "You can have eternal life through different bodies," Vorilhon has said. "My mission is only to bring eternal life to human beings."[30]

In addition to their New Age message of the future, UFO groups come under the New Age umbrella for other significant reasons. Each in its own way borrows beliefs and practices from New Age religious traditions such as reincarnation, spiritual evolution, psychic phenomena, channeling, astrology, Eastern mysticism and occultism, although not every group subscribes to each belief. Other New Age characteristics include antipathy toward Christianity, unorthodox interpretation of key biblical doctrines and rejection of Jesus Christ as the Messiah.

There are also clear dissimilarities between New Age adherents and UFO believers. The former work diligently to fit in as normally as possible in society, while the latter often strive unabashedly for their cause no matter how strange they may appear or how starkly they stand out from the crowd. Also, unlike some UFO proponents, New Age seekers generally do not abandon their families or slavishly follow any one man, woman or group to society's margins, where leaders frequently control their followers' lives on the compound—in work, rest, diet and relationships—and off it.

CONCLUSION

The September 1, 2003, issue of *Publishers Weekly* ran a major report by Judith Rosen on the shift of New Age religion from cultural backwaters to widespread popular acceptance. "Let's face it," publicity manager Katie McMillan told Rosen, "New Age is no longer becoming mainstream, it *is* mainstream" (her emphasis). Noting deep concerns such as the war on terrorism, McMillan added that "people are dealing with issues that they may not have ever had to deal with before, and they are looking for tools that will help them." Publicity director Jacqui Clark noted a further sign of the shift in the sales of New Age titles to include "Target, Wal-Mart and Costco as the norm, along with appearances on national TV shows." Rosen concludes that "despite the uncertainties, judging by the diversity of titles that have come to be known as New Age, publishers' future lists will contain a heady mix of spirituality, the soul and the sacred in everyday life, with an overlay of self-improvement that will appeal to pagan and nonpagan alike."[31] This report from the publishing industry encapsulates a major trend that has been taking place in American life since the early 1990s.

It is said that human beings are incurably religious. Sooner or later events will motivate them to face the big questions about life, death and what follows. Our post-9/11 world continues to challenge us socially and personally, its ongoing crises driving us to question and perhaps change deeply held beliefs and values. As a result, the incurably religious become soul-searchers rediscovering the importance of their spiritual lives and their relationship with God. This reality was poignantly expressed by a priest who counseled the grieving near the fallen World Trade Center. Even atheists were asking him why God had allowed it to happen. He couldn't answer that question, he told them. But he turned the tables. He asked them a question in return: What is God saying to you in this tragedy? That question became his starting point for many meaningful conversations.

The millions who follow or flirt with New Age beliefs today—whether they explore yoga or UFOs, traditional non-Christian faiths such as Buddhism or Hinduism or quasi religions such as Zukav's—need the key that will open them to the only true hope of a sure future: Jesus Christ, the One who will forgive their sin, strengthen them for their journey, answer their big questions with truth, and usher them into the genuine new age. It may seem a mission impossible, especially given more than a decade of Christian silence regarding the normalization of New Age religion. Yet the Christian community has overcome worse obstacles throughout its long history. Offering winsome and believable alternatives to "secular" New Age thinking and practice is a leading challenge today. Could the time be more perfect?

7

THE DALAI LAMA AND
TIBETAN BUDDHISM

James C. Stephens

Nearly three thousand tickets for the annual Distinguished Speaker Series at the Pasadena Civic Auditorium featuring the Dalai Lama had sold out within an hour. Since no seats were available, I decided to go down, Jay Leno fashion, and conduct some on-the-street interviews of people waiting to get a glimpse of the god-king of Tibet.

As that balmy Southern California evening arrived, the air was filled with the anticipation of an opening night in Hollywood. Black limousines carrying the Dalai Lama and his U.S. Diplomatic Security Service escort pulled up to the Mediterranean-style auditorium. A smattering of celebrities mingled with Tibetan lamas with shaved heads and dressed in maroon robes trimmed in golden yellow as the large crowd lined up to pass through the specially installed security stations.

I was standing near Heather, a slender hippyish woman in her twenties who was observing that evening's crowd and occasionally asking if a passerby had any extra tickets. Nonchalantly I asked her, "So, what brings you out here this evening?"

She replied, "Oh, I hitchhiked out here this summer from the Ozarks with my boyfriend to attend the empowerment ceremonies with the Dalai Lama. Tonight we decided to see if we could attend his public talk on [his book] *Ethics for the New Millennium*."

"Will you be disappointed if you can't get in?" I inquired.

Without hesitation she mused, "Not really. I've been watching all the well-dressed people going in and decided they probably need to hear him more than I do."

Since she was open I posed a slightly more personal question. "Hypothetically, let's say that Jesus Christ and the Dalai Lama were standing here before you and you had the opportunity to choose one to follow. Who would you select?"

She paused for a moment and then said, "The Dalai Lama." Observing my somewhat baffled look, she confessed, "Well, he is the spiritual leader of our day who's bringing everyone together. He seems to fit our times better and although I find Jesus attractive, I don't feel the same about most Christians."

When asked why the Dalai Lama was so popular, she commented, "I think he is like the Wizard of Oz, reflecting people's illusions of what they want to believe."

At first I was taken aback, but then I recognized that her comments represented a growing number of people in our society who wholeheartedly embrace Buddhism as their religion of choice. According to Robert Wuthnow, a sociologist of religion, and Wendy Codge, an ethnographer, "one out of every seven Americans has had at least a fair level of contact with Buddhism, and that one out of eight Americans reported that Buddhism had influenced their religious life." The math? Although there are only 4,000,000 Buddhists in the U.S., there are 26,125,000 adults that "favorably" include Buddhist elements—a little or a lot—in their personal lives, "leaving no doubt that the lotus is blooming in America."[1] Studies have shown that there are presently more than sixteen hundred Buddhist temples, centers and monasteries in America, many of them Tibetan. In the twelve years between 1985 and 1997, "more Buddhist meditation centers were established than the total number founded in the first eighty-five years of the twentieth century."[2]

Buddhism is being marketed to such a high degree that even Buddhists parody the Madison Avenue hype. Buddha books are big business, and magazines are a lucrative enterprise supported by pages and pages of advertisements for retreats, national conferences, tea, salad dressing, Buddha beads and sneakers. In one ad campaign, smiling Tibetan lamas open Toshiba laptops on the "rooftop of the world." In another, huge billboards along Los Angeles freeways feature the smiling image of the Dalai Lama encouraging Apple users to "Think Different." *The Simpsons* recently focused on little Lisa's conversion to Tibetan Buddhism on its Christmas special.

DOCTRINE OF ASSIMILATION

Over the last 2,500 years, the Buddhist faith has developed a highly sophisticated process of expanding its religious message and adapting to many contexts. The historic doctrine of assimilation (*honji-suijaku*) allows Buddhism to compete with highly established indigenous religions in countries where it attempts to take root.

Buddhism's first step is to approach the indigenous host culture. As Buddhism took hold in China, which at the time was primarily Confucian and Taoist, this took the form of introducing the Buddhist law (dharma) to the emperor and his court. The next step involved the translation of Buddhist scriptures into the language of the host country. In China this process took eighty years. In the West it occurred during the pinnacle of the British Empire when Rhys Davids, Max Müller, Daniel Gogerley and a host of scholars belonging to the Pali Text Society translated numerous Buddhist texts into English. These translations were incorporated into the voluminous series Sacred Books of the East and brought Buddhism to the attention of English-speaking audiences worldwide.

During the third step of the process, Buddhists seek out areas of commonality with the host culture's faith, making it appear that they have much in common with that religion.[4] In the West, we now find a plethora of books along these lines, such as *The Good Heart: A Buddhist Perspective on the Teachings of Jesus* by the Dalai Lama, *Living Buddha, Living Christ* by Thich Nhat Hanh and *The Zen Teachings of Jesus* by Kenneth S. Leong.

A careful reading of the Dalai Lama's book *Ethics for the New Millennium* reveals that it bears little resemblance to traditional Buddhist ethics. His "consensus ethics" assimilates a variety of religious viewpoints that don't require the reader to adhere to any one faith. Like a chameleon the Dalai Lama is able to blend into many religious settings, which grants him access to an enormous secular audience yearning for spiritual answers.

HISTORICAL CAUSE FOR CONCERN

The Office of the Dalai Lama has systematically developed the doctrine of "skillful means" (*upayakaushalya*) over thirteen hundred years. Tibet, an isolated and sparsely populated country with a weak standing army, is strategically located between four historical military giants: China, Mongolia, Russia and India. Consequently it has had to rely upon its religious and political prowess to survive.

Tibet was not always Buddhist. Tibetans in fact were followers of Bön (pronounced "pern"), an indigenous faith centered on shamans who worshiped fierce mountain gods and other demonic spirits.[5] In A.D. 642 the Tibetan king Srong-btsan-sgampo granted his Chinese and Nepalese wives' wish to introduce Buddhism.

A little over a hundred years later in 745, an Indian tantric named Padmasambhava journeyed to Tibet and taught that humans could reach enlightenment in one lifetime. At the request of the Tibetan king Detsan, who was Buddhist, he "waged war against and conquered all the malignant gods in Tibet, only sparing those that promised to become Defenders of the Law (*Dharmapala*)." Padmasambhava introduced the systematic practice of the tantras[6] to Tibetans, which involved the use of mantras (chants intended to invoke divine power),[7] mandalas (circular sand paintings of deities), deity yoga (symbolic sexual union with deities), mudras (occult hand gestures) and magic.[8]

Buddhists attempted to co-opt control of Tibet from the Bön rulers by challenging the power of the local gods. One researcher has discovered drawings from this period, and they reveal that when Buddhists originally tried to establish authority by building an altar on the grounds of the capital city, someone always tore the altar down.

Frustrated by their lack of success, the Buddhists consulted their oracles, which instructed them to locate spiritual power points throughout the nation, build altars there, and make offerings to local gods on mountain peaks, valleys, rivers and lakes. As the Buddhists completed their assignment, they noticed that key points on the national map formed a constellation-like image of a demoness who was "nailed down." They built the Jokhang Temple at the "heart of the woman" and were then able to assume authority over the kingdom. Consequently, some buddhologists speculate that Tibetan Buddhism is founded on the symbolic subjugation of a woman who is nailed down, alive, at the bottom of a lake near the Johkang. The location of this power center is Lhasa—"city of the gods," capital of Tibet, and the former residence of the Dalai Lama.

Later, as Muslim invaders were destroying Buddhism in Northern India, Genghis Khan in 1206 led the Mongols in a war to establish his kingdom across China and Mongolia. The Tibetan lamas seized this opportunity to convert the notorious Khan to Tibetan Buddhism before he became the emperor of China. A symbiotic patron-priest relationship served both parties well as the Tibetan grand Lama became a vassal-ruler of Tibet and spiritual advisor to the emperor.

Because of the corruption of the Tibetan monastic centers, Tsong Khapa (1357-1419) established a reform movement called the *dGe-lugs-pa* (literally "model of virtue," pronounced and often referred to as "Gelak"), whose members were recognized by their yellow hats. This is the school of Tibetan Buddhism led by the Dalai Lama. It focuses on the serious study of tantric texts such as the Kalachakra tantra,[9] which forms the foundation of the Gelak Buddhists' national myth.[10]

A key component of this movement's religious agenda is the establishment of Shambhala, a global Buddhist empire. Agvan Dorzhiev, tutor to the thirteenth Dalai Lama and an emissary to Russia, created his own "Shambhala Project," a vision of how this great Buddhist empire would come about. It would not be a spiritual kingdom as in Christianity but a literal earthly empire.[11] After the Russian revolution, Dorzhiev negotiated the political support of the Bolshevik regime in his religious vision by stating that "Buddhist doctrine is largely compatible with current Communist thinking."[12] He also counted the work of lama Geshe Wangyal as an important part of the Shambhala Project. When a group of refugees from Kalmykia, a Tibetan Buddhist republic in the former Soviet Union, were fleeing Stalin, they crossed the ocean in 1952 and settled in New Jersey—the first group of Tibetan Buddhists to see Lady Liberty. They established a temple, and in 1955 Wangyal, a key Buddhist leader from their home country, came to minister there.[13]

Who Is the Dalai Lama and What Does He Believe?

The designation "Dalai Lama" refers to the office of god-king of Tibet and literally means "ocean of wisdom." It was first ascribed to Sonam Gyatso, a Gelak Buddhist reformer, in 1543 by Altan Khan, the leader of Mongolia. Tibetan followers refer to him by the title "Kundun," meaning "the presence."

The phrase "the Lama knows" can be heard throughout all strata of Tibet's priest-dominated society. The nation's early rulers established the divine right of priest-kings and enforced absolute submission to religious authorities.[14] For Tibetan Buddhist laity, it is impossible to achieve enlightenment without the instruction of a private lama, or guru. From childhood Tibetans are taught to worship the "four jewels"—first the Lama (spiritual master), and then the Buddha, the dharma (Buddhist law) and the *sangha* (priestly community).[15]

Reincarnation, or *patisandhi* (literally "reunion" or "relinking"), is a foundational belief of Tibetan Buddhism that states that an individual's consciousness is reborn lifetime after lifetime based on the karmic conditions of his or her previous existence. Karma, it is believed, will determine when, where and in what form a person will be reborn, be it peacock, snake, elephant or king.

In each lamasery approximately thirty lamas are accorded the rank of "noble monks" resulting from their recognition as reincarnations of previous lamas. One young boy named Lhamo Thondup was born in 1935 in a small village in northeast Tibet. A group of lamas disguised as merchants were led to his home by "a series of signs and visions" in their search for the new reincarnation of the recently deceased thirteenth Dalai Lama.

At the age of three, little Thondup grabbed the prayer beads around the neck of one of the lamas, saying they were his. The beads had belonged to the thirteenth Dalai Lama.[16] This sign, along with a physical examination, led the lamas to believe Thondup was indeed the fourteenth Dalai Lama—the reincarnated version of the thirteenth Dalai Lama, who himself had been considered an incarnation of Avalokitesvara, the patron deity of Tibet who they believe can save all living beings. To obtain Thondup's release the lamas paid a large ransom to the local Muslim governor.

At age five the new Dalai Lama was enthroned in Tibet's Potala Palace, taken to the Jokhang Temple for ordination, had his head shaved, and was renamed Tenzin Gyatso. For the next eight years his tutors trained him in the monastic curriculum and the art of leading a nation. He was also schooled in the occult praxis of Tibetan Buddhism based on ritualistic chanting of sutras and the magical incantation of *Om mani padme hum*.

In October 1950, the Dalai Lama's "age of innocence was swept away as eighty thousand [Chinese] soldiers marched into Chamdo and started the 'peaceful liberation' of Tibet."[17]

Beginning at age fifteen the Dalai Lama formally assumed the reign of authority as the temporal and spiritual ruler of Tibet and directly dealt with the Chinese occupation until his escape in March 1959. Moments before leaving, the Dalai Lama ceremonially presented a long silk scarf to his personal protector deity, Mahakala.[18] He later commented, "This is the traditional Tibetan gesture on departure and signifies not only propitiation, but also implies the intention of return."

Unlike Christian salvation, in which an individual relies on the unmerited favor of God and through faith personally accepts Christ's finished work of redemption on the cross, Tibetan Buddhism incorporates a rigorous system of works righteousness through which an individual accumulates enough merit to achieve deliverance from the wheel of samsara, or cycle of rebirths. These works include reciting mantras and sutras, performing proscribed religious rites, deity yoga, utilizing Buddhist rosary beads, prayer wheels, prayer flags and mani stones, visualizing demonic entities, and making symbolic offerings.

Disciples who are on a fast track to enlightenment must attend their guru's empowerment ceremonies and engage in tantric rituals, deity yoga (the practice of being spiritually yoked to Tibetan gods) and other acts, some of which are too explicit to mention. They perform rigorous acts of asceticism to deny the flesh and in doing so hope to attain the short path of liberation and attain nirvana.

The Kalachakra tantra was first preached by Buddha, who explained the spiritual practices necessary to remove obstacles blocking the path to nirvana. The tantric texts include more than 12,000 stanzas, numerous expositions and commentaries written over the last 2,500 years. Normally, before Tibetan lamas are allowed to study tantric practices, they are required to graduate from regular monastic studies.

A reading of the Dalai Lama's commentary on the Kalachakra raises considerable alarms. He states that certain followers who have achieved a level of great altruism and compassion are permitted to kill people who are "harmful to the teaching," speak "untrue words" for worthwhile purposes, steal someone else's wealth or mate, and use intoxicants, the five ambrosias (excrement, urine, blood, semen and human flesh) and the five fleshes.[19] Whether these statements are meant to be taken literally is a question worth posing to the Buddhist community. For Christians, they represent doctrines that need to be exposed.

THE PUBLIC RELATIONS DEPARTMENT

How is it that wherever the Dalai Lama ventures, the Teflon mystique of Shangri-La follows? Originally the myth seems to have found its voice through the writings of James Hilton, the author of *Lost Horizons*, and Lowell Thomas's radio programs about his adventures in Tibet.[20] Movie director Frank Capra perpetuated the myth of Shangri-La, a mysterious hidden kingdom, when he made a movie version of *Lost Horizons* in 1937.

The Dalai Lama rarely speaks of his country's historical problems with feudalism or his political contacts with neosocialists. In *Tricycle*, a quarterly Buddhist magazine, Alex McKay documented a Nazi expedition to Tibet in 1939 involving five members of Hitler's secret service. Their anthropological studies sought to provide evidence for Hitler's "idea of racial perfection that would justify their views on world history and German supremacy."[21] This mission became a source of embarrassment to the producers of the 1997 movie *Seven Years in Tibet*, which glossed over Heinrech Harrer's connection to Adolf Hitler.

Erwin Lutzer, pastor of Moody Bible Church in Chicago, shared his concern about Tibet's connection with Nazi Germany in *Hitler's Cross*, a startling exposé. He wrote:

> Karl Haushofer became Hitler's mentor. Haushofer had made several trips to India and was well versed in eastern occultism. He also

lived in Japan for a time where he was initiated into an esoteric Buddhist sect called the "Green Dragon." Through these contacts a colony of Tibetan lamas settled in Berlin, and when the Russians took the city in 1945, they found a thousand Tibetan corpses in German uniforms. Haushofer, more than any other, challenged Hitler with the vision of world conquest.[22]

The Dalai Lama's more recent contacts with neo-Nazis are equally troubling. On several occasions he has met with Chilean diplomat Miguel Serrano, the leader of the National Socialist Party of Chile, who is an "ideologist of esoteric Hitlerism." Serrano was a student of Julius Evola, who was fascist dictator Benito Mussolini's chief ideologist and heavily influenced by Tibetan tantricism.[23]

The remarkable tenure of the Dalai Lama as god-king for life surpasses every president since Franklin D. Roosevelt. Although most nations do not officially recognize Tibet as a sovereign nation, they still allow the Dalai Lama to speak from his platform as a religious leader. They have little knowledge of Tibetan Buddhism's global agenda or its worldview. As a religious and political foreign guest, the Dalai Lama has mastered the Buddhist art of "skillful means" (upaya) and utilizes his position to propagate Tibetan Buddhism, believing the end justifies the means.

INTERNATIONAL RECOGNITION

How did the Dalai Lama rise to such a high level of worldwide acclaim? After his escape from Tibet, he concentrated on establishing a Tibetan government-in-exile in Dharamsala, India, and encouraged Tibetans to engage in nonviolent opposition to the Communist occupation. Subsequent travels to Japan and Thailand in 1967 cemented his ties with Asian Buddhists.

The United States' political ties with the Dalai Lama extend back to secret CIA operations overseen by presidents Eisenhower, Kennedy and

Johnson.[24] In 1956, the U.S. government secretly trained three hundred Tibetan Khamba warriors in the military's winter training camp in Colorado to assist the Dalai Lama. He later thanked the CIA for organizing guerilla protection during his flight into Indian exile.[25]

In 1973 the Dalai Lama was first exposed to the West when he met with Pope Paul IV and visited the Tibetan diaspora in Switzerland. He was shocked to find that the next generation of Swiss Tibetans could not speak Tibetan. On the occasion of his 1979 visit to the United States, the *New York Times* greeted him with the headline "Hello Dalai!"

During his second journey to the U.S. in July 1981, the Dalai Lama conducted a Kalachakra initiation ceremony at the Deer Park Buddhist Center in Madison, Wisconsin. Performed in the Year of the Iron Bird, this ceremony symbolically fulfilled an ancient prophecy by Padmasambhava in A.D. 745: "When the Iron Bird flies to the land of the red man, the dharma will come to the West."

After thirty years of exile in India, the Dalai Lama was invited to Sweden to receive the Nobel Peace Prize in 1989 for his nonviolent efforts to resolve the Chinese armed occupation of Tibet. He declared the following year the International Year of Tibet, which was celebrated in schools, museums and cities around the globe. Since then the Dalai Lama's notoriety has dramatically increased.

THE DALAI LAMA'S POPULARITY

The New Testament provides an important insight into why Americans have so wholeheartedly embraced the Dalai Lama: "For false Christs and false prophets will rise and show great signs and wonders to deceive, if possible, even the elect" (Mt 24:24).

As descendants from political and religious immigrants who fled from repressive regimes, Americans are characterized as a people of goodwill who have a compassionate heart for the oppressed. Slowly, as knowledge of the Chinese invasion of Tibet has grown and stories of the gruesome deaths of nearly a million Tibetans through violence or starvation have become public, Americans committed to issues of freedom and justice have taken a strong stand against the repression of Tibetans' human rights and the systematic destruction of Buddhist monasteries.

In 1990 America welcomed one thousand Tibetan refugees after the passage of the Tibetan Refugee Resettlement Act sponsored by Representative Barney Frank of Massachusetts. Since then the Free Tibet movement has been vigorously promoted by an influential Washington lobby spearheaded by the late Senator Patrick Moynihan, former ambassador to India; his daughter Maura; and philanthropist Richard Blum, president of the Himalayan Foundation and husband of Senator Dianne Feinstein. Assisted by the notoriety and financial backing of celebrities such as Richard Gere, Steven Seagal, Sharon Stone and the Beastie Boys' Adam Yauch, the cause has found a global stage.

Hollywood has become the Dalai Lama's most significant public relations department. The twentieth anniversary rerelease of *Star Wars* underscores Hollywood's public love affair with postmodern Buddhist illusion. According to director Irving Kirschner, *The Empire Strikes Back* was designed to introduce Zen Buddhism to children.[26] Yoda was the proverbial Zen master. *The Phantom Menace* focused on the council's selection of the next incarnation of a Jedi knight, which closely parallels the process by which each successive Dalai Lama is selected. Would it be unfair to say that the Dalai Lama is the contemporary embodiment of Yoda in our popular culture's consciousness?

A number of years ago, I received a knock at my office door from a neighbor who had caught a glimpse of our sign, Sonrise Center for Buddhist Studies. He introduced himself and said he was a member of the Friends of the Western Buddhist Order. He had moved to California from Seattle after being hired as director of public relations for Disney. We chatted briefly, as I explained that we were a Christian organization that studied Buddhism and that many of us were formerly Buddhists. I invited him to join our discussion, and then we went our separate ways. It wasn't a surprise when I later heard that Disney was backing Martin Scorcese's production *Kundun,* a dramatization of the Dalai Lama's life, for a cool $30 million. Scorcese previously produced the controversial film *The Last Temptation of Christ.*

The historical revisionist film *Seven Years in Tibet* attracted a large following in Europe and America. Viewers flocked to see Brad Pitt's portrayal of Nazi stormtrooper Heinrech Harrer and his ensuing adventures in Tibet featuring his stumbling intercultural relationship with the Dalai Lama. After the film's release, the number of monthly hits on the Free Tibet website increased from five hundred to forty thousand.

The first American to become a Tibetan Buddhist lama was Columbia University professor Robert Thurman, father of actress Uma Thurman. It is rumored that Thurman, who has been mentored by Geshe Wangyal and the Dalai Lama himself, is Agvan Dorzhiev's successor and closely connected to his vision of the Shambhala utopia. Often called the Billy Graham of Buddhism, Thurman openly maintains that he will celebrate the Buddhization of the United States within his lifetime.[27] In 1991, as director of Tibet House in New York City, which he cofounded with Richard Gere, Thurman sponsored a Kalachakra initiation ceremony at New York's Madison Square Garden.[28] Tibet House contains a three-dimensional Kalachakra mandala and the only life-size statue of the Kalachakra deity outside of Tibet.

After the first World Trade Center bombing in 1993, the Samaya Foundation, the Lower Manhattan Cultural Council and the New York Port Authority jointly sponsored a sculpture of the Kalachakra sand mandala in the lobby of one of the towers.[29] Namgyal monks invited many World Trade Center workers and visitors to participate in the construction of the mandala. It is said that its shape symbolized nature's unending cycle of creation and destruction and in the countless grains of its material, it celebrated life's energy taking ephemeral form, then returning to its source. At the end of the mandala's month long lifespan, the monks swept up the sand and "offered it to the Hudson River." This ritual, they believed, purified the environment.[30]

For ten days in August 1993, the Palmer House Hilton in Chicago was buzzing as six thousand delegates from a variety of religious backgrounds attended the centennial celebration of the Parliament of the World's Religions. The religious leader on whom all eyes were focused was the fourteenth Dalai Lama, the god-king of Tibet who emerged from the parliament as the pluralist pope.

Now in any city the Dalai Lama visits, lights flash, reporters' keyboards churn out the standard lines and a general cry for "Free Tibet!" can be heard. One moment the Dalai Lama seriously addresses human rights abuse in Tibet, and the next he exhibits a humorous curiosity that the public finds attractive. The oral cuisine he serves up with few variations is kindness, compassion and world peace, with a twist of don't change the faith you're born with, be tolerant and don't proselytize.

Dr. David Woodward, a Christian scholar who has sympathetically followed the plight of Tibetans for the last fifty years, says of the Dalai Lama, "It is, of course, ridiculous for him to criticize Christian witness when he himself is engaged in proselytizing Westerners."[31] The Dalai Lama's intent to proselytize was obvious to Tibet watchers during the spring of 2001, when nine thousand Oregon high schoolers were hand-picked to attend one of his talks. He encouraged the youth to become ambassadors of peace and expounded on his texts, which were required prereading.

And yet not many of his enthusiasts know who this "simple monk" really is. The Dalai Lama as a religious and political globetrotter is reticent about his contact with fringe groups. One extremist leader with whom he has cooperative ties is Shoko Asahara, leader of Aum Shinrikyo, an apocalyptic sect that also holds to a vision of a global Buddhist empire. Asahara is now being tried in Japan for the 1995 poison gas attack on a Tokyo subway that killed twelve people and injured five thousand.

Meetings between the Dalai Lama and the pope and extensive dialogue with Catholics reveal the desire of both parties to learn about and even assimilate one another's ideas—a process that fits very well within a plan for a global Buddhist empire. For example, the Dalai Lama called the late Thomas Merton a close friend who taught him "a deeper way" than the Bible.[32] The Buddhist-Christian Monastic Dialogue brought together Benedictine and Trappist monks with the Dalai Lama and other Tibetan Buddhist lamas in a discussion to explore their religious differences and similarities. Loyola Marymount University has opened its doors to lamas who built a mandala on its campus. And Bryan Borys, a Catholic professor at the University of Southern California who attended the Dalai Lama's three-day teaching in Pasadena, was reported as saying, "I think he's the closest thing to a hero that anyone has around here nowadays."[33]

The Dalai Lama's tolerance is clearly pragmatic—it wouldn't be prudent for him to offend any of his hosts, be they Mormon, Catholic or Hindu, and he skillfully avoids doing so. And yet his embrace of pluralism is also in keeping with the goals of his exclusivist school of Buddhism, which assimilates other faiths in its mission to establish the Shambhala empire. After advancing "five arguments against the existence of God" at a talk to a pro-Buddhist audience, he went on to deny the salvific claims of Christianity while holding fast to the claim that "Tibetan Buddhism will be found to make final sense, in contrast to all rival claims and other religions."[34]

As Christians we hold to the principle that we reap what we sow, but unlike Buddhists we believe in only one lifetime (Heb 9:27) and that we cannot atone for our sins alone (Eph 2:8-9). Robert B. Ekvall, a nineteenth-century anthropologist and missionary to Tibetan nomads, penned the following words to one of his converts who understood the good news of Christ's incarnation:

> It is ordered for man to die once and after that to be judged. That word *once* makes the road of life a straight line. We cannot change it. The Complete Perfection [God] that made all things, the great powerful One has ordered it. His honored order stands. We must die once. Not many times, between many rebirths, but one. After that we must be judged from the sins and the sin—leaf, branch, and root. Life is no succession of circles, but a straight line, leading from one time without end to another time without end. It is but once: once to live, once to choose, once to win or lose, once to be saved, or once to be lost.[35]

For Tibetan Buddhists, "nothing has inherent existence," and truth is relative. In the Christian view, truth is an eternally nonnegotiable matter leading to spiritual life or spiritual death. Ultimately, doctrine does affect the fruit produced through practice. Belief behaves.

Unlike the Judeo-Christian immigrants from Europe admitted through Ellis Island a century before, Tibetans arriving from Asia have a religious worldview diametrically opposed to a belief in one God. In order to maintain Tibetan community's cultural and religious cohesiveness, the Dalai Lama carefully thought through their resettlement in Los Angeles, Seattle, Minneapolis and thirteen other sites after experiencing the Tibetan diaspora's cultural deterioration in Switzerland. After studying persecuted Jews' pattern for survival, he purposely encouraged his followers to settle in cluster sites complete with a resident Buddhist lama, craftsmen, artisans and families.

When the Dalai Lama received the Simon Wiesenthal Peace Prize in 1996, the Jewish community readily identified with the genocide experienced by Tibetans and likened him to "Aaron, our man of peace." The Dalai Lama told his audience on accepting the award that his people had much to learn from the Jews about preserving a minority religious culture that faced extinction.

As I listened to the presentation, I pictured the Dalai Lama at the Wailing Wall in Jerusalem, juxtaposed to his close friendships with World War II Nazis. Christians who served Tibetan refugees in the early days expressed alarm at the Dalai Lama's rapid rise to global prominence, but secular Tibet watchers said society needed a man of peace such as the Dalai Lama. These conflicting images stirred up some unsettled feelings about the Oz of Tibet.

A passage from the prophet Daniel in 537 B.C. struck me as I contemplated the reality of a "man of peace" who would in the end demand worship of himself. I meditatively read:

> And through his policy also he shall cause craft to prosper in his hand; and he shall magnify himself in his heart, and by peace shall destroy many: he shall also stand up against the Prince of Princes; but he shall be broken without hand. (Dan 8:25 KJV)

A MODERN TROJAN HORSE?

Victor and Victoria Trimondi, two radical German social activists who were instrumental in inviting the Dalai Lama to Germany, wrote, "Only the worst villain could disagree with what he has said and written." However, after responding to his encouragement to convert to Tibetan Buddhism, they uncovered an extreme "metaphysical exploitation of women," a vile connection between magic and politics, and "the foundation for an absolutistic system in which spiritual and worldly power are united in one person, the Dalai Lama."[36]

Their findings were released in 1999 in *The Shadow of the Dalai Lama: Sexuality, Magic and Politics*, an exposé of eight hundred pages of carefully researched and reasoned arguments. The Trimondis take their readers on a painful spiritual journey that dismantles the West's idealized image of Tibet and takes off the pacifistic mask of the Dalai Lama, revealing a pantheon of warring deities and a skillful god-king who still consults the demonic Nechung oracle in all his important state decisions.[37]

The Trimondis also warn that the Kalachakra initiation is designed to manipulate believers and introduce "an aggressive military ethos" toward the establishment of a global Buddhocracy. This empire will supposedly be established after a war in the year 2327 that eliminates or forces the conversion of the followers of Muhammad, Abraham and Jesus.[38]

In light of Tibetan Buddhists' historical takeover of the Bön people, we should be asking ourselves whether we as Americans understand the worldview that is motivating Tibetans to systematically build sand mandalas across our nation. Are they really, as is commonly believed, simply sharing their art and culture to raise money to build prayer halls in Asia? Or is something more strategic going on? In October 1998, two groups of tantric Buddhist monks began a tour across America and Canada to construct one hundred mandalas, predominantly financed by the Gere Foundation and the National Endowment for the Arts. Their professed goal beyond raising funds simply was "to spread their knowledge to everyone who wants to learn about their traditions."[39]

In one of Karl Jung's last works, he remarked that mandalas are the "pre-eminent symbol for our time" and appear in "situations of psychic confusion and perplexity."[40] He went on to associate the psychological experience of UFO phenomenona with the "rotundum, the symbol of wholeness and the archetype that expresses itself in mandala form."[41]

In the blockbuster movie *Independence Day*, terrified citizens across the globe helplessly observe as alien ships attack earth in a global Armageddon. If you watch carefully, you can see that the alien ships assume the form of giant airborne mandalas, symbolically opening up as lotus flowers (a euphemistic tantric symbol for the vagina in Buddhism) and usurping power from giant buildings (phallic in structure) that penetrate the skies. Just before an alien ship destroys the White House, the camera shows for a split second a small framed picture of the Dalai Lama and the president in the Oval Office.

According to the Trimondis' website, "the Kalachakra sand mandala is a means of occult possession of the territory in which it is created,"[42] including the waters where it is dispersed, which brings to mind the lake in the story of the Buddhist takeover of Tibet. Some Buddhists theorize that the mandala brings peace, while others say it brings destruction in its wake. The Smithsonian Institution, as part of a $6.5 million Folk Life Festival featuring Tibet, displayed a mandala on the Capitol Mall in Washington, D.C., in the summer of 2000. More than 2.5 million visitors attended the exhibit, which included a Tibetan temple and prayer monument, prayer wheels, pornographic tantric idols and chanting lamas.

CAVEAT EMPTOR

In the overcrowded marketplace of ideas, where every guru, priest and religious leader is being promoted as the solution to the world's problems, I believe we need to have a "buyer beware" attitude. Maybe my apprehension arises from my own experience as a Buddhist in the seventies, when I heard all the talk about peace, compassion and kindness from leaders who in the next breath spoke condescendingly of the superiority of Buddhism. Critical thinking is absolutely necessary when we host, interact with or share our faith with people of other religious persuasions.

Christians have a duty to investigate religious systems that impact their lives and to effectively proclaim the gospel in full understanding of the context of world history. Os Guinness, born in China and edu-

cated at Oxford, issued a stern warning in 1973 that the church has yet
to heed:

> The swing to the East has come at a time when Christianity is weak
> at just those points where it would need to be strong to withstand
> the East. Without this strength, the Eastern religions will be to
> Christianity a new, dangerous Gnosticism, but this time much of
> the fight will be lost before many see the nature of the danger.[43]

I have observed Tibetan lamas in local museums teaching young children to make mandalas, the children innocently unaware of their proximity to malevolent spirits. Even Tibetan lamas recognize that dangerous
demons manifest during the construction of mandalas, and they perform
ritual offerings to prevent their own possession by demonic spirits. The
late Mas Toyotomi, a Japanese American who served with Japanese Evangelical Missions Society, warned, "Satan's subtle strategy is to camouflage
idolatry in such a way that even Christians do not recognize it as such.
Because there is practically no preaching against idolatry in America, they
are vulnerable to the temptations of modern sophisticated idolatry."[44]

The watchman's warning is clear (Ezek 33:4). The Tibetan Buddhist
World Peace Vase Project recently completed its first global target, America.[45] Tantric vases have now been buried in every state, key national
parks, significant mountain peaks, capital cities, and major lakes and
waterways. Tibetan tantric lamas continue to build mandalas at American universities, museums, buildings and temples, and they are financed
by major foundations.

In the Old Testament, God abandoned Israel because it was filled with
idols and influences from other nations. Rather than serving God and
loving him, the Israelites "mingled with the nations and adopted their
customs" (Ps 106:35), which were detestable to the Lord. So the Lord
"handed them over to the nations, and their foes ruled over them" (Ps
106:41). As Christians, it is our duty to flee idolatry and to expose the

deeds of darkness. Our battle is not against Tibetans, for whom Jesus Christ gave his life, but rather it is on their behalf as we wrestle against the ruling spirits of darkness that have kept them in spiritual bondage for centuries (Eph 6:12).

As the apostle Paul observed the spirituality of the people of Athens at Areopagus near the Acropolis, he found an altar with the inscription, "To an unknown god." He presented the gospel and told them, "What therefore you worship in ignorance, this I proclaim to you" (Acts 17:23). To people who profess to be followers of Buddhism, I call attention to the following Buddhist scripture:

> Verily, there is an Unborn, Unoriginated, Uncreated, Unformed. If there were not this Unborn, Unoriginated, Uncreated, Unformed; Escape from the world of the born, the originated, the created, the formed would not be possible.[46]

This "Uncreated" is Jehovah God, unborn because he is the unchanging I AM. He is above time and desires that humanity not be ignorant of his path of deliverance (Jn 20:30-31). The greatest mystery of all is that he would physically reveal himself through his incarnation as Immanuel, which means "God with us." To seekers who have eyes to see and ears to hear, all creation manifests his handiwork and the heavens speak of his glory. Tibetan Buddhists recognize the power of speech, and if they seek the "Uncaused Cause," the Creator who spoke the heavens and the earth into existence from nothing will reveal himself to them.

There is a dualism that marks a profound distinction between God and his creation, which is in sharp opposition to the Buddhist monism that holds all creation to be divine. Without the Uncreated Cause there is no deliverance from the cycle of sin initiated by our own ancestors, which connected us intrinsically to their fall. The Dalai Lama himself has said he is not perfect. But there is a promise of deliverance from that cycle of sin through the only perfect Master who "committed no sin, nor was any deceit found in his mouth" (1 Pet 2:23). His name is the Lord Jesus Christ, and his boundless merit can be appropriated only by faith. He offers an invitation:

> I am the door. If anyone enters by Me, he will be saved. . . . The thief does not come except to steal, and to kill, and to destroy. I have come that they may have life, and that they may have it more abundantly. (Jn 10:9-10 NKJV)

8

NEOPAGANISM

John Peck

In some respects neopaganism is more like a subculture than a religious movement. It lacks any specific structure; it has developed its own networks, mythologies and disagreements—many of them quite profound; and it has cultivated its own art forms, especially in music, film, painting, poetry and fiction. It is widespread, with representative groups in all five continents, but it is statistically difficult to quantify. Some have estimated that there are approximately six thousand witches and druids in the United Kingdom, and estimates of the number of neopagans in the United States range from forty thousand to over two hundred thousand. And the numbers are growing.

DEFINITIONS AND TYPES

For our purposes here, neopaganism may be characterized as the conscious attempt to revive religious attitudes and practices common around the world before the appearance of the major religions of today. Beneath its many forms are certain fairly consistent characteristics: (1) seeing nature as divine (in this respect neopagan thinking tends to be pantheistic); (2) reverence for a goddess commonly identified as Mother Earth (usually an equal consort of a high god) alongside an animistic view of the cosmos as indwelt by lesser spirits; (3) a working belief in ritual and symbolism as a means of access to the divine powers of nature, especially the earth and sky; (4) a prevailing interest in religious and mystical antiquity, especially prehistorical and late medieval.

Clearly many of these attributes correspond with New Age thinking, but most pagans insist that there is a definite distinction. While pagans may experience possession by their gods, there is no spiritistic practice quite comparable to channeling. In addition, paganism is deliberately realistic; there is no dichotomy between spirit and matter. The earth and the body are divine, so the cruel and the benign elements of nature share equally in that divinity. Neopagans tend to assert that New Age feminism is not truly egalitarian and gives no scope for women to match men in the public arena.

The goals of the two movements are also different. New Age activity aims at individual self-fulfillment; neopagans focus more on changing people and situations. Hence Buddhism is more at home in the New Age movement (though it does also have a niche in neopaganism), while polytheisms and their mythologies are more at home in neopaganism. Finally, there is little neopagan millennarian interest. One hardly hears any reference, for instance, to "the age of Aquarius."

There are two types of neopagan practice, which often overlap. One is largely concerned with worship and meditation and focuses on the god, goddess or spirits of the cosmos. It is thus naturally polytheistic or polydemonistic. The other is often referred to as the practice of "magick," spelled archaically to distinguish it from popular ideas of magic as illusionist showmanship or wonders wrought with a mere wave of a wand. It is an esoteric mysticism, offering special knowledge and power to its initiates through several levels of spiritual experience. Its purpose therefore is to enhance the spiritual vision of practitioners, equipping them to use the special powers and gifts that manifest themselves. One prominent form of this second type is called "hermetic," predominantly deriving its inspiration from Greek, Arabic and Egyptian symbolism. (Much of this symbolism also appears in Freemasonry, though I have found little "mag-ick" in this tradition—and my father was a grand master.)

The most visibly influential of the neopagan traditions is Wicca, an al-ternative term to *witchcraft* introduced by Aleister Crowley in the 1920s largely to counteract popular prejudice—though many sympathizers quite happily identify the two. Some, however, make a distinction, say-ing Wicca refers to people who follow more recent traditions offered by Gardner and Crowley, while witches are those who follow older practices believed to derive from antiquity. Wicca claims to adapt ancient tradi-tions to the needs of the modern age. It starts with the worship of nature but readily understands nature in terms of modern physics, and it incor-porates new symbolism into its rituals. There are eight annual festivals (*sabbats*), punctuated by the solstices and equinoxes and lesser holidays connected with phases of the moon. Wiccans also participate in initia-tion rites and additional ceremonies such as "handfasting," a form of quasi marriage. Wicca insists on the freedom of each individual and group to "choose its own path"; no single viewpoint or belief is abso-lutely true.

Obi-Wan Kenobi of *Star Wars* expresses this philosophy when his spirit explains to Luke Skywalker that what he had just said was true "from his own perspective," though untrue from Luke's. (In many ways, *Star Wars* is a neopagan myth in which the ultimate struggle is between a mentality of control and power and one of live and let live.) A group, then, is normally supposed to function democratically, by consensus, so that even a priestess has no special authority. Underlying this mindset is the belief that the feminine principle of the goddess focuses on face-to-face personal relationships rather than authority backed by power. Con-trol is regarded as a male preoccupation. A Wiccan group is often re-ferred to as a "coven" or "circle." In the United States, Wiccans have found voice through organizations such as Covenant of the Goddess and Church of All Worlds. In the U.K. there is a Pagan Federation that is pre-

dominantly Wiccan, though it has acted as a mouthpiece for the whole
movement under the energetic presidency of Leonora James. There are
analogous organizations around the world.

Neopaganism's many forms often arise from local histories. The modern Wicca movement arose in England out of a belief that country folk
rituals and the practices of the witch trial victims of the sixteenth
through seventeenth centuries were survivals of a primal religion. Celtic
neopaganism harks back to the primitive religions of Scotland and Ire-
land; Druidism looks back chiefly to Welsh origins. Some Druids are
barely distinguishable from Wiccans, but others are more devoted to earlier rituals and see their function shamanistically, as guardians of the culture's historical identity in much the same way as ancient Druids were
believed to be. (Historically, the Druids had widespread influence: Julius
Caesar's invasion of Britain was a punitive expedition to eliminate the
Druidic support for resistance movements in Gaul.)

There are three grades of involvement in Druidism. Bards are keepers
of the stories, ballads, epics, myths and language of the community.
Ovates are the practitioners of spiritual life—they deal with birth, death,
rebirth, healing, divination and communication with ancestors. The
third grade, Druids, are the professionals: administrators, judges,
priests. All require lengthy and exacting training. Druid groups are often
called "groves."

Druids worship a pantheon of gods and godesses, and they believe in
an otherworld from which people come to be born and to which they
are reborn at the end of their earthly life. Druids have a special interest
in the number three, which they express in special symbols—the Awen
(/|\) and the Triskele (three joined bent legs). Druids hold three fire fes-
tivals during the year but reject as ancient Roman propaganda the association of human sacrifice with historic Druidism. The modern Druid
movement began in the U.K. with the establishment of the Order of
Bards, Ovates, and Druids. In the United States the two best-known

groups are the Reformed Druids of North America and ADF, an acronym for a Celtic title meaning "Our Own Druidism." One of the best-known Druids is the latter group's arch-Druid emeritus, Isaac Bonewits.

The European continent has seen similar movements, such as the northern tradition of Asatru, whose followers often refer to themselves as "heathen." These neopagans accept the pantheon of classical Norse mythology: the gods of the tribe, of the earth and of destruction; goddesses such as Freya and Ostara (Saxon *Eostre*, origin of the word *Easter*); and male gods such as Odin and Thor (origin of *Wednes-day* and *Thurs-day*). They believe in an afterlife of bliss or torment, and worshipers now share drink offerings instead of offering animal sacrifices. Asatruers meet in "hearths" or "kindreds." In addition to celebrating the usual festivals, in early February they hold a Charming of the Plough. Groups can be found throughout Scandinavia, and in Iceland, Asatru is a legally recognized religion. In North America the best-known group is the Ring of Troth.

Native American spirituality is strongly shamanistic. Its special reverence for the land is quite alien to the "white" concept of ownership, though its followers now include a significant number of white Americans. Some groups such as Earthkeepers particularly foster an earth-centered spirituality intrinsic to Native American religions but draw from other traditions in the world as well. Recently the movement has begun to identify itself more closely with "first nation" religions (that is, religions of the indigenous peoples flourishing before Western colonization in the nineteenth century)—especially from the East—as survivals of original paganism.

Other North American neopagan movements are inspired by Eastern mysticism, in particular tantrism and shamanism. Shamanism, originally from Central Asia, now eclectically draws from all established Western traditions. The shaman is especially gifted and experienced in the ways of the gods and spirits and is available for counsel in times of need. In addition to the above groups is a long list of lesser known neopagan organizations, including Dianic witches, the Green Circle, crone groups, the Circle of Awen, the Hyksos, and groups with a special interest in astrology, tarot, and faerie lore, among others.

Philosophical Characteristics

Neopagans dislike formal, organized statements of belief, but they almost universally accept a "grand narrative," a belief that human beings originally lived in relative peace with each other and harmony with the natural world through reverence for a mother goddess. She was the divine creatrix, the source of all life, the prototype of the sensual delights of mother love, and the ultimate nurturer. The primal communities were then conquered by a people (sometimes identified as Indo-Aryan) who worshiped a male high god predominantly interested in exercising power. (Feminists see analytical discourse and hierarchical structures as twin characteristics of this invading patriarchalism.)

Mother goddess worship survived in various muted forms under names such as Astarte, Ishtar, Aphrodite, and in the Christian tradition the cult of the Virgin Mary. However, some zealous Christians perceived this primal spirituality as a threat. The classic period of persecution is recalled as the "burning times," when for some two centuries (fifteenth through seventeenth) the church is said to have engaged in an attempt to eradicate paganism as the work of Satan and laid a stigma on witchcraft that has survived to the present day.

As a result neopagans have reacted against analytical thinking, which they see as an attack on the intuitive experience of true nature-mysticism. They are also in general suspicious of hierarchical structure, which they believe utilizes such thinking as a tool for domination. Most neopagans regard each person as responsible for finding his or her own path of self-realization. Hence they tend to avoid the word *religion*, believing it implies a hierarchical structure of thought and adherence to the authoritative revelation associated with the major world religions. At the same time it is not uncommon for neopagans to be represented in interfaith dialogues.

In place of analytical abstract thought, pagan thinkers stress imagination and intuition as a route to "real" reality. They assert that appropriate rituals can empower and give material substance to the imagination, which can then, through the exercise of a trained will, bring about changes in the real world. To the outsider, this belief system suggests an uncomfortable blurring of fact and fantasy, especially when neopagans support the validity of myth independently of historical fact. On occasion, too, they disregard factual accuracy, as paganism historian Ronald Hutton occasionally complains. Indeed, a group known as the Discordians saw themselves as the "jokers," the "fools" of the movement in the tradition of medieval court jesters, who were paid to act and talk nonsensically. This gave them leave to make fun of even the monarch with impunity even though it might imply criticism (compare the Fool in Shakespeare's *King Lear,* esp. Act 1, scene 4). The neopagan attitude corresponds with the view that nature is an organic whole of which human beings in both their subjective and objective experience are an equally valid part, and what others call "good" and "evil" are simply complementary elements.

Two implications are significant. The first is that humans share in the natural cycle of birth, growth, death and rebirth. Hence there is a widespread (though not universal) belief in reincarnation. The second implication is that nature and the cosmos are maintained by analogical relationships—for example, electrons orbiting round a nucleus correspond with planets orbiting around a sun. In particular, the human individual is seen as the microcosm of the total cosmos. A mystical goal, especially of ritual magick, is the union of the human with the cosmos, of the human soul with the world soul. This goal is often termed "gnosis," which gives rise to the tendency to characterize the tradition as gnostic. Insofar as classical Gnosticism of the first three centuries offered an esoteric insight into reality only to the initiated elite, this is justified, but the content of the gnosis is profoundly different. Classical Gnosis in the Hellenistic tradition was of a reality "out there," distinct from our human subjectivity. Magickal gnosis is a radical knowledge of one's "true self," which at the same time is identified with the whole.

Neopagans claim that the Western distinction between subjective and objective experience is illusory. It follows from the pantheistic character of such thinking that they do not believe in evil in the Judeo-Christian sense; nature is essentially and paradoxically dualist. Darkness and light are two sides of the same coin. Hence the cruelty of nature is not evil but simply the "dark side" of its nurturing, protecting care. Neopagans are particularly sensitive about Satan, since they have traditionally been accused of worshiping him. For them, Satan is real and powerful only in the imagination of people who believe in him.

History

One difficulty in establishing the history of paganism is that neopagans are predominantly interested in practice, which is orally transmitted, rather than beliefs and organizations, which more naturally become matters of record. This difficulty is compounded by neopagans' felt need for secrecy in view of possible social disapproval. (Anthropologists might observe that where ethically directed religions lose their momentum, communities tend to lapse back into a basic animism.)

Different types of neopaganism trace their history to different origins. Wicca has traced its roots back to the witch hunts of the fifteenth through seventeenth centuries; Druidism has origins in the late fifteenth century but claims much earlier roots in thirteenth-century Wales and even the "lost continent" of Atlantis; magick traces lines of practice back through Masonry and Rosicrucianism to gnostic mysticism of the middle ages. Other sources of inspiration are Jewish kabbalistic and Muslim Sufic mysticism.

Many of paganism's accounts of origin are historically uncertain, often seriously inaccurate. For example, Druids' assumptions of primal goddess worship on Atlantis are based on a few artifacts that in themselves provide no positive information to contradict an opposing theory of primal monotheism. In addition, recent scholars have seriously challenged the theory of religious survivals promulgated by Frazer's *Golden Bough,* in which he argues that modern religions are formed by motifs derived from a primal animism—for example, the belief in angels is a survival of primitive ancestor worship. But most significantly, modern studies of documents from the witch trials of the fifteenth through seventeenth centuries contradict assumptions still current among most people—that the church was the prime instigator, seeing witches as female practitioners of the "old" pre-Christian religion; that governmental authorities opposed them as being threats to the current patriarchal hierarchy; and that as many as nine million suffered death. In fact, witchcraft regularly used Christian symbolism, church leaders often sought to mitigate the hysteria, and witch trials were usually initiated by local communities, not by the authorities. During the two hundred years, no more than forty thousand people were executed in all of Europe, usually for attempting to harm someone by witchcraft.

Neopaganism as a modern phenomenon seems to find its ideological origins in the Romanticism of the early nineteenth century, which reacted against the "dark satanic mills" of the Industrial Revolution and the Enlightenment's scientific rationalism. Romanticism also expressed a nostalgic hankering after the nature-bound simplicities of agricultural life. During the nineteenth century various kinds of nature-mysticism arose, the most significant groups being the Hermetic Order of the Golden Dawn and the Ordo Templi Orientis. A new interest in Eastern religion also resulted in the formation of a Western Buddhist Order. Neopagan themes are apparent in the works of composers such as Chopin and Wagner.

Some outstanding thinkers articulated the ethos of the movement. Carl Jung's theory of archetypes provided powerful support for the use of symbols and ritual. Frazer's *Golden Bough* was enormously significant, especially as expounded by Egyptologist Margaret Murray. The theosophist Rudolf Steiner was a dominant exponent of hermetic mysticism. Aleister Crowley, a fairly prolific author better appreciated after his death, was a deliberately notorious proponent of ritual magick, which he sometimes referred to as the "left hand path." Among his more significant writings are *The Book of Lies* (1917) and *Magic in Theory and Practice* (1929). Crowley violently rejected any kind of conventional Christianity and was especially interested in sex as an element of ritual power, an indication of his interest in tantrism. He defined magick as "the art or science of causing change in conformity with the will," and "the study and use of those forms of energy which are (a) subtler than the ordinary physico-mechanical types, (b) accessible to those who are (in one sense or another) initiates."[1]

Crowley had some influence on his contemporary Alexander Gardner, whose *Book of Shadows* (1964) has been as near a witchcraft textbook as is possible in so amorphous and creative a movement (there is a whole Wicca tradition referred to as "Gardnerian"). Another founder of a "school" was the publicity-minded Alex Sanders, who modified Gardner's tradition by allowing male priests in the coven and making way for the acceptance of homosexuals. Sanders's collaborator and Gardner's successor and critic was Doreen Valiente, who did much to improve Wicca's image in the 1960s after a period of public hostility in the 1950s. Also prominent among the feminist pagans is American writer Miriam Simos, who goes by the name Starhawk and is known particularly for her book *The Spiral Dance: A Rebirth of the Religion of the Great Goddess* (1979).

An interesting feature of neopagan history is the role that fiction has played (not always favorably) in the growth of public awareness of the movement. Crowley and Gardner both produced novels, and other influential writers have been John Buchan, Robert Graves, Dennis Wheatley and even D. H. Lawrence. In the last decade some groups of a younger generation have seen the neopagan experience as specially explicable in terms of modern physics, especially quantum, chaos and probability theories. They have found the Internet a particularly happy medium for interchange of ideas and mutual understanding.

SOCIOLOGY

Neopagans' dislike of formal structure means that their organizations have no spokespeople or officers who officially represent the entire group. Even the priests are no more than first among equals, marked out merely by function. Wiccan groups tend to be small and scattered, and to form and re-form with great fluidity. Individual Wiccans sometimes practice in isolation, then occasionally and perhaps only temporarily join a group with which they feel some spiritual affinity. The fact that many people are suspicious of their occult practices tends to keep neopagans on the fringes of social life, especially the magickal groups whose esoteric tradition is available only to screened initiates. Television programs such as *Sabrina, the Teenage Witch* may do something to bring them into the public mind, but in a form that most witches would hardly recognize or appreciate.

PRACTICE

All neopagans use symbolism, and therefore ritual, to generate experiences of spiritual power or energy, while firmly rejecting the idea that any particular ritual is superior. Indeed, some groups create their rituals. The test of a particular ritual is whether it works, that is, whether it generates effective mystical experience for the practitioner. A few groups practice forms of self-denial as a route to mystical experience, and some use hallucinogenic drugs, but members stress that they do not use them recreationally.

The turn of the seasons has a strong significance for neopagans; the movement of the sun and the phases of the moon determine appropriate occasions for ritual activity, though the actual days vary with different groups. Thus Samhain, a dominant Celtic festival, is celebrated on Halloween by some, on the next day by others, and even several days later by others. Most groups, however, do observe the main "moments" of the year—the equinoxes and the solstices, which each have their own mystical significance. Such times are regarded as occasions when the veil between the seen and unseen worlds becomes thin.

Wicca has an enormous variety of rituals, and new ones are continually appearing. For the purpose of this book, we will examine some of its most common characteristics. Witches may work in isolation or in covens. Either way, the "work" begins with the use of a ceremonial dagger (*athame*) to mark out a circle on the ground as consecrated space. The group or individual then invokes the four "guardians" of earth, air, fire and water. Rituals make extensive use of symbols—candles, stones, a sword, bread, wine, an altar, water, flowers, fruit—anything is regarded as potentially usable for sacred purposes. The pentacle (a five-point star in a circle) is an almost universal badge. Next comes liturgical chanting, discourse, prayers and declamations.

The rituals are aimed at building up a "cone" of energy, making it possible to call on chosen gods or spirits to make themselves present in the circle and, perhaps, in individual participants who are then understood to be their embodiments. In the latter case, there is the expectation that the gods will speak to the individual or the coven (called a "charge"). Rituals are also developed to deal with the larger issues of society. It is said that during the Battle of Britain witches engaged in intensive rituals to obstruct Hitler, and they were so demanding that some practitioners died in the process.

Often the form of the ritual arises from a myth associated with the particular deity or spirit—for example, Persephone's visit to the underworld or the story of Gilgamesh. Wicca involves some erotic rituals and sexual themes are often significant, but most Wiccans are acutely conscious of their reputation, and so far as investigators have seen, there is virtually no orgiastic promiscuity. Sacrifice of any kind is fairly rare, and most Wiccans greet suggestions of human sacrifice with amused contempt.

Wicca, along with most forms of paganism, has the characteristics of a mystery religion, with special levels of spiritual enlightenment. There are commonly three stages of initiation with increasing levels of responsibility. The first ritual often involves blindfolding and vows of lifelong commitment, with a rite apparently modeled on Freemasonry. The second level involves learning to use the "tools" of the craft—its symbols and rituals—effectively. The third level equips a participant to form his or her own coven. The ceremonies are conducted by a priestess, who represents the earth goddess; there is usually also a priest of the god, and they initiate each other into their function. The ritual for the initiation of the priestess is often referred to as "drawing down the moon."

Welsh Druidism has an older, more magickal style with nine levels of initiation, and it claims affinities with witchcrafts in Brittany, Italy, ancient Greece and Asia Minor. Druidism is an esoteric tradition with secret lore often handed down through families from mother to daughter. Its rites reflect a sense of the duality of nature: male-female, light-dark, birth-death, god-goddess, lord-lady. Some rituals are designed to call on a deity to "touch" a devotee, inducing a condition of trance.

An ecstatic state in Native American practice typically occurs in the sweat lodge. The initiate, with fasting and meditation, begins the spiritual exercise by building a small hut, gathering stones and firewood, and pouring water on hot stones to fill the hut with steam. The devotee stays inside for a spiritual purification, a rebirth experience that leads to communion with the earth and its gods. Among other things, this practice produces a powerful bonding effect with the community and other participants.

Another characteristic of Native American spirituality is the sun dance, a complex tribal ritual worship of the sun lasting four days, involving the building of a sacred teepee, the ceremonial use of a live buffalo and also a buffalo skull, sacrifices and tests of endurance of self-inflicted suffering. A participant described it to me as follows:

> The females don't pierce as the males do, but they have small strips of their arm taken as an offering in return for prayers granted usually. It is a very spiritual affair and lasts four days. The dancers don't eat or drink during this time. . . . It is not usual for most people to know where and when this takes place.

Special Interests

Neopaganism is essentially a nature spirituality, and it is thus a radical reaction against modern Western culture, characterized as it is by the control and exploitation of nature. Obviously they are highly interested in ecological issues, and "green" movements have enthusiastic support from neopagans. Much of their ritual activity is aimed at empowering nature to resist destruction.

Neopaganism also assumes a polarity between male and female humanity, roughly expressed as a tension between rational intellect and intuition. It is a general conviction in the movement that the present control-oriented culture is the climax of a history of male domination. Now, they believe, is the time to work for a renewal of the primal blessedness and restore the natural balance of the sexes. Not all neopagans are militant feminists—indeed they do not think in terms of a power struggle at all. But they do believe that womanhood has special access to the powers of the spirit. Witchcraft has long been seen as the purview of women, and most neopagans believe that prejudice against them arises from a perceived threat to the male-oriented status quo.

The individualism of our modern Western culture has its own reflection in neopaganism, which lays great stress on individual choice, mode of operation and lifestyle. The reaction against rationalism and artificial social relationships results in a higher value on individual spiritual development. One of the leading themes of neopagan spirituality is that "you will not find that which you seek outside of you if you cannot first find it within." Such enlightenment involves reaching past self-analysis to direct confrontation with the inner self, on Jungian lines. A typical expression of this process is found in the *Star Wars* series: Luke Skywalker is bidden to "listen to his heart," but one stage of his preparation for doing so effectively is to enter into an imagined conflict with Darth Vader, the embodiment of evil in a black helmet-mask. Luke triumphs and stands over the corpse—only to find, when the mask is removed, his own face.

RELIGION AND ETHICS

Aleister Crowley laid down as a basic neopagan morality the creed "An' it harm none, do what thou wilt." Crowley's intention, however, goes beyond the Augustinian dictum "Love, and do what you like" or the Buddhist ethic of ahimsa, or harmlessness. His meaning is particularly dependent on a unique idea of the will, which he defines as the instinctive, uncalculated intention of the trained initiate. The individual will is an instrument of cosmic power, the personal aspect of the cosmic will. Crowley further asserts that the individual will is compounded by a "rule of three"—that is, what you do to another person will return to you threefold; it becomes part of the law of your existence. Morality, then, is basically prudential and rejects any notion of revealed morality authorized by a deity. If human duty exists at all, it consists simply of finding one's "real," divine self and responding to its direction. It is understandable, then, that in handfasting the couple sometimes pledge themselves only "as long as they truly love each other."

Neopagans, in their reaction against rationalism, insist that "truth" is not a category that interests them; everyone has to find what works for him or her to achieve the chosen goal of personal authenticity. The only condition is that those goals cannot prevent others doing the same. The result is inevitably a comprehensive eclecticism. People join others with whom they are comfortable sharing a joint quest. This takes neopaganism out of any recognizable category of organized religion.

RELATIONSHIP TO CHRISTIANITY

Historically, Christians have had varied attitudes toward earlier manifestations of what is now termed paganism. Many of the early scientists, who were founding members of the Royal Society (established under royal patronage in 1662 as a forum for scientific research and debate, and still flourishing today), were also members of the Rosicrucian order, a kind of freemasonry stressing the importance of character-development as a prerequisite for service to mankind. Most Druids in the last century were active Christians. Past ages regarded magic as a fact of life, much as we regard x-ray technology; the only question was whether it was used benignly or maliciously. Magicians were accepted as functionaries within the Christian community—Merlin being the historic prototype.

Neopaganism, however, is a different animal, growing as it has on the back of the increasing secularism of the past two centuries, reacting against technological alienation from nature, and looking nostalgically back to lost sensitivities. The witch hunt myth has combined with these factors to produce an antagonism toward major religions. Christianity in particular is seen as male-dominated, hierarchical, rationalistically preoccupied with propositional statements, and repressive of authentic human self-expression. Wiccans hold as many misconceptions about Christianity as Christians do about witchcraft. Christian response to neopaganism is, of course, widely varied, from the ecumenical liberalism that sees neopagan ritual as a kind of disguised Christianity, to the fundamentalism that refuses to acknowledge anything in the movement except satanic engagement with evil spirits.

A conservative evangelical stance implies submission to the judgment of Scripture, which carries several implications. First, Christian discipleship is not merely incompatible with but directly opposed to any attempt to contact discarnate spirits, however benign. Spirits are not even to declare gospel truth (Mk 3:11; Acts 16:17). The experiences of the apostle Paul at Ephesus and his subsequent letter to the Ephesians are especially relevant here. Pagans may insist that they don't worship idols and images, but in biblical terms, any lifestyle that recognizes no authority beyond this universe is idolatrous and so condemned by Scripture.

Secondly, some neopagan rhetoric has to be challenged. Its implicit claim to tolerance—"An' it harm none, do as thou wilt"—means little if "harm" is true only for the individual. In addition, it is impossible to forecast with any certainty what will or will not ultimately cause harm. As Viscount Samuel, an early twentieth-century English liberal politician, once remarked, "It is easy to be tolerant if you have no principles." Christian tolerance is surely to be found in the exhortation to honor all people, being willing to listen and learn from them, even when their convictions oppose our own. After all, falsehood is parasitic; it thrives on neglected truth.

Finally, neopagan use of the word *responsible* is suspect, too. It sounds good to insist that everyone is individually "responsible" because it carries connotations of mature conscientiousness. But being responsible means being answerable—that is, prepared to give account of one's behavior to a higher authority.

Some neopagan thinking, however, demands our consideration. In particular, Christians need to take more account of the power of the imagination in the activity of faith to give authority to persons or things, quite apart from any intrinsic value they might have. In addition, Christians need to acknowledge the possibility of powers in the world that are not accessible to modern scientific investigation but not necessarily occult either. After all, our present use of radiation would have been regarded at one time with considerable suspicion. Above all, we need to face the underlying reasons for the attractiveness of neopaganism: the increasing distrust, even fear, of modern science and the disillusionment with politics and lawmaking. Our failures in personal relationships are significant, too. For all our technological achievements, marriages in so-called "primitive" societies survive; two-thirds of ours don't. Our devotion to analysis and technique, expressed in books such as *How to Win Friends and Influence People*, isn't working. And we are becoming increasingly aware that if we don't look after this planet, our descendants might curse us for making it uninhabitable.

Many neopagans see the Christian religion as an establishment showing little concern for nature, but Scripture imparts its own ecological vision of human responsibility, even though many Christians are poorly informed of that fact. Christianity describes a universe with an organic, personal quality of interconnectivity "in Christ" (Jn 1:3; Col 1:16). It redefines authority as service. It is essentially about a personal relationship, starting with God. And it has its own feminism: male domination is a disorder brought about by sin, as is the identification of woman as merely reproductive, as Phyllis Trible has pointed out. This is why the Bible rejects fertility religions and uses masculine titles for God along with feminine attributes (Ex 19:4; Dt 32:11; Is 49:15—the phrase "tender mercy" comes from the Hebrew *rechem*, or "womb"; see also Mt 23:37; Jas 1:18).

In neopagan ethics, there is no forgiveness; the decisions of the cosmos are irreversible. Neopagans see forgiveness, with some justification, as lessening our sense of responsibility. But in the cross, and only there, human beings can receive forgiveness in a way that does not spoil them. It changes them into beings that are fully responsible. Christ offers us a life that we cannot discover ourselves, but he also lets us forget ourselves in devotion to a Creator who gave himself for us in love.

BIBLIOGRAPHY

Margot Adler, *Drawing Down the Moon: Witches, Druids, Goddess-Worshippers, and Other Pagans in America Today* (New York: Penguin/Arkana, 1997).

Hilda Davidson, *Myths and Symbols in Pagan Europe* (Manchester, U.K.: Manchester University Press, 1988).

James R. Lewis, ed., *Magical Religion and Modern Witchcraft* (Albany: State University of New York Press, 1996).

James Lovelock, *Gaia: A New Look at Life on Earth* (Oxford: Oxford University Press, 1982).

Starhawk, *The Spiral Dance: A Rebirth of the Ancient Religion of the Great Goddess* (San Francisco: Harper & Row, 1989).

Graham Harvey, *Listening People, Speaking Earth: Contemporary Paganism* (London: Hurst & Co., 1997).

Graham Harvey and Charlotte Hardman, *Pagan Pathways: A Guide to the Ancient Earth Traditions* (London: HarperCollins/Thorsons, 2000).

Tony and Aileen Grist, *The Illustrated Guide to Wicca* (New York: Sterling, 2000).

Kenneth Meadows, *Earth Medicine: Revealing the Hidden Teachings of the Native American Medicine Wheel* (Rockport, Mass.: Element, 1991).

Sogyal Rinpoche, *The Tibetan Book of Living and Dying* (San Francisco: HarperSanFrancisco/Random House, 1992).

WEBSITES

About Neopaganism

<www.webofoz.org>

<www.ukpaganlinks.co.uk/links/organisations.shtml>

About Druids

<www.druidorder.demon.co.uk>

About Welsh Witchcraft and Druidism

<www.tylwythteg.com/wfwfaq.html>

About Asatru

<www.thetroth.org>

About Native American Spirituality

<www.theearthkeepers.com>

About the Great Witch Hunt

An important essay, "Recent Developments in the Study of the Great European Witch Hunt" by Jenny Gibbons, is found by a link on Covenant of the Goddess homepage: <www.cog.org>.

9

THE BAHA'I WORLD FAITH

Francis J. Beckwith

The Baha'i World Faith is a religion whose apparently eclectic and open nature is perfectly suited for our contemporary age, one in which tolerance, inclusiveness and diversity are the reigning values. This is why converts to Baha'ism—especially those who have been educated in Western liberal democracies—find the faith's precepts affirmed and reinforced by their pluralistic sensibilities.

The fundamental teaching of Baha'ism is that all the major religions derive from the same source and that God has been manifested in virtually every era of human history in the person of a great religious leader such as Jesus or Muhammad. Although Baha'ism is no more tolerant, inclusive or diverse than Christianity (or any other dogmatic faith), that is not readily apparent upon a superficial analysis of the faith. This chapter will examine the Baha'i World Faith, including its history and doctrine, and then critically assess three apparently inclusive and tolerant aspects of the faith that its converts and admirers find so attractive.

HISTORY

The Baha'i Faith (or Baha'ism) originated in mid-nineteenth century Persia—what is now Iran.[1] It is a world religion with its roots in Islam and, in its early days, could rightly have been described as a sect of that religion. But Baha'ism is now considered a religion independent of Islam, in the same way that Christianity, though having its roots in Judaism, is not a sect of that faith.

On May 22, 1844, Mirza Ali Muhammad, a Shiite Muslim, declared himself to be the "Báb," which literally means "gate." He claimed to be the rightful successor of the prophet Muhammad's son-in-law Ali, who had led the Shiite sect of Islam after Muhammad's death. (The larger group of Muslims, the Sunnis, recognize no successor to Muhammad). According to the Shiites, Muhammad had twelve descendants, beginning with Ali, who were known as Imams (literally "leaders"). In A.D. 873 the twelfth and final descendant, Imam Mahdi, vanished. Following his disappearance the Shiites claimed that he would return again at the end of time. The Báb, who is one of the manifestations of God in Baha'i theology, claimed to be the return of this twelfth Imam, thus provoking the wrath of the Shiites.

In addition to theological teachings, the Báb promoted radical social and religious changes inconsistent with Islamic thought of his time. He was a strong advocate of improving the social standing of women, including permitting them to speak with men and allowing them to attend mosque at night for devotions.[2] According to one Baha'i writer, the Báb's writings instructed his followers to "be distinguished by brotherly love and courtesy. Useful arts and crafts must be cultivated. Elementary education should be general. . . . The poor are to be provided for out of the common treasury, but begging is strictly forbidden, as is the use of intoxicating liquors for beverage purposes."[3]

However, some of the Báb's reforms would appear today to be far from liberating. For example, the Báb forbade "the study of jurisprudence, logic, philosophy, dead languages, and grammar (except as necessary for understanding the *Bayan* [a collection of the Báb's writings])."[4] He called for the destruction of all Muslim books except the Qur'an.[5] He also taught that kings who convert to Bábism must proselytize non-Bábís and remove unbelievers from their territories.[6] It should be noted, however, that the Báb's pronouncements are no longer binding on present-day Baha'is since Bahá'u'lláh, and not the Báb, is considered the current manifestation of God. In addition, some Baha'is argue that the Báb's apparently oppressive laws were necessary due to the historical and political circumstances he faced.[7]

The Bábí movement did not last long. After years of persecution, of both he and his followers, the Báb was killed in 1850 in a public execution. But the Baha'i faith claims that the Báb had made arrangements for a successor, for he predicted a leader even greater than the Báb would arise.

Mirza Husayn Ali was a follower of the Báb and claimed in 1863 to be the one the Báb had predicted as his successor. Changing his name to Bahá'u'lláh (which literally means "the glory of God"), Husayn Ali declared himself to be a manifestation of God. Those Bábís who embraced Bahá'u'lláh's claims and teachings came to be identified as Baha'is. However, some Bábís continued to follow Subh-I-Ezel, the younger half-brother of Bahá'u'lláh, who some argue Báb had designated as his successor.[8] The two groups fought each other. Some of their encounters turned violent and resulted in fatalities. The government finally interceded in 1868, extraditing both Subh-I-Ezel and Bahá'u'lláh to prison, the former to Cyprus and the latter to Akka.[9] Subh-I-Ezel's sect slowly faded away while Bahá'u'lláh's group gained momentum and attracted more and more disciples.

Bahá'u'lláh clarified and expanded on the Báb's teaching and presented to the world a unique set of theological and political beliefs that formed the foundation of the Baha'i World Faith. After Bahá'u'lláh's death in 1892, leadership was placed in the hands of his son, Abbas Effendi, who later became known as Abdul-Baha. Unlike his father or the Báb, Abdul-Baha never claimed to be a manifestation of God, though he is considered an authoritative interpreter of the faith.[10] He was instrumental in bringing Baha'ism to Europe and North America, and his travels included a coast to coast visit to the United States in 1912 that introduced him to many American religious groups and university students and faculty. Abdul-Baha passed away in 1921. He was succeeded by his grandson, Shoghi Effendi. Since his 1957 death, the leadership was no longer held by a descendant of Bahá'u'lláh but rather by the Universal House of Justice (UHJ), a representative body whose members are elected by Baha'is from every portion of the globe.

This transition of leadership did not go unchallenged within the Baha'i community. Arising out of the controversy was the Orthodox Baha'i Faith. Organized by excommunicant Mason Remy, this group differs little from the Baha'i World Faith in its doctrines. Its chief dispute with the main body concerns the line of leadership. Orthodox Baha'is deny that the Universal House of Justice is Shoghi Effendi's proper successor. They believe that Remy was the true successor.[11]

The international headquarters of the Baha'i World Faith is in Haifa, Israel. Its U.S. headquarters is located in Wilmette, Illinois, and is well-known for its opulent nine-sided temple, which represents the nine great religious leaders believed to be manifestations of the one God.

As of December 2001, according to the official Baha'i website <www.bahai.org>, there are some five million Baha'is worldwide with an impressive geographic spread. Second only to Christianity in how widespread it is, the Baha'i Faith is "established in 235 countries and territories throughout the world." Baha'is "come from over 2,100 ethnic, racial, and tribal groups."

DOCTRINE

The Baha'i Faith derives its doctrines from the writings and talks of the Báb and Bahá'u'lláh, with the latter taking precedence over the former.[12] Bahá'u'lláh dictated more than a hundred books and tablets, the "most weighted and sacred" work being the Kitab-i-Aqdas ("Most Holy Book"). Baha'i beliefs are also derived from the interpretations of Bahá'u'lláh's works by Abdul-Baha, Shoghi Effendi and the Universal House of Justice. Although they believe that the scriptures of other religions, such as the Qur'an and the Bible, are valuable, Baha'is maintain that they should be interpreted in light of the teachings of the most recent manifestation of God, Bahá'u'lláh. For example, in the Kitab-i-Iqan Bahá'u'lláh reinterprets the Christian Scriptures' clear affirmation that the dead will undergo a literal physical resurrection upon the return of Christ (1 Cor 15:51-53). "According to Baha'i teaching," writes Baha'i scholar J. E. Esslemont, "the Resurrection has nothing to do with the gross physical body. That body, once dead, is done with. It becomes decomposed and its atoms will never be recomposed into the same body."[13]

Many people are attracted to the Baha'i Faith because of social and political ideals that call for a one world government to institute the following precepts and general policies: unfettered search for truth, oneness of mankind, the reconciliation of science and religion, universal peace, an international language (Esperanto), education for all, equal opportunity for both men and women, work for all, elimination of extremes of wealth and poverty, unity of freedom, unity of religion, unity of nations and unity of races.

Although the Baha'i Faith is popularly known for these high ideals, it does have a distinct set of beliefs about God, revelation and humanity that clearly distinguish it from other world religions but also serve as the philosophical foundation for its high ideals. Its primary and basic belief is that the major world religions derive from the same source. This tenet is based on the doctrine that the great religious figures in human history were manifestations of the same God, an invisible and unknowable essence. Baha'ism teaches that the manifestations reflect, though do not directly reveal, the glorious attributes of God.[14] An analogy often used by Baha'is is that the manifestations are to God what the sun's rays and reflection are to the sun.[15] Baha'ism also teaches that "knowledge" of God may be acquired through general revelation, that one may recognize God's handiwork by observing and reflecting on both human nature and the natural world.[16]

It is difficult to find in Baha'i literature a definitive list of divine manifestations. The closest we have to such a list is from a letter from the Universal House of Justice to a Baha'i that quotes Shoghi Effendi: "The nine religions to which you have referred include both the Bábí and Baha'i Dispensations, Bahá'u'lláh being the Ninth Prophet in the series. The other Prophets included are Zoroaster, Krishna, Moses, the Christ, Muhammad, Buddha, the Prophet of the Sabeans whose name is unrecorded, the Báb and Bahá'u'lláh."[17] However, Baha'i leaders have presented different lists over the years. For example, the official Baha'i website claims that "the Messengers have included Abraham, Krishna, Zoroaster, Moses, Buddha, Jesus, and Muhammad."[18] Abdul-Baha in 1908 asserted that the manifestations of God were Abraham, Moses, Christ, Muhammad, the Báb and Bahá'u'lláh.[19] In October 1912 he claimed that the manifestations were Moses, Jesus, Zoroaster, Krishna, Buddha, Confucius, Muhammad, the Báb and Bahá'u'lláh.[20] The Báb included Adam as one of the manifestations,[21] while Bahá'u'lláh has said that the list includes Noah, Hud,[22] Salih,[23] Abraham, Moses, Jesus, Muhammad and the Báb.[24]

According to a booklet published by the Baha'i Publishing Trust, the nine revealed religions of the world are the Sabean religion, Hinduism, Judaism, Zoroastrianism, Buddhism, Christianity, Islam, the Bábí religion and the Baha'i religion.[25] In a 1965 Collier's Encyclopedia article, Hugh E. Chance, who in 1963 was elected to the first Universal House of Justice, listed the nine religions as Hinduism, Zoroastrianism, Buddhism, Confucianism, Taoism, Judaism, Christianity and the Baha'i religion.[26] According to Baha'i apologist Peter Terry, one reason for these differing lists is that "the Guardian [Shoghi Effendi] did not indicate that only nine Manifestations were authentic, but rather he stated that only nine living religions derived from authentic Manifestations are presently in existence."[27]

According to Baha'i doctrine, each manifestation brings to his era new laws and revelations that would have been too difficult for the people of previous dispensations to understand. This is why Baha'ism teaches that special revelation is not static (perhaps even relative), and that revelation binding for previous eras cannot be rightly applied to the present or future unless it is included in the revelation of the current manifestation. Teachings subject to change are those believed to be nonessential to the essence of true religion. These include moral, ceremonial, dietary and doctrinal teachings. Truths apparently not subject to change are those believed to be fundamental to true religion: the oneness of God, the brotherhood of humanity, and the doctrine of relative (or progressive) revelation through God's manifestations. Therefore Baha'is do not consider the inconsistencies among different religious systems to be problematic.

Unlike the orthodox versions of Islam, Judaism and Christianity, which teach that the universe had a beginning and was created by a personal God out of nothing (creatio ex nihilo), Baha'ism seems to teach that the universe is without beginning and is a perpetual emanation from God's being. According to Esslemont, "Bahá'u'lláh teaches that the universe is without a beginning in time. It is a perpetual emanation from the Great First Cause."[28] Yet some Baha'i literature speaks of God in terms that seem consistent with classical monotheism and creatio ex nihilo. For example, the Baha'i Faith asserts on its website: "The Baha'i belief in one God means that the universe and all creatures and forces within it have been created by a single supernatural Being. This Being, Whom we call God, has absolute control over His creation (omnipotence) as well as perfect and complete knowledge of it (omniscience)."[29]

Concerning the afterlife, the Baha'i Faith teaches that the depictions of heaven and hell in other religions ought to be read symbolically. It does, however, teach that there is disembodied conscious existence in the afterlife. Those who cared for their souls in this mortal realm will be able to enjoy the next world and continue to make progress. Those who neglected their souls will forever be in an unhappy state, though it is possible that unbelievers will receive a pardon in the afterlife if they change.[30]

THREE CHALLENGES TO BAHA'I TEACHINGS

Baha'i teachings raise numerous philosophical and theological questions. The following are three areas in which a Christian may raise questions in dialogue with a Baha'i: the claim of nonexclusiveness, Baha'i affirmation of the unity of religions, and the relativity of religious truth. These three areas are important because they seem to be the most attractive to non-Baha'is.

The claim of nonexclusiveness. Because it claims that the founders of the world's major religions were manifestations of God, the Baha'i Faith appears to be nonexclusive in its view of other religions. Many people find this posture attractive, and some Baha'is cite this apparent nonexclusivity as evidence of Baha'ism's truth.

For example, Baha'i apologist Esslemont writes, "The different religious communities have failed to unite in the past, because the adherents of each have regarded the Founder of their community as the one supreme authority, and His law as divine. Any Prophet Who proclaimed a different message was, therefore, regarded as the enemy of truth. . . . It is obvious that while this state of matters exists no true unity is possible."[31] Esslemont provides us with a solution: "Bahá'u'lláh, on the other hand, teaches that the Prophets were bearers of authentic messages from God; that each in His day gave the highest teachings that the people could then receive, and educated men so that they were able to receive further teaching from His successors."[32] But this solution of Esslemont's promotes the same exclusivism he is claiming to combat.

First, Esslemont is saying that the best way for all religions to unite is for their adherents to become Baha'is. But each religion already makes that same appeal about itself to outsiders: "Agree with us and we won't disagree anymore." Second, Esslemont's solution is really claiming that Bahá'u'lláh is correct about the world religions and if you disagree with him you are incorrect. But how does this position differ from Esslemont's appraisal of other religions that assert that "any Prophet Who proclaimed a different message was, therefore, regarded as the enemy of truth"? For there is no doubt that if Bahá'u'lláh is telling the truth and we disagree with him, then we are in fact enemies of truth. So Esslemont's position does not differ in any significant way from the religious positions he is attacking and from which he wants to distinguish Baha'ism. Thus, Baha'ism is no more open or inclusive than any other world religion, including Christianity.

Baha'i affirmation of the unity of religions. In order to avoid the impact of the incoherence in affirming that all the major world religions are ultimately derived from the same God, Baha'i leader Shoghi Effendi once said that the manifestations only disagree on "non-essential aspects of their doctrine."[33] But there are at least two problems with this response.

It is a criterion without any content. No matter what inconsistent concepts of God one presents to the Baha'i, she can dismiss them out of hand simply on the basis that "they are nonessential aspects." And who decides which doctrines in other religions are nonessential? The Baha'is, of course. The truth of the Baha'i religion depends on the manifestations' being unified in some theological sense. But the Baha'is declare certain aspects of the "unified" religions to be essential or nonessential based on what Bahá'u'lláh and the authoritative interpreters have decided is relevant. Why should we accept Bahá'u'lláh's criteria if the purpose of citing religious unity is to convince us that Bahá'u'lláh is God's manifestation for this age and to become Baha'is? In other words, because the question is whether Bahá'u'lláh is God's manifestation for this age, it does no good to appeal to the authority of Bahá'u'lláh to convince us of this point. Hence, only by assuming that Bahá'u'lláh is a manifestation of God (thus assuming the truth of Baha'ism) can the Baha'i make her point.

This faulty reasoning is similar to that which occurs in a film starring French comedian Sacha Guitry:

> Some thieves are arguing over the division of seven pearls worth a king's ransom. One of them hands two to the man on his right, then two to the man on his left. "I," he says, "will keep three."

The man on his right says, "How come you keep three?"
"Because I am the leader," he replies.
"Oh. But how come you are the leader?"
"Because I have more pearls."[34]

Table 1. The Doctrine of God Taught by the Manifestations

Manifestation	Important Elements in His Doctrine of God
Moses	God is personal. Strict, uncompromising monotheism. God existed prior to creating the universe; that is, the universe is not eternal (Gen 1—3; Deut 6:4).
Krishna	Polytheistic, but ultimately pantheistic and impersonal. The universe is therefore eternal.
Zoroaster	One good god and one evil god. Religious dualism.
Buddha	God is not relevant. Essentially agnostic.
Confucius	Polytheistic.
Muhammad	God is personal, unable to beget a son. Strict, uncompromising monotheism.
Jesus Christ	God is personal, able to beget a son. Strict, uncompromising monotheism.
Bahá'u'lláh	God is the creator of the universe. The universe is either created ex nihilo or is an emanation of God. God is unknowable, yet revealed in part by manifestations.

There is no basis for distinguishing true from false manifestations. Although Baha'is affirm Shoghi Effendi's credo that the world's religions disagree only on nonessential aspects, it stretches credibility to the limit to suppose that the nature of God is one of these nonessential aspects. This is, however, precisely what the Baha'is must claim, since the manifestations disagree with one another on the nature of God. How can the

Baha'is claim that any individual is a manifestation of God if all the manifestations describe God differently? That is, if God's nature is either unknowable, as Bahá'u'lláh and his authoritative interpreters have claimed, or inconsistent beyond coherence, then how can the seeker of truth separate false manifestations from true ones or discover if any of them speaks for the true God? Baha'is obviously do not accept every alleged prophet as a manifestation of God—neither Joseph Smith nor Sun Myung Moon made the cut. How then can they justifiably exclude someone from being a manifestation when the God being manifested is either unknowable or described in terms inconsistent with the teachings of prior manifestations? Just as an "object" with incompatible properties, such as a "square-circle," is really no object at all, a God with inconsistent properties is really no God at all. Therefore, if the Baha'i manifestations teach irreconcilable concepts of God, as they apparently do (see table 1), there is rational warrant to reject the Baha'i Faith as the true religion.

A Baha'i reply. Peter Terry replies to the above two points in several ways, the following of which are the strongest. First, he argues that Confucius was not a manifestation, because Shoghi Effendi said so. However, Abdul-Baha, another authoritative interpreter, said Confucius *was* a manifestation (see note 20). Second, he maintains that the concept of God is an essential truth and although the original teachings of Buddha, Zoroaster and Krishna are largely lost,[35] these leaders were apparently known by Baha'i leaders to have taught monotheism.[36] For that reason, he says, Baha'is are justified in saying that these manifestations taught a concept of God consistent with Judaism, Islam and Christianity.

Such reasoning is flawed. On the one hand, if Terry is arguing that because we do not have the original teachings of these manifestations, Baha'is are justified in believing they were monotheists, he is committing the fallacy of argument from ignorance. For in the absence of evidence it is just as likely that these manifestations taught polytheism or dualism. So it is not clear why a non-Baha'i should accept these religious leaders as manifestations if Baha'is themselves admit to having little or no evidence of what they taught concerning the nature of God. On the other hand, if Terry's argument is primarily appealing to Baha'i authorities such as Abdul-Baha—and to no historical evidence outside those authorities—then we have the same problem as in the question of nonessential aspects. Terry cannot appeal to the authority of individuals to convince non-Baha'is to accept the authority of those individuals. The argument is viciously circular.

A final problem with Terry's case is that the evidence does not seem to matter. If there was overwhelming evidence that Confucius, Buddha and the like were not monotheists,[37] it would likely be reinterpreted to conform to Baha'i teachings. Take for example Terry's assessment of Bible passages that seem to affirm the incarnation of the Second Person of the Trinity in the historical person of Jesus of Nazareth, which "have been interpreted by many Christians to be in support of" this doctrine. Such verses, according to Terry, "have simply been interpreted differently by Muslims, Bábís and Baha'is, and in accord with their Scriptures, which claim to vouchsafe a more complete Revelation of the divine Will to humanity than that found in the Gospels."[38] So, if there is no evidence against the Baha'i view, then the Baha'i view must be right—again, an argument from ignorance. But if there is evidence against the Baha'i view, then the Baha'i view is still right, for the Baha'i interprets the contrary evidence in light of the Baha'i view—more circular reasoning. Thus, at the end of the day, the evidence does not really matter for Baha'is.

The relativity of religious truth. The Baha'i Faith sometimes seems to teach that there is no absolute unchanging religious truth. Shoghi Effendi writes, "The fundamental principle enunciated by Bahá'u'lláh . . . is that religious truth is not absolute, but relative."[39] Depending on what he means, this principle is either self-refuting or trivial.

It is self-refuting. A self-refuting argument is one that cannot fulfill its own criterion. Philosopher J. P. Moreland cites some examples: "'I cannot say a word of English' is self-refuting when uttered in English. 'I do not exist' is self-refuting, for one must exist to utter it. The claim 'there are no truths' is self-refuting. If it is false, then it is false. But if it is true, then it is false as well, for in that case there would be no truths, including the statement itself."[40]

The statement "all religious truth is relative," which is accepted by the Baha'is as a religious truth, is itself either a relative or an absolute religious truth. If the statement is relative, it is not absolutely binding and could change tomorrow, but that means that it is possible that absolute religious truth does exist. On the other hand, if the statement "all religious truth is relative" is an absolute religious truth, then the statement "all religious truth is relative" cannot be true, for it is itself a nonrelative religious truth. Thus the Baha'i doctrine of relative religious truth is self-refuting and incoherent.

It is trivial. It is likely that Shoghi Effendi employed a poor choice of words when articulating the Baha'i view of religious truth. Perhaps all he meant to say was that some unchanging eternal truths do exist, but other religious truths are relative to time and place. The Baha'i Faith instructs us to abandon such relative truths and replace them with new ones from the latest manifestation. But it is not clear how this view differs from the one held by Christians, that God has progressively revealed himself over time. According to the Christian view, God has provided special revelation through specific people and events in history, first recorded in the Old Testament and later in the New Testament, and this revelation tells the story of the death and resurrection of his Son, the genesis of the early church and the formation of its theology. According to the dominant view held by the Christian church, certain commands and laws were relative to certain ages—for example, ceremonial and dietary laws—while other truths revealed in Scripture are just that: truths, propositions about the nature of God, the universe and humanity, which are always and everywhere true.

Thus, on this second interpretation of Shoghi Effendi's "relative revelation" doctrine, the Baha'i view of revelation is trivial, for it is not in principle different from the one embraced by Christians and adherents of other monotheistic faiths.

CONCLUSION

Although much more can be said about the Baha'i Faith, I believe that the above analysis adequately conveys the history and tenets of the faith as well as some of the legitimate questions that Christians can raise in dialogue with Baha'is.

The Baha'i Faith affirms doctrines that are appealing to the contemporary mind, doctrines that seem to affirm people's intuitions about nonexclusivism, religious unity and revelational relativism. But as we have seen, there are deep philosophical and theological problems with Baha'i teachings on these matters. Consequently Christians, when they come to truly appreciate these problems, may confidently share their faith with Baha'is without fear of being accused of being less tolerant or more dogmatic than the adherents of Baha'ism—or any other worldview or religion.

THE NATION OF ISLAM

Craig S. Keener and Glenn Usry

Until the early part of the twentieth century, most African Americans lived in the rural South with its legacy of subjugation and discrimination. Beginning with World War I, the promise of a better life and the availability of manufacturing jobs resulted in a massive migration of blacks from the rural South to the industrialized, urban north. As these migrants settled in the urban ghettoes of the northern cities, many of them were attracted to a variety of sects and new religious movements.

The origins of the Nation of Islam movement can be traced to the ghettoes of Detroit and the arrival there of Wallace D. Fard in the summer of 1930. Fard began to preach a message of black supremacy, claiming that all African Americans were Muslims in their origins and all whites were "blue-eyed devils." His form of black nationalism and his interpretation of black civilization appealed to poor ghetto blacks, and he continued to gain converts.

In 1934 Fard mysteriously disappeared and one of his devotees, Elijah Muhammad, assumed the mantle of leadership. The Nation of Islam (black Muslims) continued to espouse a philosophy of individual self-help, racial separation and moral discipline. Malcolm X, later to become one of Elijah Muhammad's primary disciples and spokespersons, joined the Nation of Islam in 1949 and soon brought national attention to the organization. The conversion of two sports celebrities, Muhammad Ali and Kareem Abdul-Jabbar, testified to the growing popularity of the movement. Later, Malcolm X resigned from the Nation of Islam following a dispute with Elijah Muhammad. After a pilgrimage to Africa and Mecca, Malcolm X renounced the teachings of Muhammad. Soon thereafter, while giving a speech in Harlem, he was assassinated.

Louis Farrakhan took over the leadership of the Nation of Islam and under his direction it became a powerful force within the African American community. His influence was especially visible when, in October of 1995, he organized the Million Man March in Washington, D.C.

Whatever else the Nation of Islam may teach today, its original principles stem from Elijah Muhammad, whose views have circulated widely even outside the movement. He was one of the primary voices in the African American community circulating claims that Christianity was a "white" religion. Yet he was not representing orthodox Islam but a new religion that is less than a century old. His influence remains strong in the in-house teachings of the Nation of Islam under Louis Farrakhan, and still more prominently among some smaller sects that preserve his teachings without apology.

ELIJAH MUHAMMAD'S VIEW OF HIMSELF

Elijah Muhammad believed that he was destined to be the true leader of American blacks. He claimed that anyone who opposed his economic program, for instance, could "not be considered a man or woman who wants to see his or her people out of the chains of want and suffering."[1] Black people's problem was that they lacked a teacher, he said, but now he, Elijah Muhammad, had come from God himself. "Why not believe and follow me?" he asked.[2] Sample some of his other claims:

- "I am the first man since the death of Yakub commissioned by God directly."[3]

- "We have a Savior that is born. . . . We have a Savior today. He is with me. He is able to feed you. He is able to clothe you."[4]

- "He [Allah] has made me a door. . . . You will come by me, and if you reject me, you will not go. I have been given the keys to heaven."[5]

- "You have been taught for the past 34 years from the mouth of Almighty God, Allah, through His Messenger."[6]

- "[Allah] did not raise me as a Messenger like the Prophets of old, but he raised me as a Messenger, a Warner and a Reminder to the Nations of that which was prophesied to take place in these last days."[7]

- "My mission is to give life to the dead. What I teach brings them out of death and into life. . . . There will be no other Messenger. I am the last and after me will come God Himself."[8]

Elijah Muhammad also claimed that the final messenger of Allah must be black and come among North American blacks; thus it was to Elijah Muhammad that Allah had revealed the end-time truth.[9] Elijah complained against apostates who preached against him, the messenger, while claiming to still follow Islam, and he warned his followers to beware of false prophets—anyone who would lead them not to respect Allah's messenger; such would perish in hell.[10] The only two unforgivable sins, he said, were failure to accept Allah as God and failure to accept his messenger. If someone rejected the messenger, that person became an enemy of Allah.[11]

Because Elijah's own son Wallace Muhammad was moving toward orthodox Islam along with Malcolm X, Elijah warned that a messenger's son may not believe him.[12] (Some of W. D. Fard's followers from the beginning repudiated Elijah as Fard's messenger as well.[13]) In response to the defection of his son and Malcolm X, Elijah announced that those who claimed to follow Allah but rejected his messenger were Allah's enemies.[14] Thus Elijah concluded that Malcolm X was a hypocrite who never "had really believed in Islam."[15] Malcolm X's charges about his sexual sins, he said, were groundless and motivated by evil.[16]

Elijah Muhammad was hardly subtle about claiming to be the final messenger—a role that orthodox Islam has traditionally reserved for the seventh-century prophet Muhammad, whom they regard as the last of the great prophets. Those familiar with the New Testament will recognize that Elijah Muhammad took many of his claims from Jesus—some of which orthodox Muslims associate with Jesus, more of which they associate with the seventh-century Muhammad, and some of which they associate with no one but Allah himself. Yet Elijah Muhammad made the claims he did because he believed he had met Allah in the flesh, Master Wallace D. Fard.

ISLAM VERSUS THE NATION OF ISLAM

Elijah Muhammad sometimes spoke as if his Nation of Islam were the same as Islam elsewhere, and that Asia, Africa and the Caribbean all followed the basic message he taught.[17] Yet the Nation of Islam is a new religion quite distinct from historic forms of Islam, and Elijah Muhammad came to understand the distinction quite well.

On more than one occasion he sought to correct the "misunderstandings" of orthodox Muslims, claiming that various prophecies traditionally applied to the first Muhammad really applied to himself instead. "There are many Arabs throughout the world who cannot bear witness to anyone that another messenger would rise up after Muhammad, who was here nearly 1,400 years ago," he said. "This is due to their misunderstanding of the Holy Qur-an."[18] Likewise, he claimed that the lives of Moses and Jesus were merely examples, or types, of the final messenger who would arrive at the time of the end.[19]

Elijah Muhammad would not depend simply on the teachings of his ancient predecessor, he said. The final messenger must be a black American, but not one "trying to learn from what Muhammad said to the Arabs nearly 1,400 years ago." He claimed that the Qur'an and Bible both showed another scripture to be given in the time of judgment.[20] As far as the orthodox Muslims in the world who disagreed with him, Elijah Muhammad asserted that they were weak and loved Allah's enemies (white people).[21] In the end it would not matter, he said, for orthodox Muslims could not stop him: "Neither Jeddah nor Mecca have sent me! I am sent from Allah. . . . I am not taking orders from them, I am taking orders from Allah (God) Himself."[22]

Elijah Muhammad's teachings frequently contradict central tenets of historic Islam, the most notable being his claim that his teacher was Allah in the flesh. Orthodox Islam rejected the Christian claim that Jesus was divine precisely because Islam denies that God could be flesh. According to Elijah, white devils propagated the lie that God is spirit rather than man.[23] Around 1930 Wallace Fard allegedly told Elijah Muhammad, "My name is Mahdi; I am God."[24] Thereafter Elijah preached the deity of Fard, one of the most repetitive refrains of his *Message to the Blackman in America.*[25] Allah's appearance as Fard in July 1930 is Elijah Muhammad's twelfth and final affirmation of faith.[26] In the future millennium, everyone will "obey One God: Fard Muhammad the Great Mahdi, or Allah in Person."[27] In addition, one must submit to Fard as Allah to be successful.[28]

Elijah Muhammad is aware that orthodox Islam disagrees with this central tenet of his faith but responds that he is the first to fully understand the Qur'an: "Many of the Orthodox Muslims do not want to believe that Allah has appeared in the Person of Master Fard Muhammad or that He has made manifest the truth that has been hidden from their religious scientists—the truth of God and of the devil as revealed to me. Though they do have the Holy Qur-an, many of them do not understand the meaning of it."[29]

Elijah Muhammad has suggested that God the Creator no longer personally exists but continues instead in his people, the black race.[30] Malcolm X openly reported that, according to Elijah Muhammad, Fard declared black people to be gods and himself to be Messiah, God in person.[31] According to Malcolm X's report, the Nation of Islam teaches that all blacks are God—Allah being the supreme black man, but other blacks being divine as well.[32]

Again, historic Islam rejected Christianity precisely because it taught that Jesus was God's Son and God in flesh; Islam declared instead that God had no son and could not become flesh. Historic Islam is no closer to the Nation of Islam on this central point than it is to Christianity.

ELIJAH MUHAMMAD ON THE RESURRECTION

At times Elijah Muhammad mixes components of Christianity and Islam, but always in ways that exalt Master Fard. For instance, while Elijah ridicules the notion that Jesus' death could have had atoning value,[33] he declares that Fard offered his life to restore blacks to their proper role.[34]

But when it comes to the doctrine of the resurrection, which is central to both historic Christianity and Islam, Elijah goes his own way. For him the final "resurrection" is simply the awakening of mentally dead black Americans through his own teaching.[35] In summarizing the beliefs of Islam, he does not hesitate to redefine the end-time resurrection: "The New Testament and Holy Qur-an's teaching of a resurrection of the dead can't mean the people who have died physically and returned to the earth, but rather a mental resurrection of us, the black nation, who are mentally dead to the knowledge of truth."[36] He adds that because black Americans need mental resurrection most, they will be resurrected before anyone else.[37] He further claims that he is resurrecting the dead and that an Arab with an Arabic Qur'an could not do it.[38]

Elijah Muhammad regards as impossible, even ridiculous, the idea that a person can be restored after death. "There is no such thing as dying and

coming up out of the earth. . . . I say, get out of such slavery teachings.
. . . When you are dead, you are DEAD."[39] He in fact attributes any belief
in an afterlife purely to slavery teaching,[40] ignoring the afterlife doctrines
of both orthodox Islam and virtually all traditional African religions.

The only proof Elijah offers for this proposition is that the contrary
position lacks proof; no one has ever come back from the dead.[41] Two
Christian responses to this argument are in order. First, orthodox Islam
and Christianity generally reserve the resurrection for the end of the age,
making it difficult to provide specimens to show that it has already taken
place. Any of Elijah's own teaching about the end times, including the
"mental resurrection," could be dismissed on the same grounds. But second, Christians claim that one resurrection, that of Jesus, has already occurred in history (1 Cor 15:20). Suffice it to note here that orthodox
Christianity and Islam stand closer on the doctrine of resurrection than
Elijah Muhammad stands to either of them.

ISLAM AND THE NATION OF ISLAM ON OTHER DOCTRINES

For Elijah Muhammad, the Qur'an is no longer inerrant. Although "the
Bible and the Holy Qur-an are filled with truth," only portions of them
remain accurate; "the [white] enemy has tampered with the truth in both
books: for he has been permitted to handle both books."[42] One can employ this approach to explain away anything in a holy book if that person
resorts merely to his own claims without evidence.

Probably the most obvious distinction between Elijah Muhammad's
Nation of Islam and orthodox Islam is their differing view of white
people. Whereas many blacks have been attracted to the Nation of Islam because of its consistent portrayal of whites as "devils,"[43] this portrayal conflicts with historic Middle Eastern Islam, the ethnic foundation of which is Arab. Malcolm X repudiated such racism after his
conversion to orthodox Islam.[44] Elijah acknowledged that "some" orthodox Muslims did not agree that the white race were devils, but, he

claimed, they "are gradually coming over with me in the understanding for the first time in their history." He says white reporters must have misrepresented the words of the general secretary of Mecca, which implied otherwise.[45] He claims that because Allah taught him that whites are a race of devils, his followers are not free to repudiate this doctrine.[46]

According to Elijah Muhammad, whites are devils by nature; there is no way out for them.[47] People should stop preaching that God loves all people, he warns. God certainly does not love whites; in fact, he hates them.[48] In Elijah's understanding, the Bible teaches that hell is the final destination for all whites, "an appointed people for hell fire from the beginning of their creation."[49] Furthermore, biblical promises for the righteous can apply only to blacks.[50] Of course, not all blacks are righteous, he continues; some 90 percent who still love whites will have to go to hell with them.[51] Whites constitute the Adamic race in the Bible, a devil race formed by the evil scientist Mr. Yakub to avenge himself against the pure and upright black world.[52]

Thus the only solution to the racial problem is separation from whites—if possible into a black state. Such separation is a more important spiritual matter than prayer.[53] In this belief the Nation of Islam formed the mirror image of white supremacists, sometimes consciously.[54] For Elijah Muhammad, love of enemies was foolishness, for God himself hates his enemies.[55] He asserted that whites taught love of enemies to keep the blacks from complaining against them.[56] Thus Martin Luther King Jr. was "making a fool of himself" and wanted to fool black people into loving devils. Only if King and his followers accepted Islam and demanded a territory for blacks would Elijah join forces with them.[57]

One problem this ideology creates is that Master Fard, whom Elijah Muhammad believed to be Allah, was a Turk—not black or an African. But this white appearance, Elijah concludes, was merely a disguise. Master Fard explained to Elijah that his father was really black but chose a white woman to marry "so that she would give birth to a son looking white."[58] Because Fard was half black and half white, he could "go among both black and white without being discovered or recognized."[59] Likewise Elijah claims that the prophet Muhammad as an Arab was black but Jesus and Moses as Jews were white.[60] He ignores the fact that Middle Eastern Jews and Arabs probably had similar complexions and that Muhammad and most of his companions were not portrayed as black in the earliest Arab artwork.

Mustafa El-Amin offers a detailed yet gracious differentiation of the Nation of Islam from historic Islam in *The Religion of Islam and the Nation of Islam: What Is the Difference?* Once a disciple of Elijah Muhammad, El-Amin followed his son Imam Warith D. Muhammad into historic Islam after Elijah Muhammad's death in 1975.[61] After Malcolm X renounced the Nation of Islam as a corruption of Islam, the Nation reportedly plotted to kill him.[62] Elijah Muhammad's son Wallace moved the Nation of Islam in a more orthodox direction, which Malcolm had espoused, but Louis Farrakhan and other breakaway groups led as many as one hundred thousand followers back to the more sectarian varieties that preserved Elijah Muhammad's teachings.[63]

CHALLENGES TO CHRISTIAN TEACHING

Elijah Muhammad's words might be more credible to Christians if he did not misrepresent Christianity and the Bible so severely. Protestant and Eastern Orthodox Christians, for example, might be surprised to learn that the head of all Christians (and of the white race) is the pope in Rome.[64] That the pope is Christians' "god" would probably surprise Catholics as well.[65] Black preachers are said to be simply pawns of white people,[66] more an enemy to their people than the white devils themselves.[67] Black Christians, Elijah claimed, are doomed to hell.[68]

Elijah Muhammad's successor, Louis Farrakhan, rarely speaks negatively of Jesus in public, but one wonders how often he speaks of the historical Jesus and how often he really means the final messenger of whom the historical Jesus was merely a "type"—i.e., Master Fard, who Elijah declared would be "the Christ, the second Jesus."[69] Elijah announced that this Jesus made his appearance on July 4, 1930, and "His work is now in effect."[70] Elsewhere Elijah Muhammad claims that the historical Jesus was an example pointing to the final messenger at the end-time resurrection, namely Elijah Muhammad himself.[71]

Elijah Muhammad instructed his followers to "forget about ever seeing the return of Jesus," the man who was on the earth two thousand years ago. Rather they should look for the one he prophesied, Allah in the flesh, the "Son of Man," "Christ," "Comforter"—that is, Wallace D. Fard.[72] This figure would come "from the East" (Mt 24:27), which Elijah interprets as the land of Islam.[73] In context this passage actually refers to a coming of Jesus so public and indisputable that it will light up the sky "from east to west," a good ancient way of saying the whole sky (Mt 24:23-27). The coming will also be of the biblical Jesus alone (Mt 24:3, 5, 23-24).

But if the second Jesus, W. D. Fard, is what matters, what then of Christianity? The Nation of Islam asserts that Allah will overthrow both Buddhism and Christianity.[74] Christians worship Jesus, Elijah Muhammad says, falsely claiming that he is the son of Allah "born without the agency of man, thus accusing God of an act of adultery."[75] (By contrast, although orthodox Islam denies that Jesus is God's Son, it does acknowledge the Virgin Birth.)

Lest one think that Elijah would tolerate the presence of the black church before its overthrow, we should remember that he warned blacks to "get away from the old slavery teaching that Jesus, who was killed 2,000 years ago, is still alive somewhere waiting and listening to their prayers."[76] Jesus was merely a prophet and, like other dead prophets, cannot hear prayers.[77] Furthermore, he says, Jesus is dead and cannot return because resurrection cannot happen.[78] (By contrast, orthodox Islam generally denies that Jesus has died.) According to Elijah, "infidel teachers" speak of Jesus' resurrection, but "this is the greatest falsehood ever told," and the only proof Christians offer is the "spirit" they feel.[79]

Elijah regards the Bible as only partly holy;[80] he says that God himself calls it "the Poison Book" because whites tampered with its contents.[81] He claims that the Bible has deceived people, and because it has been misunderstood, it is the "graveyard" of black people, from which they must be mentally resurrected.[82] Why then would Elijah Muhammad bother quoting from the Bible? Only because, as he points out, many blacks would not hear him otherwise.[83] Thus Elijah affirms the Bible's "truth" while feeling free to reinterpret it because it has been "tampered with."[84]

And he does come up with some unusual interpretations. The twenty-four elders of Revelation, for example, are the "Islamic scientists."[85] Every twenty-five thousand years, the period of time necessary to realign the earth's poles, twenty-four black scientists write a new history such as the Bible or the Qur'an.[86] Like some errant teachers of Christian prophecy, Elijah interprets the Bible as if it were written specifically for his generation and his mission. For example, the "lost nation" in the wilderness supposedly predicted in the Bible can only be the black community in North America.[87] Presumably he refers to biblical promises of Israel's restoration, which some Christian interpreters also apply to the church, but he takes these prophecies out of context to fit only black Americans.

Where a biblical text does not suit Elijah's purpose, he ignores the contradiction: "lost sheep of the house of Israel" (Mt 10:6) become black Americans,[88] even though Jesus was borrowing Old Testament language for the Jewish people (Is 53:6; Jer 50:6; Ezek 34:5). At different points he interprets the beast in Revelation as "the white man," the United States, or Christianity[89]—the latter being somewhat of a stretch given that the beast persecutes Jesus' followers (Rev 17:6).

Elijah interprets some passages of the Bible in a way that allows him to criticize Scripture without acknowledging other, more carefully re-searched interpretations. For instance, he asserts that "Lead us not into temptation" must imply "a lack of confidence in God to lead us aright," and the prayer for bread "this day" instructs people to seek physical nourishment before spiritual.[90] But the "temptation" line in the Lord's Prayer is simply a prayer for protection in testing, similar to Jewish prayers with which Jesus' disciples may have already been familiar. As to "this day," God is practical in recognizing our daily need for food, but the context is clear that disciples should seek God's kingdom first (Mt 6:9-10, 33). Elijah fails to read the Bible in context and then blames the results of that failure on the Bible itself.

RESPONSES TO THE NATION OF ISLAM'S CLAIMS

None of these interpretations are particularly surprising given Elijah's logical system: he fits the evidence to previously held conclusions. No one who reads Scripture in context is likely to find such interpretations persuasive. Here is another example of his logic: in the word *Europe*, "EU stands for hills and cavesides of that continent and ROPE means a place where that people were bound in."[91] This suggestion presup-poses that the first Europeans spoke English, a language that did not then exist, and ignores the actual use of the word at least as early as ancient Greece. Nevertheless, he opines, "the truth is plain enough for a fool to see and say that it is the truth."[92] Although not as glaring as his interpretive errors, historical and scientific errors also appear in his arguments.[93]

Some of Elijah's speculations are more interesting. He describes a wheel-shaped plane, a "humanly built planet" that contains fifteen hun-dred bombers to destroy the world's cities, which people can see in the sky twice a week.[94] It seems remarkable that astronomers who have mapped distant galaxies invisible to most telescopes have never noticed this phenomenon. In addition, many of his predictions have failed to come to pass: he expected America to be destroyed in 1965, 1966 or very soon thereafter.[95]

Many people, of course, misinterpret the Bible or make factual errors, and such errors need not discredit their central message. What is more disturbing is the apparent character of Elijah Muhammad's God—neither supremely loving nor supremely powerful. When this God could not get all the people to speak one language, "he decided to kill us by destroying our planet," but he failed to kill humanity. The cataclysm did, however, form the moon.[96]

Perhaps most disturbing of all for Christians are Elijah Muhammad's words about Christ. By claiming that most of the gospel records refer not to the historical Jesus but to the future Jesus, a later prophet, Elijah Muhammad and his successor Louis Farrakhan fall directly into a trap that Jesus warned about:

> Be on your guard so that no one leads you astray. Many are going to come with my name, claiming, "I'm the Christ," and will lead many people astray. . . . If someone says to you, "The Christ is over here," or, "He's over there," don't believe them. False Christs and false prophets will rise up and show great signs. . . . Thus if someone tells you, "He's there, out in the country," or, "Over here, inside this building," don't believe them. When the Son of Man really returns, it will be like a lightning flash that lights up the whole sky. (Mt 24:4-5, 23-27)

Many other leaders have fallen into this trap. For example, David Koresh, leader of the Branch Davidian sect in Waco, Texas, expected a final manifestation of the Christ figure. From 1983 until the U.S. government's fatal raid on his compound, in fact, he claimed that he was this final messenger.[97] Many other people, including Sun Myung Moon, have made the same claims. Unlike Jesus, however, few of them have been able to pull off a resurrection, especially with eyewitnesses prepared to die for the claim that they saw him.

WHERE ELIJAH MUHAMMAD WAS RIGHT

Many of Elijah Muhammad's social claims were correct. In a capitalist society people need land or other kinds of capital, such as education, to advance.[98] He denounced white plans to sterilize blacks, which were under way on a small scale in some hospitals in his day.[99] No one can legitimately dispute his demands for freedom, justice and equality[100] or his complaint that whites often turn a deaf ear to cries for justice while making blacks sound like troublemakers for complaining.[101] We should note, however, that the black church and its Bible had voiced such concerns for justice long before Elijah did.[102] We should also note that though he ridiculed Christians for not being radical enough, he opposed King's marches in the face of police opposition. He also condemned Malcolm X as a poor fool for seeking the United Nations' help to address America's race problem. Elijah said that only God could help America and that he would not act until people turned to Islam.[103]

Elijah's moral convictions often correspond with those of Christians. He complained that most sports, entertainment and gambling were white games that wasted the black community's resources.[104] Some nineteenth-century black Christians had likewise warned against gambling and other practices that undercut support for the whole community.[105] He also condemned the great sexual sin of the United States[106] and warned that white America was packaging sexuality to seduce blacks to hell with them.[107]

Elijah Muhammad was correct to denounce white Christians for their frequent failure to embrace black Christians as equals,[108] although Islam's history is no less stained. The Bible would also agree with Elijah Muhammad that whites have an evil nature and nothing less radical than being "born again" can change them, but unlike Elijah, the Bible paints that same portrait of all humanity.

Elijah Muhammad may also have been correct to predict judgment on the United States for its sins, even if his picture of absolute destruction may be overstated.[109] But then again, Christians such as David Walker and John Wesley offered the same sorts of prophecies against the United States in times when it was far less popular to do so. More recent Christian writers such as David Wilkerson, founder of Teen Challenge and pastor of Times Square Church in New York, have also announced judgment on this nation.[110] So Christians can agree with Elijah Muhammad on various points while disputing his claims about God, Christ and his own identity.

CONCLUSION

Black Muslims have demonstrated success in rehabilitating ex-convicts and improving the lives of members. Many blacks believe that Louis Farrakhan has been a positive force in the African American community. The Nation of Islam stresses empowerment, and it provides structure and external discipline to young African American men.

Yet despite such features, the Nation of Islam has glaring problems in its theology and ideology. As Richard Abanes observes, "When all is said and done, the belief system taught by the Nation of Islam is nothing but white supremacy in reverse. Black Muslims—like the white racists they so despise—propagate racial division, racial superiority, and a patently false view of history."[111]

11

EVALUATING
NEW RELIGIOUS MOVEMENTS

LaVonne Neff

Change is threatening. It is especially alarming to those who are in control—leaders in religion, politics or business, people with established positions in their communities, the middle-aged. Change is also appealing. It is particularly attractive to those who have little to lose—the poor, the jobless, the friendless, the young.

When new religious practices or movements come knocking on the door of established religions, the old guard often panics. It's good that they do. Most of today's trends are tomorrow's jokes, and nothing is stranger than an outdated pop religion. Most new religions include teachings that contradict the gospel as Christians understand it. A few pop religions are downright dangerous: we can't help thinking of the Jonestown massacre, the Waco immolation, the Heaven's Gate mass suicide.

On the other hand, new religious movements are not necessarily evil. Even if a group criticizes what Christians consider the true faith, it may not be dangerous. Some critical groups have, in the long run, built up the Christian church by giving it more zeal, fresh insights, stronger commitment. Look at the record: First-century Christians criticized traditional Judaism. Sixteenth-century Lutherans broke with the Renaissance papacy, while Mennonites stood apart from all institutionalized churches. Eighteenth-century Methodists combated the moral laziness they saw in Anglicanism. And yet today all of these groups are in the big tent of mainstream religion.

How then can Christians tell if a group is silly, unchristian, evil—or appropriately critical? To separate the harmful innovators from the necessary reformers, we need to look at two aspects of a group's life.

First, we must compare the group's teachings with basic Christian doctrine. In spite of differences between Baptists and Bible churches, Willow Creek and St. Symphorosa, Christians of all denominations and congregations still share certain basic beliefs. Strip these away and what you have left is not Christianity.

Second, we must look at how the group affects people's lives. We humans are not disembodied intellects. We have emotional and physical needs. We live in a web of relationships that include family, coworkers, friends and neighbors. Good religion is doctrinally sound, and it also has a positive effect on people's everyday lives.

DOES THE GROUP TEACH ORTHODOX CHRISTIANITY?

In this book various authors have looked at a selection of contemporary religious movements in the light of biblical Christian teachings. Since each group abandons Christian orthodoxy at a different point, each chapter has looked at a different part of the Christian faith. But it is important when evaluating religious movements to keep in mind the overall picture of Christianity found in all Christian churches.

The earliest Christians asked baptismal candidates three questions: Do you believe in God? Do you believe in God's Son, Jesus Christ? Do you believe in the Holy Spirit? The answers to these questions soon developed into creeds—formal statements of the church's beliefs. The Nicene Creed is recited every Sunday in Orthodox, Roman Catholic and some Protestant churches. The similar but shorter Apostles' Creed, also used by Catholics, is often preferred by Protestants. Some Protestants do not use creeds, but all agree with the trinitarian teachings summarized in these ancient documents. A religious group that disagrees with the church's classic position as stated in the creeds is not part of orthodox Christianity.

We will use the Apostles' Creed as a starting point in our discussion of orthodoxy:

> I believe in God, the Father almighty,
> creator of heaven and earth.
> I believe in Jesus Christ, his only Son, our Lord.
> He was conceived by the power of the Holy Spirit
> and born of the Virgin Mary.
> He suffered under Pontius Pilate,
> was crucified, died, and was buried.
> He descended to the dead.
> On the third day he rose again.
> He ascended into heaven,
> and is seated at the right hand of the Father.
> He will come again to judge the living and the dead.
> I believe in the Holy Spirit,
> the holy catholic Church,
> the communion of saints,
> the forgiveness of sins,
> the resurrection of the body,
> and the life everlasting. Amen.

I believe in God, the Father almighty, creator of heaven and earth. Some religions, such as Buddhism, have no god. Others, such as Hinduism and various New Age movements, have many gods and goddesses. These divinities are usually considered part of the world, not separate from it. Being present in everything that exists, they do not distinguish between good and evil. They may not be personal; in fact, Eastern religious movements often see individual personality as something to overcome. The ultimate goal of Eastern religion is to merge one's personality with the One, the impersonal state of being at one with all things. Western new religions are more active: their practitioners are likely to expect gods and goddesses to help them achieve their own goals.

By contrast, Christians, Jews and Muslims believe in one God, who is the powerful Creator of everything that exists. Existing eternally, God is greater than all creation, yet God is revealed through created things. God is continuously involved in maintaining and directing the universe. To use philosophical terms, God is both transcendent (above creation) and immanent (within creation).

This God is not merely a force or a power. God is a person who relates to other persons and wants them to relate to him. He is completely loving and totally good in all that he does. In fact, human ideas of love and goodness come from God. (It is impossible to speak in normal English about a person without using gendered pronouns, but Christians do not believe God has a physical body with genitals. Because Jesus called God "Father," we traditionally use masculine pronouns to refer to God, but God also has maternal qualities. It would also be accurate—though shocking to some—to use feminine pronouns and say that because God is a person, she relates to other people and wants them to relate to her. The one pronoun we cannot use for our personal God is *it*.)

The God of the Bible is not a philosophy to understand or a tool to use, but a person to love and worship.

I believe in Jesus Christ, his only Son, our Lord. Some of the groups discussed in this book agree with Christians that God is both transcendent and immanent, both personal and loving. They disagree, however, about Jesus.

Many religions and religious movements recognize Jesus as a great teacher. Eastern-inspired groups may describe him as an avatar, an incarnation of the One. Western groups are more likely to see him as a wise man or even as the most important of God's created beings. But no group can be considered Christian unless it understands Jesus to be fully divine, in every way equal to God the Father and God the Holy Spirit.

Christians agree with the words of the Nicene Creed that describe Jesus as "eternally begotten of the Father, God from God, Light from Light, true God from true God, begotten, not made, of one Being with the Father." At the same time Christians believe that Jesus is entirely and permanently human. He is not God in temporary human clothing. He is not a divinely enlightened man. He is fully God and fully man—a mystery that Christians accept even though they cannot explain it. Furthermore, Jesus' nature is unique. He is not one of a succession of God-men. He is the only person in all history to be both divine and human.

Christians also believe that Jesus is the world's Savior. God, who is totally good, created good people in a good world. Although God has permitted evil to invade our world for a time, someday everything bad will be destroyed and the world will once again be good. This would be welcome news except for one fact—we humans are not so good ourselves. All of us have sins, flaws, problems; whatever we call our faults, they have turned the world into a dangerous place. Does this mean that we will be destroyed when God cleans up the universe?

We don't have to be. Our good and loving God sent Jesus to save us from the evil that is in our world and that is in each of us. "For our sake," says the Nicene Creed, "he was crucified under Pontius Pilate; he suffered death and was buried." In a way that we can never fully understand, Jesus took the sins of the world upon himself. Protestants often call this "substitutionary atonement"—God accepts Jesus' death in place of our own. In the words of the Catholic liturgy, "Dying he destroyed our death; rising he restored our life." Eastern Orthodox Christians emphasize the union of divinity and humanity that Jesus' death and resurrection makes possible. All Christians agree that because Jesus died and rose again, we too can be raised to eternal life with God.

What can we do to receive eternal life? Most religions prescribe human acts to assure eternal bliss or at least absence of pain. The Christian approach stands in sharp contrast: "The free gift of God is eternal life in Christ Jesus our Lord" (Rom 6:23 NRSV). We cannot earn a place in heaven by good actions, sacrifices, rituals or prayers. We do not need to earn a place, because God has already reserved one for us. Our eternal happiness is a gift of God's grace, not something we have earned. "By grace you have been saved through faith, and this is not your own doing; it is the gift of God" (Eph 2:8 NRSV).

I believe in the Holy Spirit. Most new religions, though they often speak of Spirit or spirits, do not believe in the Holy Spirit of traditional Christian teaching. "Spirit" is usually depersonalized. Perhaps it is a collective spirit residing in all things; perhaps it is an expression of the individual rather than part of the Holy Trinity. In some writings "Spirit" seems simply to be an effort to give God a nonsectarian name.

Christians, by contrast, believe that the Holy Spirit is personal, one of the three persons of the Godhead. The Spirit is separate from the created world but works in the world—with all people in general, pointing out sin and turning them to Jesus; with the Christian church in particular, giving people gifts that will strengthen it; and with individuals, assuring them of their salvation and making them resemble Jesus, their Lord. In the beginning God's Spirit created the world, and throughout all ages God's Spirit renews it.

Some groups that call themselves Christian tend to limit the Holy Spirit's work. They believe the Spirit is active in a special way in their own group but not in the church or the world as a whole. They charge that the church is spiritually lazy, doctrinally impure or morally corrupt, and they warn that the Spirit will not tolerate such wickedness. Come to our group, they say: our doctrine is pure, our discipline rigorous. Here and only here you will be blessed.

Such groups may not be un-Christian in most of their teaching. They do not deny the infinite-personal God after the manner of many Eastern religious movements. They do not dispute the Christian view of the nature and work of Christ after the manner of many Western religious movements. Their criticisms of the church may be well founded. Are such groups prophetic movements raised up by God to purify the church, or are they schismatics that will divide the church and harm their own members?

Answering this question requires a great deal of discernment. Nobody welcomes prophets, and it is tempting to dismiss all criticism—especially when it is most necessary—as divisive and sub-Christian. On the other hand, even divinely inspired prophetic movements risk degenerating into splinter movements if they lose sight of their original purpose of building up the body of Christ. Does the group reject the work of the Holy Spirit in the rest of the Christian church? Or does it see itself as working with the Holy Spirit on behalf of the entire church? The answer to these questions often marks the dividing line between prophecy and schism.

Good doctrine is important, but it is not the only measure of a group's health. Of equal importance is the impact the group has on people's lives.

DOES THE GROUP STRENGTHEN AND SUPPORT ITS MEMBERS?

Some Christians make a serious mistake: they assume that if they can prove a group's teachings false or absurd, they can then persuade people to leave the group. Such an approach will work with some people, but most have needs that far outweigh their perceived need for truth. People do not usually base their attraction to the Latter-day Saints, for example, on a conviction that Joseph Smith was a hieroglyphics expert. Instead, they are attracted by the Mormon way of life with its emphasis on traditional American values.

In evaluating religious movements, it is important to consider the effects such groups have on individuals who join them. Jesus told his listeners to distinguish false prophets from true ones the same way they would tell bad trees from good ones: "You will know them by their fruits" (see Mt 7:15-20). Good results will not sanctify bad doctrine, but bad results serve as warning lights even where teaching appears sound. In some cases, looking at the group's effect on its members' lives may be the only way to distinguish between a damaging schismatic group and a prophetic Christian movement. What happens to members' personalities, relationships, job commitments, community involvement? Is the group's overall effect on those who come in contact with it—members and nonmembers—positive or negative? Is it an agency of healing, restoration and reconciliation? Consider the following questions:

1. Does a member's personality generally become stronger, happier, more confident as a result of contact with the group? Or does the person become fearful, depressed or fatigued?

2. Do members of the group seek to deepen and strengthen their family commitments? Or are their contacts with family limited and monitored?

3. Does the group encourage independent thinking and the development of discernment skills? Or do members quote extensively from the leader, parrot a party line or refuse to consider evidence from sources outside the group?

4. Does the group allow for individual differences of belief and behavior, particularly in areas of less-than-central importance? Or must members adhere to the leaders' prescriptions in areas such as diet, dress, schedule, entertainment choices and even friendships?

5. Does the group encourage high moral standards both among members and between members and nonmembers? Or are immoral behaviors encouraged or even required as means of proselytizing or for the leaders' benefit?

6. Does the group's leadership invite dialogue, advice and evaluation from outside its own immediate circle? Or is it suspicious of the press, theologians, people of other faiths or anyone else who might criticize it?

7. Does the group allow for development in theological beliefs? Or does it believe that its original belief system is complete and unchangeable?

8. Are group members encouraged to ask the hard questions without threat of reprisal of any kind? Or does the group discourage questioners by discipline, expulsion or social exclusion?

9. Do group members appreciate truth wherever it is found, even if it is outside their group? Or do they believe that all truth has been or will be revealed to them personally?

10. Is the group honest in dealing with nonmembers, especially as it tries to win them to the group? Or does the group have a public face that differs considerably from the realities lived by members?

11. Does the group foster relationships and linkages with the larger society—connections that are more than self-serving? Or are its primary connections made primarily in order to gain converts, money or good publicity?

12. Does the group listen to its members? Are the leaders held accountable for their decisions? Or is the group led by one or two charismatic leaders who make the rules and, often, become objects of worship? Any group that idolizes its human leader is in grave danger of losing its soul, however pure its theology may have been when the group first formed. Any group that worships and obeys its leader is dangerous.

HOW NEW RELIGIOUS MOVEMENTS CAN HELP THE CHURCH

The teachings of most new religious movements are incompatible with those of traditional Christianity. A few—the ones that virtually worship their leaders and tightly control their members—can be dangerous. And some may be just what the Christian church needs.

Throughout its history the church has benefited from religious movements. From the desert fathers to medieval monastics to nineteenth-century missionaries to twentieth-century campus evangelists, groups of visionaries have raised the church's standards and renewed its enthusiasm. Critics have kept the church honest, whether they are fighting against militarism, slavery or bad stewardship in high places; or for the poor, women's rights or the Bible.

Most of today's new movements do not have Christian roots. A change in immigration trends since 1965 has resulted in a change in our country's religions. There are now six million Muslims, four million Buddhists and more than a million Hindus living in the United States. (Compare this with approximately two million Episcopalians—the denomination that once epitomized the power of mainline Protestant Christianity in America.) America is the most religiously diverse nation on earth, but diversity should not threaten Christians. New religious movements, along with newly imported ancient religions, can actually help Christians grow strong.

Other religions can help Christians draw closer to one another. When a suburb's houses of worship are all Christian—Catholic, Methodist, Presbyterian, Episcopal, Baptist, Lutheran and several nondenominational congregations—it's easy to identify with one part of Christianity and ignore the folks in other denominations, or even fight with them. If that suburb adds, say, a Latter-day Saints ward, a Hindu temple, a Jewish synagogue, a Muslim mosque, a Buddhist temple and a number of active practitioners of Wicca, suddenly Catholics and Bible church members realize they have more in common than they had suspected.

Warning: Some Christians close ranks, assert their own superiority and become bigots or even persecutors of those who disagree with them. When Christians join forces, it should be to praise God and help others, not to hurt or exclude.

Other religions can help Christians pay closer attention to their own beliefs and practices. A generation or two ago, it was possible for an American Christian to get through school without ever making close friends with someone of another race or religion. This is no longer likely, and when teenagers from vastly different backgrounds get together, questions are bound to arise. Why won't you eat pork? Why don't you drink alcohol? Why do you wear that funny underwear? Do you really think my family is going to hell? Why do you have three gods? Why do you bow to idols? Isn't witchcraft the same as worshiping Satan? Why do you pray to a god who died? Questions like these exercise the theological muscles.

Warning: Some Christians decide that since so many nice people hold such differing beliefs, belief must not be all that important. Our friends of other faiths want us to respect them, but they do not expect us to water down our own convictions on their behalf.

Other religions can help Christians understand the needs and longings of our contemporaries. Why are books of Buddhist philosophy suddenly so popular? Why are quite a few African American Christians converting to Islam? Why are stressed young professionals studying yoga? Why do women with graduate degrees meet in groves to dance by the light of the moon? If these people are seekers, what exactly are they looking for? Are Christians seeking some of the same things? Does the Christian church have anything to offer that will appeal to today's seekers?

Warning: Christianity is not a market-driven religion. No poll can tell us what we ought to believe or how we ought to practice our faith. But unless we understand what people are seeking, we won't know how best to attract them to Jesus.

Other religions can remind Christians of what we may have forgotten.
Many religious movements have strong points that Christians should sit
up and notice. Wiccans want to live in harmony with nature. Baha'is
long for world peace. Mormons work to build strong families. Jehovah's
Witnesses are eager to tell others about their faith. Devotees of hatha
yoga practice discipline. Christians share such goals. If another group
seems more effective in reaching their objectives than we are, can we
take lessons from them?

Warning: If we really want to learn, we have to listen.

Some Christians feel an obligation to turn every encounter with people of other faiths into an opportunity to witness. If the Christian happens to be a parent or concerned friend of someone who has joined a
new religious movement, the Christian should pray earnestly for the gift
of silence.

Why did our son, our daughter, our friend, leave Christianity for
this other group? We will not learn the answer by talking. What are this
person's needs, hopes, passions? The only way to find out is by listening. What is this person gaining from being in this religious movement? Again, insight comes to those whose ears are open and whose
mouth is shut.

Why are some people attracted to new religions rather than to the
Christian church? Can the church listen to what seekers are saying? Can
it create a welcoming environment where questioners feel they will be
heard and respected, whatever they say? Can it at the same time preach
and practice its own Christian faith, including the parts about loving
those who stray?

New religions will not evaporate in the heat of Christian argument.
They may, however, lose some of their appeal where the Christian
church is alive and well. Two thousand years ago Paul wrote to the Christians in imperial Rome, a hotbed of new religious movements: "Do not
be conformed to this world, but be transformed by the renewing of your

minds, so that you may discern what is the will of God—what is good and acceptable and perfect" (Rom 12:2 NRSV). If new religions and spiritual movements nudge Christians to renew their minds and transform the church, their persistent presence will turn out to be not a threat but a blessing.

NOTES

Chapter One: What Is a New Religious Movement?

[1]Robert Wuthnow, "Presidential Address 2003: The Challenge of Diversity," *Journal for the Scientific Study of Religion* 43, no. 2 (2004): 159-70.

[2]Ibid., p. 160.

[3]Ibid., p. 164.

[4]Martin E. Marty, *A Nation of Behavers* (Chicago: University of Chicago Press, 1976), p. 130.

[5]Charles Strohmer, *The Gospel and the New Spirituality* (Nashville: Thomas Nelson, 1996), p. xiii.

[6]Ronald Enroth, "Cult/Countercult," *Eternity*, November 1977, p. 35.

[7]Alan W. Gomes, *Unmasking the Cults* (Grand Rapids, Mich.: Zondervan, 1995), pp. 47-48.

[8]James W. Sire, *Scripture Twisting* (Downers Grove, Ill.: InterVarsity Press, 1980), p. 20.

[9]Irving Hexham, Stephen Rost and John W. Morehead II, eds., *Encountering New Religious Movements* (Grand Rapids, Mich.: Kregel, 2004), p. 17.

[10]Thomas Robbins, "Religious Movements, the State, and the Law: Reconceptualizing 'The Cult Problem,'" *New York University Review of Law and Social Change* 9, no. 1 (1980-81): 33.

[11]Robert S. Ellwood, *Alternative Altars* (Chicago: University of Chicago Press, 1979).

[12]Rodney Stark and William Sims Bainbridge, *The Future of Religion: Secularization, Revival and Cult Formation* (Berkeley: University of California Press, 1985), p. 25.

[13]William Sims Bainbridge, "After the New Age," *Journal for the Scientific Study of Religion* 43, no. 3 (2004): 381.

[14]John Lofland, *Doomsday Cult* (Englewood Cliffs, N.J.: Prentice-Hall, 1966), p. 1.

[15]Robert Wuthnow and Wendy Cadge, "Buddhists and Buddhism in the United States: The Scope of Influence," *Journal for the Scientific Study of Religion* 43, no. 3 (2004): 363.

[16]Ibid.

[17]Wuthnow and Cadge, "Buddhists and Buddhism," p. 364.

[18]Eileen Barker, "What Are We Studying? A Sociological Case for Keeping the 'Nova,'" *Nova Religio: The Journal of Alternative and Emergent Religions* 8, no. 1 (2004): 88-102.

[19]Ibid., p. 92.

[20]The material that follows draws heavily on the cited work of Barker.

[21]Ibid.

[22]Ibid., p. 93.

[23]Ibid., p. 95.

[24]Andrew Holden, *Jehovah's Witnesses: Portrait of a Contemporary Religious Movement* (London: Routledge, 2002), p. 11.

[25]Barker, "What Are We Studying?" p. 95.

[26]Ibid.

[27]Ibid.

[28]Ibid., p. 96.

[29]John A. Saliba, *Understanding New Religious Movements* (Grand Rapids, Mich.: Eerdmans, 1995), p. 10.

[30]Ellwood, *Alternative Altars*, p. 19.

[31]Nori J. Muster, "Authoritarian Culture and Child Abuse in ISKCON," *Cultic Studies Review* 3, no. 1 (2004): 3.

[32]Barker, "What Are We Studying?" p. 97.

[33]Ibid.

[34]Ibid., p. 98.

[35]Ibid.

[36]"'Boston Movement' Founder Quits," *Christianity Today*, March 2003, p. 26.

[37]Barker, "What Are We Studying?" p. 98.

Chapter Two: Jehovah's Witnesses

[1]David Reed, *Jehovah's Witness Literature* (Grand Rapids, Mich.: Baker, 1993), p. 9.

[2]Alan Gomes, *Unmasking the Cults* (Grand Rapids, Mich.: Zondervan, 1997), p. 22.

[3]Robert Bowman, *Jehovah's Witnesses* (Grand Rapids, Mich.: Zondervan, 1995), p. 10.

[4]*The Watchtower*, September 15, 1910, p. 4,685.

[5]*Jehovah's Witnesses: Proclaimers of God's Kingdom* (New York: Watchtower Bible and Tract Society [hereafter WBTS], 1993), p. 59.

[6]*The New World* (New York: WBTS, 1942), p. 104.

[7]*1975 Yearbook of Jehovah's Witnesses*, p. 194.

[8]*Awake!*, October 8, 1968, p. 13.

[9]*The Watchtower*, October 15, 1980, p. 31.

[10]*The Watchtower*, May 15, 1984, p. 5.

[11]Rich Abanes, *Cults, New Religious Movements, and Your Family* (Wheaton: Crossway, 1998), p. 243.

[12]*The Watchtower*, March 1, 1983, p. 25.

[13]*The Watchtower*, January 15, 1983, p. 22.

[14]*The Watchtower*, September 15, 1911, p. 4,885.

[15]See *Reasoning from the Scriptures* (New York: WBTS, 1985), pp. 191-99.

[16]Jehovah's Witnesses concede this fact.

[17]See *Reasoning from the Scriptures*, pp. 405-26.

[18]*Should You Believe in the Trinity?* (New York: WBTS, 1989), pp. 14-20.

[19]Robert Reymond, *Jesus, Divine Messiah: New Testament Witness* (Phillipsburg: P&R, 1990), p. 247.

[20]*Should You Believe in the Trinity?*, p. 15.

[21]*Aid to Bible Understanding* (New York: WBTS, 1971), p. 1,395.

[22]*Should You Believe in the Trinity?*, p. 20.

[23]*Reasoning from the Scriptures*, pp. 380, 407.

[24]*You Can Live Forever in Paradise on Earth* (New York: WBTS, 1982), p. 83.

[25]*The Watchtower*, April 1, 1947, p. 204.

[26]*Reasoning from the Scriptures*, p. 76.

[27]James Beckford, *The Trumpet of Prophecy* (New York: Halsted, 1975), p. 185, 160.

[28]*You Can Live Forever*, pp. 22-23.

[29]*The Watchtower*, July 15, 1963, pp. 443-44.

[30]Randall Watters, "Should I Divorce My Jehovah's Witness Mate?" *Free Minds Journal*, March-April 1993 <www.freeminds.org/psych/divorce.htm>.

[31]Randall Watters, "The Introduction of Phobias (Deep Rooted Fears) and Other Development Traits in the Jehovah Witness Child," Free Minds, Inc. <www.freeminds.org/psych/kid-phob.htm>.

[32]*The Watchtower*, August 15, 1950, p. 263.

[33]*Studies in the Scriptures*, vol. 2 (New York: WBTS, 1888), pp. 98-99.

[34]*Millions Now Living Will Never Die* (New York: WBTS, 1920), pp. 88-90.

[35]*Awake!*, October 8, 1966, p. 19.

Chapter Three: Yoga and Hinduism

[1]William James, *The Varieties of Religious Experience: A Study in Human Nature, Being the Gifford Lectures on Natural Religion Delivered at Edinburgh* (London: Longman's & Co., 1902), p. 410.

[2]Amma, *Swami Muktananda Paramhamsa* (Ganeshpuri, India, 1971), p. 32.

[3]Ibid.

[4]See Acharya Rajneesh, *From Sex to Superconsciousness* (Bombay: Jeevan Jagruti Kenotra, 1971).

[5]Cited in Brooks Alexander, "Tantra: The Worship and Occult Power of Sex," *SCP Newsletter* 2, no. 2 (1985).

[6]Bhagwan Sri Rajneesh, *Neo-Sanyasa* 2, no. 4 (1973): 20.

[7]Shirley MacLaine, *Going Within: A Guide for Inner Transformation* (New York: Bantam, 1990).

Chapter Four: Unification Church

[1]For biographical data on Moon's early years see Michael Breen, *Sun Myung Moon* (West Sussex: Refuge, 1997).

[2]See Massimo Introvigne, *The Unification Church* (Salt Lake City: Signature, 2000).

[3]See David Bromley and Anson Shupe Jr., *"Moonies" in America* (Beverly Hills: Sage, 1979).

[4]For a sympathetic portrayal of Moon's tax case see Carlton Sherwood, *Inquisition* (Washington: Regnery Gateway, 1991).

[5]See James A. Beverley, "King of the Spirit World: The Post-Mortem Role of Heung Jin in the Unification Church," in Malcolm Greenshields and Tom Robinson, eds., *Orthodoxy and Her-*

esy in *Religious Movements* (Lewiston, N.Y.: Edwin Mellen, 1992).

[6]See Sun Myung Moon, "New Hope Farm Declaration" (April 3, 1995), <www.unification.net/misc/newhopefarm.html>. For critical perspectives on Moon's South American ventures see Tom Gibb, "Brazil Probes Moonie Land Purchases," *BBC News* (February 28, 2002), available at <www.bbc.co.uk>.

[7]For data on Chung Pyung see the Unification website at <eng.cheongpyeong.org>.

[8]Nansook Hong, *In the Shadow of the Moons* (Boston: Beacon, 1998). See also James A. Beverley, "Moon Struck," *Christianity Today* (November 16, 1998). In a conversation I had with Hong in Toronto she reversed her opinion expressed in an interview with Mike Wallace that Moon was a con artist. Upon further reflection she stated that she thought he was totally convinced of his messianic status.

[9]James A. Beverley, "Son's Death Shakes Up Unification Church," *Christianity Today* (December 13, 1999).

[10]For details on the Milingo affair see the reports at <www.cesnur.org> and <www.archbishopmilingo.org>.

[11]See Moon's comments in "The Dividing Peak of Restoration" (January 15, 1978), <www.unification.org/ucbooks/Mspks/1978/780115.html>.

[12]Moon, "The Stony Path of Death" (April 27, 1980), <www.unification.org/ucbooks/Mspks/1980/800427.html>.

[13]Moon, "Restoration from the Origin and Rebirth Are for Myself" (September 20, 1992), <www.unification.org/ucbooks/Mspks/1992/920920.html>.

[14]Moon, "Critical Turning Point of the Dispensation of God" (December 31, 1978), <www.tparents.org/Moon-Talks/sunmyungmoon78/SM781231.htm>.

[15]See Moon, "CAUSA Seminar Speech" (August 29, 1985), <www.unification.org/ucbooks/Mspks/1985/850829.html>.

[16]Ed Mignot, "Marriage Rituals in Tongil," *Areopagus Trinity* 2, no. 4 (1989): 36-37.

[17]Moon, "The Providence of God in Relation to the Human Viewpoint" (August 21, 1974), <www.tparents.org/Moon-Talks/sunmyungmoon74/SM740821.htm>.

[18]Moon, "The Way Our Blessed Family Should Go" (August 28, 1971), p. 28. Moon's sermons are usually published in English and Korean and are available from Unification headquarters. They are not always available on the internet.

[19]Moon, "Resoration from the Origin and Rebirth Are for Myself" (September 20, 1992), pp. 29-30.

[20]Lynn Kim, quoted in Darrol Bryant and Susan Hodges, eds., *Exploring Unification Theology* (New York: Rose of Sharon, 1978), p. 31.

[21]George Chryssides, *The Advent of Sun Myung Moon* (New York: St. Martin's, 1991), p. 32.

[22]Moon, "The Pinnacle of Suffering" (June 26, 1977), <www.tparents.org/Moon-Talks/sunmyungmoon77/770626.htm>.

[23]Moon, "What the Unification Church Is Trying to Solve After Taking the Responsibility of Jesus on Earth" (December 26, 1971), <www.tparents.org/Moon-Talks/sunmyungmoon71/SM711226.htm>.

[24]Moon, "Human Life" (December 1, 1974), <www.tparents.org/Moon-Talks/sunmyungmoon74/SM741201.htm>.

[25]Moon, "Address to the Prayer and Fast Participants" (July 29, 1974), <www.tparents.org/Moon-Talks/sunmyungmoon74/SM740729.htm>.

[26]Moon, "The Way Our Blessed Family," p. 12.

[27]Moon, "What the Unification Church is Trying to Solve After Taking the Responsibility of Jesus on Earth" (December 26, 1971), <www.tparents.org/Moon-Talks/sunmyungmoon71/SM711226.htm>.

[28]Moon, "Critical Turning Point."

[29]Moon, "The Completion of the Providence and Parents' Day" (April 15, 1980), <www.tparents.org/Moon-Talks/sunmyungmoon80/800415.htm>.

[30]Moon, "Providential Time Limits" (April 17, 1975), p. 12.

[31]See Sang Hun Lee in Hideo Oyamada et al., *The Establishment of a New Culture and Unification Thought* (Tokyo: Unification Thought Institute, 1991), p. 9.

[32]Moon, "Blessed Couples' Conference" (February 21, 1991), <www.tparents.org/Moon-Talks/sunmyungmoon91/SM910221a1.htm>.

[33]Moon, "God's Day and the Unification of the New Nation," in *Today's World* (February 1992), pp. 46-47.

[34]Moon, "Today in the Light of Dispensational History" (February 23, 1977), <www.tparents.org/Moon-Talks/sunmyungmoon77/770223.htm>.

[35]Moon, "Good Day" (July 3, 1977), <www.tparents.org/Moon-Talks/sunmyungmoon77/770703.htm> and "Day of All Things" (June 13, 1980), <www.tparents.org/Moon-Talks/sunmyungmoon80/800613.htm>.

[36]Moon, "The Blessing" (February 20, 1977), <www.tparents.org/Moon-Talks/sunmyungmoon77/770220.htm>.

[37]Moon, "The Will of God and Thanksgiving" (February 12, 1978), <www.tparents.org/Moon-Talks/sunmyungmoon78/780219.htm>.

[38]Moon, "Destiny and Judgment" (January 31, 1982), <www.unification.org/ucbooks/Mspks/1982/820131.html>.

[39]Moon, "The Age of Repentance" (September 1, 1978), <www.tparents.org/Moon-Talks/sunmyungmoon78/780901.htm>.

[40]Moon, "Territory of Goodness" (October 14, 1979), <www.tparents.org/Moon-Talks/sunmyungmoon79/791014.htm>.

[41]Moon, "About Myself" (February 27, 1983), <www.tparents.org/Moon-Talks/sunmyungmoon83/830227.htm>.

[42]Moon, "Our Family in Light of the Dispensation" (March 1, 1977), <www.tparents.org/Moon-Talks/sunmyungmoon77/770301.htm>.

[43]Moon, "The 23rd Anniversary of the Unification Church and the History of God's Dispensation" (May 1, 1977), <www.tparents.org/Moon-Talks/sunmyungmoon77/770501.htm>.

[44]Moon, "Territory of Goodness."

[45]Moon, "Perfection of Restoration by Indemnity Through Human Responsibility" (March 1, 1983), <www.unification.org/ucbooks/Mspks/1983/830301.html> and "Ideal Home Church" (December 21, 1986), <www.unification.org/ucbooks/Mspks/1986/861221.html>.

[46]Moon, "Road Toward the Ideal" (September 7, 1986), <www.unification.org/ucbooks/Mspks/1986/861221.html>.

[47]Moon, "The Dividing Peak of Restoration" and "Territory of Goodness."

[48]Moon, "God's Day 1990 Morning Address" (January 1, 1990), <www.tparents.org/Moon-Talks/sunmyungmoon90/900101a.htm>.

[49]Moon, "The Final Warning Concerning Good and Evil" (December 26, 1976), <www.tparents.org/Moon-Talks/sunmyungmoon76/761226.htm>.

[50]Moon, "Home Church and the Completion of the Kingdom of Heaven" (January 1, 1979), <www.tparents.org/Moon-Talks/sunmyungmoon79/SM790101.htm>.

[51]Moon, "With Whom Shall I Live?"

[52]Moon, "Our Church and Korea as Seen from the Providence of God" (February 19, 1989), <www.tparents.org/Moon-Talks/sunmyungmoon79/SM790101.htm>.

[53]See Tim Folzenlogen's September 12, 1985, letter to Sun Myung Moon in Special Collections, Unification Theological Seminary Library, Barrytown, New York.

[54]For concerns about spiritual grandiosity see comments in Dick Anthony, Bruce Ecker and Ken Wilber, eds., Spiritual Choices (New York: Paragon, 1987), pp. 69, 167-68, 190, 341.

[55]See David Bromley and Anson Shupe, Strange Gods (Boston: Beacon, 1981).

[56]For an example of recent scholarly exchange about brainwashing, see Benjamin Zablocki and Thomas Robbins, eds., Misunderstanding Cults (Toronto: University of Toronto Press, 2002). Also note Jack Hitt, "The Return of the Brainwashing Defense," The New York Times (December 15, 2002).

[57]Eileen Barker, The Making of a Moonie (Oxford: Basil Blackwell, 1984).

[58]For information on the program see the website of the Family Federation for World Peace and Unification at <www.familyfed.org>.

[59]For a very helpful and extensive listing of such "front" groups see the data on the Unification Church at <www.freedomofmind.com>. The site features the work of Steve Hassan, an ex-Unificationist and one of the most influential exit counselors dealing with new religions. Other significant ex-member sites are at <www.xmoonies.com> (Craig Maxim) and <www.allentwood.com> (Allen Tate Wood).

[60]Thomas G. Walsh, Gordon L. Anderson and Theodore Shimmyo, eds., Hope of All Ages (Tarrytown: Interreligious and International Federation for World Peace, 2002).

Chapter Five: Latter-day Saints

[1]See Richard N. and Joan K. Ostling, Mormon America: The Power and the Promise (San Francisco: HarperSanFrancisco, 1999), pp. 130-46.

[2]For a very readable history from a faithful Latter-day Saints perspective, see Coke Newell, Latter Days: An Insider's Guide to Mormonism, the Church of Jesus Christ of Latter-day Saints (New York: St. Martin's, 2000; St. Martin's Griffin, 2001), pp. 65-224. For a comprehensive non-Latter-day Saints account, see Richard Abanes, One Nation Under Gods: A History of the Mormon Church (New York: Four Walls Eight Windows, 2002).

[3]Joseph Smith, History of the Church 4:461.

[4]See H. Michael Marquardt and Wesley P. Walters, Inventing Mormonism: Tradition and the Historical Record (Salt Lake City: Smith Research Associates, 1994). For a Mormon reference work containing Smith's different versions of the First Vision, see Dean C. Jessee, ed., The Papers of Joseph Smith (Salt Lake City: Deseret, 1989).

[5]The classic work on this subject is by LDS writer Juanita Brooks, *The Mountain Meadows Massacre* (Norman, Okla.: University of Oklahoma Press, 1991; orig. 1962).

[6]The clarion call for evangelicals to engage this new scholarship was a paper first circulated on the Internet: Carl Mosser and Paul Owen, "Mormon Scholarship, Apologetics and Evangelical Neglect: Losing the Battle and Not Knowing It?" *Trinity Journal* 19, no. 2 (Fall 1998): 179-205. The book coauthored by Latter-day Saints scholar Stephen E. Robinson and evangelical scholar Craig L. Blomberg, *How Wide the Divide? A Mormon and an Evangelical in Conversation* (Downers Grove, Ill.: InterVarsity Press, 1997), also showed—and provoked—a growing interest among evangelicals in LDS scholarship. Two recent essays critiquing Book of Mormon apologetics are included in the important book *The New Mormon Challenge: Responding to the Latest Defenses of a Fast-Growing Movement*, ed. Francis J. Beckwith, Carl Mosser and Paul Owen (Grand Rapids, Mich.: Zondervan, 2002).

[7]Parenthetical page references in this section are to *Gospel Principles* (Salt Lake City: Church of Jesus Christ of Latter-day Saints, 1997). The entire text is also available online at <http://www.lds.org/library/display/0,4945,11-1-13-1,00.html>.

[8]Quoting a famous 1844 funeral oration known as the King Follett Discourse, in *Teachings of the Prophet Joseph Smith*, ed. Joseph Fielding Smith (Salt Lake City: Deseret, 1938), pp. 345-46.

Chapter Six: Astral Religion and the New Age

[1]Some names and occupations in this story were changed.

[2]This was the period when spirit mediums began calling themselves "channelers," saying they contacted "guides," "wise persons," "energies" or "ascended masters" but not spirits in the biblical sense. Ancient alchemical and shamanistic practices came to be called "transformational therapies" and astrology shed its occult coat to become a form of "archetypal counseling." Occult forms of healing appeared in rubric that allowed them, tentatively at first, a place alongside valid forms of alternative health care and complementary medicine. Eastern mystical meditation appeared as "grounding," "stilling," "centering," "going within."

[3]Charles Strohmer, *The Gospel and the New Spirituality: Communicating the Truth in a World of Spiritual Seekers* (Thomas Nelson, 1996). See pp. 83-116, especially pp. 101-16, for a model that helps illustrate the commingling of modernism with the cosmopolitan spirituality of the New Age.

[4]Few Christian thinkers and writers investigated what was going on behind the scenes in the 1970s. Even when secular publishers turned out notable works like Fritjof Capra's *The Tao of Physics* in 1976, Christians saw it as anomalous. Gary North's *None Dare Call It Witchcraft* (New Rochelle, N.Y.: Arlington House, 1976; revised and retitled *Unholy Spirits: Occultism and New Age Humanism*, 1986), was a rare, intelligent exception in the 1970s to Christian lack of interest in the Aquarians.

[5]Mark Albrecht, *Reincarnation: A Christian Appraisal* (Downers Grove, Ill.: InterVarsity Press, 1982); Paul C. Reisser, Teri K. Reisser and John Weldon, *The Holistic Healers: A Christian Perspective on New Age Health Care* (Downers Grove, Ill.: InterVarsity Press, 1983); Douglas R. Groothuis, *Unmasking the New Age* (Downers Grove, Ill.: InterVarsity Press, 1986); F. LaGard Smith, *Out on a Broken Limb* (Eugene, Ore.: Harvest House, 1986); Norman L. Geisler and J. Yutaka Amano, *The Reincarnation Sensation* (Carol Stream, Ill.: Tyndale, 1987); Reisser,

Reisser and Weldon, *New Age Medicine: A Christian Perspective* (InterVarsity Press, 1987); Charles Strohmer, *What Your Horoscope Doesn't Tell You* (Carol Stream, Ill.: Tyndale, 1988); Groothuis, *Confronting the New Age* (Downers Grove, Ill.: InterVarsity Press, 1988); Russell Chandler, *Understanding the New Age* (Dallas: Word, 1988); Amano and Geisler, *The Infiltration of the New Age* (Carol Stream, Ill.: Tyndale, 1989); Elliot Miller, *A Crash Course on the New Age Movement* (Grand Rapids, Mich.: Baker, 1989).

[6]Books such as David Burnett's *Dawning of the Pagan Moon* (Nashville: Oliver Nelson, 1992) and *Unearthly Powers* (Nashville: Oliver Nelson, 1992) covered areas such as the New Age's relationship to neopaganism, animism and folk religions. Yet even John P. Newport's fairly exhaustive *The New Age Movement and the Biblical Worldview* (Grand Rapids, Mich.: Eerdmans, 1998) largely re-articulates the 1980s Christian apologetic, albeit the final pages of each chapter outline helpful biblical alternatives to New Age views in areas such as art, science, business, education and so on, which Christians could build on.

[7]Wouter J. Hanegraaff, *New Age Religion and Western Culture* (Albany, N.Y.: State University of New York Press, 1998). In particular, chapters 14 to 16 of this comprehensive scholarly study are especially helpful in understanding what Hanegraaff calls the "secularization of esotericism."

[8]Hanegraaff, *New Age Religion and Western Culture*, p. 106.

[9]Gary Zukav, *Soul Stories* (New York: Simon & Schuster, 2000), p. 23.

[10]Ibid., pp. 23, 27.

[11]Ibid., p. 41.

[12]Ibid., pp. 36-37.

[13]Zukav, *The Seat of the Soul* (New York: Simon & Schuster, 1989), p. 34.

[14]Zukav, *Soul Stories*, p. 53.

[15]Zukav, *Seat of the Soul*, p. 35.

[16]Ibid., p. 41.

[17]Ibid., p. 46.

[18]Ibid., p. 43.

[19]Richard Corliss, "The Power of Yoga," *Time* (April 23, 2001). See also Nadya Labi, "Om a Little Teapot . . ." *Time* (February 19, 2001), reporting on the trend of yoga for stressed-out children.

[20]Accompanying Corliss's *Time* story is a large drawing of the human body. The left side of the drawing details an Eastern mystical view of yoga, with the locations and descriptions of the chakras (seven alleged psychic energy centers through which the life force, *prana*, is said to flow through the body); the right side details a Western science view of yoga, showing numerous organs and physical systems (brain, heart, kidneys, muscles and so on) and how they might benefit from yoga.

[21]Sharon Begley, "Religion and the Brain," *Newsweek* (May 7, 2001). The term *neurobiology* seems to have been coined by Andrew Newburg and Eugene d'Aquila in their book *Why God Won't Go Away* (New York: Ballantine, 2001).

[22]On the two-hour ABC-TV prime time special about UFOs, "Seeing Is Believing" (February 24, 2005), Peter Jennings noted that 80 million Americans now believe in UFOs.

[23]It was during the flying saucer craze of the 1950s that interest in UFOs became intertwined with spirituality, quasi-theological speculation and occult interpretations. Books like *Flying Saucers Have Landed* (1953), by Desmond Leslie and George Adams, engaged in theosophical

speculation, following influential writers like Charles Fort and Richard Shaver, whose material was richly steeped in occult mythologies. In the 60s and 70s, sci-fi writers like Erich von Daniken and Brad Steiger "continued to blur the distinction between science and religion, empirical reality and the occult" (Irving Hexham, Karla Poewe, "UFO Religion," *The Christian Century*, May 7, 1997).

[24]Charles Strohmer, *America's Fascination with Astrology: Is It Healthy?* (Greenville, S.C.: Emerald House, 1998).

[25]William M. Alnor, *UFO Cults and the New Millennium* (Grand Rapids, Mich.: Baker, 1998). Unless otherwise indicated, the details about UFO groups stated in this section have been compiled from Alnor's book. The analyses and conclusions, however, are mine.

[26]Strieber's three bestsellers, *Communion, Transformation,* and *Breakthrough* describe him as inhabited by alien "visitors" who are using him as their agent to initiate a new age on the earth after it endures an apocalyptic period.

[27]Alnor, p. 110.

[28]Ibid., p. 113.

[29]News story from Kyoto, Japan, August 3, 2001; see Apologetics Index: <www.gospelcom.net/apologeticsindex/news1/an010806-21.html>.

[30]Ibid.

[31]Judith Rosen, "Casting a Wider Spell," *Publishers Weekly*, September 1, 2003.

Chapter Seven: The Dalai Lama and Tibetan Buddhism

[1]"Buddhists and Buddhism in the United States: The Scope of Influence," *Journal for the Scientific Study of Religion* (September 2004) <http://tricycleblog.blogspot.com/2004/08>. Also, a map of Buddhism in America may be viewed at <www.sonrisecenter.org>.

[2]Don Morreale, *The Complete Guide to Buddhist America* (Boston: Shambhala, 1998).

[3]Os Guinness, *The American Hour: A Time of Reckoning and the Once and Future Role of Faith* (New York: Free Press, 1993).

[4]Alicia Matsunaga, *The Buddhist Philosophy of Assimilation* (Tokyo: Voyager's, 1969).

[5]Geoffrey Parrinder, *A Dictionary of Non-Christian Religions* (Philadelphia: Westminster Press, 1971), p. 48.

[6]Tantras, according to Christmas Humphreys's *Popular Dictionary of Buddhism* (London: Arco Publications, 1962), pp. 192-93, are "writings dating from the sixth century A.D. in India . . . whose meaning is handed down from Guru to Chela. Both symbolize the basic duality of manifestation in figures, in sculpture or in pictures, composed of some deity or aspect of Reality with a female partner locked in sexual embrace. . . . [In] the Tantras of Tibet the female represents Wisdom (*Prajna*), and the male the active 'use' or compassionate 'skill in means' of that wisdom."

[7]A mantra, according to Humphreys, is "a magical formula or invocation used in Tantric Bsm. In Tibet and in the Shingon School of Japan. The practice is based on a scientific knowledge of the occult power of sound. The most famous Mantra is Om Mani Padme Hum."

[8]T. O. Ling, *A Dictionary of Buddhism: A Guide to Thought and Tradition* (New York: Charles Scribner & Sons, 1972), pp. 245-52.

[9]The Kalachakra (god of the wheel of time) tantra is a ritual empowerment initiated by a Ti-

betan Buddhist master such as the Dalai Lama who initiates a disciple or group of disciples into the Shambhala kingdom of the Adi-Buddha (universal religious monarch). This is accomplished through a series of secret, active empowerments based on Buddhist myths. See also Marku Tsering, *Sharing Christ in the Tibetan Buddhist World* (Upper Darby, Penn.: Tibet Press, 1988), p. 59.

[10]Ankul Chandra Banerjee, *Aspects of Buddhist Culture from Tibetan Sources* (Calcutta: Firma KLM, 1984).

[11]John Snelling, *Buddhism in Russia: The Story of Agvan Dorzhiev, Lhasa's Emissary to the Tsar* (Rockport, Mass.: Element Books, 1993), pp. xii, 78.

[12]Ibid., p. 193.

[13]Ibid., p. 256.

[14]Hajime Nakamura, *Ways of Thinking of Eastern Peoples* (Honolulu: University of Hawaii Press, 1985), p. 327.

[15]Ibid., p. 318.

[16]Gill Farrer-Halls, *The World of the Dalai Lama: An Inside Look at His Life, His People, and His Vision* (Wheaton, Ill.: Quest Books, 1998).

[17]Ibid., p. 77.

[18]According to Alice Getty, Mahakala, also known as Dharmapala, "the great black one," is "the tutelary god of Mongolia who was not popular until the sixteenth century, when the Dalai-lama was summoned to the court of Altan Khan, and so influenced the king that all non-Buddhist idols were burned, and the six-armed Mahakala was proclaimed Protector of the Mongolian Buddhists."

[19]Jeffrey Hopkins, *Kalachakra Tantra Rite of Initiation for the Stage of Regeneration: A Commentary on the Text of Kay-drup-ge-lek-bel-sang-bo by Tenzin Gyatso, the Fourteenth Dalai Lama, and the Text Itself* (London: Wisdom Publications, 1989), pp. 350-51.

[20]Orville Schell, *Virtual Tibet: Searching for Shangri-La from the Himalayas to Hollywood* (New York: Henry Holt, 2000).

[21]Alex McKay, "Hitler and the Himalayas: The SS Mission to Tibet 1938-1939," *Tricycle: The Buddhist Review* (Spring 2001): 65.

[22]Dusty Sklar, *The Nazis and the Occult* (New York: Dorset, 1977), pp. 23, 54.

[23]Victor and Victoria Trimondi, *The Shadow of the Dalai Lama: Sexuality, Magic and Politics in Tibetan Buddhism* (2000), <www.trimondi.de/SDLE/contents.htm>. English translation prerelease is through the courtesy of the Trimondis. H-M-R Medienagentur.

[24]Dan Wooding, "How God Helped Save The Dalai Lama of Tibet," e-mail, August 10, 1999.

[25]Jonathan Mirsky, "Mission Impossible: An Account of the C.I.A.'s Secret Operations in Tibet" *New York Times,* July 18, 1999.

[26]J. Yutaka Amano and Norman L. Geisler, *The Religion of the Force* (Dallas: Quest Publications, 1983).

[27]Trimondi, *Shadow of the Dalai Lama.*

[28]Farrer-Halls, *World of the Dalai Lama.*

[29]Eric Darton, *Divided We Stand: A Biography of New York's World Trade Center* (New York: Basic Books, 1999).

[30]Ibid.

[31]Excerpt from the author's e-mail correspondence with Dr. David Woodward, March 2001.

[32]My eyewitness account in Chicago at the 1993 Parliament of the World's Religions.

[33]Theresa Watanabe, "Dalai Lama: Humble Man Inspires Awe," *Los Angeles Times,* October 12, 1999.

[34]Gavin D'Costa, "The Near Triumph of Tibetan Buddhist Pluralist-Exclusivism" in *The Meeting of Religions and the Trinity* (Maryknoll, N.Y.: Orbis, 2000), pp. 72-95.

[35]Robert B. Ekvall, *Tents Against the Sky* (Westchester, Ill.: Good News, 1978), pp. 249-50.

[36]Trimondi, *Shadow of the Dalai Lama.*

[37]The Nechung oracle is a human being who is specially designated to receive demonic impartation and verbally instruct the Dalai Lama on key decisions.

[38]Trimondi, *Shadow of the Dalai Lama.*

[39]Monk's Tour website address <http://www.monkstour.org/en/welcome.htm>.

[40]C. G. Jung, *Mandala Symbolism* (Princeton, N.J.: Bollingen Foundation, 1959).

[41]Ibid., p. vi.

[42]Günter Röschert, "The Buddhism of the Dalai Lama—a Trojan Horse for the West?" (October 1999), posted on *The Shadow of the Dalai Lama,* Victor and Victoria Trimondi, <http://www.trimondi.de/en/med01.html>.

[43]Os Guinness, *The Dust of Death: A Critique of the Counterculture* (Downers Grove, Ill.: InterVarsity Press, 1973), p. 209.

[44]James C. Stephens, "Looking at Buddhist America and Keys to World Evangelization," *The International Journal of Frontier Missions* (1993): 111.

[45]"World Peace Vase Programme," Siddhartha's Intent International, <www.siddharthasintent.org/peace/index.html>.

[46]Nyanantiloka, *Buddhist Dictionary: Manual of Buddhist Terms and Doctrines* (Colombo, Ceylon: Frewin & Co., 1972), p. 106.

Chapter Eight: Neopaganism

[1]Ronald Hutton, *The Triumph of the Moon: A History of Modern Pagan Witchcraft* (Oxford: Oxford University Press, 1999), p. 174.

Chapter Nine: The Baha'i World Faith

[1]This brief summary of Baha'i history is derived from several sources: Shoghi Effendi, *God Passes By* (Wilmette, Ill.: Baha'i Publishing Trust, 1970); J. E. Esslemont, *Bahá'u'lláh and the New Era,* 5th ed. (Wilmette, Ill.: Baha'i Publishing Trust, 1980); Lewis M. Hopfe, *Religions of the World,* 5th ed. (Encino, Calif.: Glencoe, 1991), pp. 442-43; Vernon Elvin Johnson, "An Historical Analysis of Critical Transformations in the Evolution of the Baha'i World Faith" (Ph.D. diss., Baylor University, 1974); William McElwee Miller, *The Baha'i Faith: Its History and Teachings* (Pasadena, Calif.: William Carey Library, 1974); John Boykin, "The Baha'i Faith," in *A Guide to Cults and New Religions,* ed. Ronald Enroth (Downers Grove, Ill.: InterVarsity Press, 1983), pp. 26-27.

[2]*Seyyed Ali Mohammed dit le Bâb, Le Beyan Persan,* traduit du Persan par A.-L.-M. Nicolas, 4 vols. (Paris: Librairie Paul Geuthner, 1911-1914), VIII, 10, as cited in Johnson, "Historical Analysis," p. 160.

[3]Esselmont, *Bahá'u'lláh and the New Era*, p. 21.

[4]*Seyyed Ali Mohammed did le Báb*, IV, 10, as cited in Johnson, "Historical Analysis," p. 158.

[5]Ibid., VI, p. 6. In his analysis of my book, *Baha'i: A Christian Response to Baha'ism* (Minneapolis: Bethany, 1985), Peter Terry misrepresents my depiction of this Bábí prohibition: "[Beckwith] indicates that the Báb called for all books to be destroyed, with the exception of the Qur'an. Actually, He called for all books but those associated directly with divine Revelation, including the Qur'an and His own Writings to be destroyed" (Peter Terry, "Truth Triumphs: A Baha'i Response to Misrepresentations of the Baha'i Teachings and Baha'i History" [December 1999], available at <bahai-library.org/unpubl.articles/truth.triumphs.html>). Actually, all I claimed in my book, as I do in this essay, is that the Báb called for the destruction of all Muslim books except the Qur'an (see Beckwith, *Baha'i*, p. 6), which of course is true. This is not to say that Terry does not raise legitimate criticisms of my book. He does.

[6]*Seyyed Ali Mohammed did le Báb*, VII, 16; IX, 2, as cited in Johnson, "Historical Analysis," p. 159.

[7]Shoghi Effendi, for example, writes: "The severe laws and injunctions revealed by the Báb can be properly appreciated and understood only when interpreted in the light of His own statements regarding the nature, purpose and character of His own Dispensation. As these statements clearly reveal, the Bábí Dispensation was essentially in the nature of a religious and indeed social revolution, and its duration had therefore to be short, but full of tragic events, of sweeping and drastic reforms. These drastic measures enforced by the Báb and His followers were taken with the view of undermining the very foundations of Shiite orthodoxy, and thus paving the way for the coming of Bahá'u'lláh. To assert the independence of the new Dispensation, and to prepare also the ground for the approaching Revelation of Bahá'u'lláh the Báb had therefore to reveal very severe laws, even though most of them, were never enforced. But the mere fact that He revealed them was in itself a proof of the independent character of His Dispensation and was sufficient to create such widespread agitation, and excite such opposition on the part of the clergy that led them to cause His eventual martyrdom" (Letter of Shoghi Effendi to the NSA of India, February 17, 1939, reprinted in *Shoghi Effendi, Dawn of a New Day* [Dehli: Baha'i Publishing Trust, 1970], pp. 77-78, as quoted in Terry, "Truth Triumphs").

[8]Edward G. Browne, "Báb, Bábís," in *Encyclopedia of Religion and Ethics* (1928 ed.), p. 301, as quoted in Boykin, "The Baha'i Faith," p. 27. See also Johnson, "Historical Analysis," pp. 173-234; Miller, *The Baha'i Faith*, pp. 70-137.

[9]Brown, "Báb, Bábís," p. 302, as quoted in Boykin, "The Baha'i Faith," p. 27. Baha'i scholars have a different take on this conflict. For example, Esslemont writes, "Bahá'u'lláh's half brother, Mirza Yahya, also known as Subh-I-Azal, arrived in Baghdad, and soon afterwards differences, secretly instigated by him, began to grow, just as similar divisions had arisen among the disciples of Christ. These differences (which later, in Andrianople, became open and violent) were very painful for Bahá'u'lláh, whose whole aim in life was the promotion of unity among the people of the world" (Esslemont, *Bahá'u'lláh and the New Era*, p. 27).

[10]According to Esslemont, "Before the death of Bahá'u'lláh He repeatedly put in writing a Covenant appointing his eldest son Abdul-Baha, Who He often refers to as 'The Branch,' or 'The Most Great Branch,' as the authorized interpreter of the teachings, and declaring that any ex-

planations or interpretations given by Him are to be accepted as of equal validity with the words of Bahá'u'lláh Himself" (Esslemont, *Bahá'u'lláh and the New Era*, pp. 128-29).

[11]See Johnson, "Historical Analysis," pp. 362-80.

[12]This brief summary of Baha'i doctrine is derived from several sources: Effendi, *God Passes By*; Esslemont, *Bahá'u'lláh and the New Era*; Hopfe, *Religions of the World*, pp. 444-47; Johnson, "Historical Analysis"; Miller, *The Baha'i Faith*; Abdul-Baha, *Some Answered Questions*, trans. Laura Clifford Barney (Wilmette, Ill.: Baha'i Publishing Trust, 1930); William S. Hatcher and J. Douglas Martin, *The Baha'i Faith: The Emerging Global Religion* (New York: Harper & Row, 1984); Abdul-Baha and Bahá'u'lláh, *Baha'i World Faith* (Wilmette, Ill.: Baha'i Publishing Trust, 1956); George Townsend, *The Heart of the Gospel or the Bible and the Baha'i Faith* (Oxford: George Roland, 1951); Boykin, "The Baha'i Faith," pp. 28-32.

[13]Esslemont, *Bahá'u'lláh and the New Era*, p. 222. Esslemont draws this conclusion after reproducing a lengthy quote from the Kitab-i-Iqan. For a biblical defense of the Christian doctrine of resurrection, see Norman L. Geisler, *Battle for the Resurrection* (Nashville: Thomas Nelson, 1989). See also Robert Gundry, *Soma in Biblical Theology with an Emphasis on Pauline Anthropology* (Cambridge: Cambridge University Press, 1976); Ronald J. Sider, "The Pauline Conception of the Resurrection Body in I Corinthians XV. 35-54," *New Testament Studies* 21 (1975).

[14]Abdul-Baha, *Some Answered Questions*, pp. 168-69.

[15]Ibid., p. 169.

[16]Esslemont, *Bahá'u'lláh and the New Era*, pp. 202-3.

[17]From a letter dated September 15, 1983, to a Baha'i adherent, available at <bahai-library.org/uhj/krishna.qayyum.html>.

[18]<bahai.org/article-1-4-0-1.html>.

[19]Abdul-Baha, *Some Answered Questions*, p. 189.

[20]Abdul-Baha, *The Promulgation of Universal Peace* (Wilmette, Ill.: Baha'i Publishing Trust, 1982), p. 346. My inclusion of Confucius in my book *Baha'i* has been challenged by Terry: "Dr. Beckwith then lists Confucius among the Manifestations of God recognized by Baha'i. This is also erroneous, given the statement by Shoghi Effendi: 'Confucius was not a Prophet. It is quite correct to say that he is the founder of a moral system and a great reformer.' (From a letter dated 26 December 1941, written on behalf of Shoghi Effendi to the National Spiritual Assembly of Australia and New Zealand; LG:1988:#1684.) Undoubtedly Dr. Beckwith has encountered references to Confucius as a Prophet in Baha'i literature, but perhaps he is not aware of the fact that statements by individual Baha'i do not constitute Baha'i doctrine, that this is confined to the statements of the Founder, the Interpreter and the Guardian of the Faith" ("Truth Triumphs"). But as we have seen, Abdul-Baha *is* an authoritative interpreter, appointed by Bahá'u'lláh (see Esslemont, *Bahá'u'lláh and the New Era*, p. 55). Terry writes: "The doctrinal statements of individual Baha'is are not representative of the authenticated Baha'i doctrines—these can be found in the Baha'i canon, that is, the Writings of Bahá'u'lláh, and the infallibly-guided interpretation of those Writings by Abdul-Baha and Shoghi Effendi" ("Truth Triumphs"). But this means that Shoghi Effendi and Abdul-Baha—two infallible authorities—disagree on whether Confucius is a manifestation. This is no small matter for Baha'ism.

[21]*Seyyed Ali Mohammed dit le Báb*, III, 3, as cited in Johnson, "Historical Analysis," p. 154.

[22]According to Johnson, "Hud is an ancient Arabian prophet after whom the eleventh surah of the Qur'an is named. According to the Qur'an, he was sent to his people of the tribe of A'ad" (Johnson, "Historical Analysis," citing Qur'an VII, 65; XI 50; XXVI, 124; XCVI, 21).

[23]According to Johnson, "Salih, is another Arabian prophet sent to the tribe of Thamud" (ibid., citing Qur'an VII, 75; XI, 61; XXVI, 142; XCVI, 45).

[24]Bahá'u'lláh, The Kitab-i-Iqan: The Book of Certitude, 2nd ed., trans. Shoghi Effendi (Wilmette, Ill.: Baha'i Publishing Trust, 1950), pp. 7-65.

[25]One Universal Faith (Wilmette, Ill.: Baha'i Publishing Trust, n.d.), p. 5.

[26]Hugh E. Chance, Collier's Encyclopedia, 1965 ed., s.v. "Baha'i Faith."

[27]Terry, "Truth Triumphs."

[28]Esslemont, Bahá'u'lláh and the New Era, p. 204.

[29]<www.bahai.org/article-1-4-0-2.html>.

[30]Esslemont, Bahá'u'lláh and the New Era, pp. 188-95.

[31]Ibid., p. 121.

[32]Ibid.

[33]Shoghi Effendi, Call to the Nations (Chatman, U.K.: W & J Mackay, 1977), p. xi.

[34]Quoted in Irving M. Copi, Introduction to Logic, as quoted in James B. Freeman, Thinking Logically: Basic Concepts for Reasoning (Englewood Cliffs, N.J.: Prentice-Hall, 1988), p. 106.

[35]Terry, for example, writes: "Abdul-Baha and Shoghi Effendi have indicated that the original teachings and writings of the Buddha are lost, and that what remains does not accurately represent what Gotama Buddha Himself taught" ("Truth Triumphs").

[36]Terry, for example, quotes Abdul-Baha: "Buddha also established a new religion. . . . The beliefs and rites of the Buddhists and Confucianists have not continued in accordance with their fundamental teachings. The founder of Buddhism was a wonderful soul. He established the Oneness of God, but later the original principles of his doctrines gradually disappeared, and ignorant customs and ceremonials arose and increased, until they finally ended in the worship of statues and images. . . . The meaning is that the Buddhists and Confucianists now worship images and statues. They are entirely heedless of the Oneness of God, and believe in imaginary gods like the ancient Greeks. But in the beginning it was not so; there were different principles and other ordinances" (Abdul-Baha, Some Answered Questions, pp. 189-90, as quoted in Terry, "Truth Triumphs").

[37]I am not conceding the point that there is no evidence that these religious leaders were not monotheists. I believe there is such evidence, and it is convincing. But because such an analysis is outside the scope of this chapter, my point here is to show that the evidence—whether or not it exists—makes no difference to Terry and other Baha'is who reason in similar ways. For an interesting philosophical discussion of the issue of truth and religious differences, see Mortimer Adler, Truth in Religion: The Plurality of Religions and the Unity of Truth (New York: MacMillan, 1990).

[38]Terry, "Truth Triumphs." It is interesting to note that these "reinterpretations" are rarely if ever argued for. That is, the interpreter—whether it is Bahá'u'lláh, Abdul-Baha or Shoghi Effendi—simply asserts what the passage is supposed to mean without any real scholarly defense of his hermeneutic. Despite its noble call for the "unfettered search for truth," the formative leaders of the Baha'i Faith virtually never got their hands dirty arguing for their

position. They simply offered new interpretations of the scriptures of other religions, especially Christianity and Judaism, without serious argument. Ironically, that smacks at the sort of dogmatism that the "unfettered search for truth" was supposed to remedy.

[39]Shoghi Effendi, *Call to the Nations*, p. xi.

[40]J. P. Moreland, *Scaling the Secular City* (Grand Rapids, Mich.: Baker, 1987), p. 92.

Chapter Ten: The Nation of Islam

[1]Elijah Muhammad, *Message to the Blackman in America* (Newport News, Va.: United Brothers Communications Systems, 1992), p. 202.

[2]Ibid., p. 232.

[3]Ibid., p. 171. If he means here the scientist Mr. Yakub, evil creator of the white race, he means he is the first in about six thousand years, which would rule out Jesus and orthodox Islam's prophet Muhammad.

[4]Ibid., p. 234. Technically the "savior" is W. D. Fard.

[5]Ibid., p. 235.

[6]Ibid., p. 244. W. D. Fard left in the early thirties, and Elijah Muhammad's quote is from 1965.

[7]Ibid., p. 247.

[8]Ibid., p. 306.

[9]Ibid., pp. 251, 264, 295.

[10]Ibid., pp. 252-64.

[11]Ibid., pp. 306-7.

[12]Ibid., p. 254; see also p. 257 on his brother, who rejected his mission in 1935. Elijah promises judgment on apostates, including family members, in *Muhammad Speaks* (April 24, 1964) in Atiyah Majied, *The Teachings of Both the Holy Qur'an and Bible* (Hampton, Va.: U.B. & U.S. Communications Systems, 1994), pp. 320-29.

[13]See C. Eric Lincoln, *The Black Muslims in America*, 3rd ed. (Grand Rapids, Mich.: Eerdmans, 1994), pp. 180-81.

[14]Muhammad, *Message*, pp. 307-8.

[15]*Muhammad Speaks* (September 11, 1964), in Majied, *Teachings*, p. 334.

[16]Ibid., p. 335.

[17]Muhammad, *Message*, p. 100, perhaps dating from the earlier period in his thought.

[18]Ibid., p. 250.

[19]Ibid., pp. 187-88.

[20]Ibid., p. 251. Elijah Muhammad felt that the new Muhammad must come to black Americans because they alone had not yet received a prophet (p. 249)—but if this were true, how could Islam have been the original religion of blacks?

[21]Ibid., p. 295.

[22]Ibid., p. 329.

[23]Ibid., pp. 6-10, 19.

[24]Ibid., p. 17.

[25]Ibid., pp. 16-17, 42, 156, 172, 179, 233, 242, 246, 259, 267, 281, 294, 325, 340; for worship to Fard, see pp. 147, 156. Muhammad is also a divine name (p. 47).

[26]Ibid., p. 164.

[27]Ibid., p. 142. Mixing in some language from Christian tradition, he adds that Fard is "our Lord and Saviour" (p. 142); Fard accepted names like "Son of Man, Jesus Christ, Messiah, God, Lord, Jehovah," and especially "Mahdi" (p. 294).

[28]Ibid., pp. 146-47.

[29]Ibid., p. 187.

[30]Ibid., p. 9. "The black man is the first and last, maker and owner of the universe" (p. 53; see also p. 244); the plural of Genesis 1:26 refers to the black race who created whites (pp. 53-54).

[31]Malcolm X with Alex Haley, *The Autobiography of Malcolm X* (New York: Grove, 1965), pp. 207-8.

[32]Lincoln, *Black Muslims,* p. 69.

[33]Muhammad, *Message,* pp. 54, 91. Elijah Muhammad claims that no father would kill his son to atone for others' sins; but Jesus' first followers claimed this act as the amazing measure of God's love toward us (Jn 3:16-17; 17:23; Rom 5:6-10).

[34]Ibid., p. 137.

[35]Ibid., pp. 19, 249, 264, 289. Hell refers to mental death (p. 269), heaven to the Islamic brotherhood in the present life on earth (pp. 70, 304).

[36]Ibid., p. 97; cf. also p. 82.

[37]Ibid., p. 163.

[38]Ibid., p. 189.

[39]Ibid., p. 168; cf. also p. 32.

[40]Ibid., p. 304.

[41]Ibid., p. 168.

[42]Ibid., p. 90.

[43]Ibid., pp. 23-24.

[44]Malcolm X, *Autobiography,* p. 169. Elijah Muhammad complains about this public repudiation in *Muhammad Speaks* (September 11, 1964), in Majied, *Teachings,* p. 335.

[45]Muhammad, *Message,* p. 328. Elsewhere he claims that the Qur'an itself declares whites to be the enemies of God's people.

[46]Ibid., p. 313.

[47]Ibid., pp. 320-21.

[48]Ibid., pp. 228, 270.

[49]Ibid., p. 323. The allusion to Matthew 25:41 certainly ignores the context: there the righteous are those who receive Christ's servants (25:42-45; see also Mt 10:40-42). Most scholars in history and today regard the "sheep" here as disciples. The popular view that this text refers to treatment of the poor or those in need would fit Jesus' other teachings but not the context, and even in this case it would refer to all the poor, not simply those of one race.

[50]Ibid., pp. 90, 128. In the latter instance he cites Revelation 16:6, but the "saints" this verse cites are those who follow Jesus (14:12; 17:6), as are its "prophets" (19:10). This passage also refers to martyrs, Jesus' followers (12:11, 17; 17:6; 19:2, 10; 20:4).

[51]Ibid., p. 231.

[52]Ibid., pp. 110-19, 244; Malcolm X, *Autobiography,* pp. 165-68. This was apparently a case of evil genius; even in his childhood Yakub was noted for his unusually large head (Muhammad, *Message,* p. 112).

[53]Muhammad, *Message*, pp. 36, 56, 162, 203-4.

[54]Cornel West, *Race Matters* (Boston: Beacon, 1993), pp. 99-100. Despite the disagreements, see the many agreements between the Ku Klux Klan and Nation of Islam doctrine in Muhammad, *Message*, pp. 330-41, especially on Christianity being a white religion (pp. 330-32).

[55]Muhammad, *Message*, p. 96.

[56]Ibid., p. 231.

[57]Ibid., pp. 217-18, 236, 318.

[58]HEM, p. 183, in Majied, *Teachings*, p. 209.

[59]Muhammad, *Message*, p. 20.

[60]Ibid., p. 94.

[61]Mustafa El-Amin, *The Religion of Islam and the Nation of Islam: What Is the Difference?* (Newark, N.J.: El-Amin Publication, 1991). See also Adib Rashad, *The History of Islam and Black Nationalism in the Americas*, 2nd ed. (Beltsville, Md.: Writers', 1991). Historic Islam itself is very diverse; see, for example, Dale Eickelman, *The Middle East: An Anthropological Approach*, 2nd ed. (Englewood Cliffs, N.J.: Prentice-Hall, 1989), pp. 256-73.

[62]See Malcolm X, *Autobiography*, pp. 308-9. Suspicious circumstances seem to imply that some white officials who could have stopped the assassination failed to intervene (see Lincoln, *Black Muslims*, pp. 26-31). One would not have expected much protection from the FBI, given their files and general lack of protection for black Americans during the civil rights movement.

[63]Lincoln, *Black Muslims*, pp. 263-71. The "million-man" agenda began not with Farrakhan but with his mentor, Elijah Muhammad: "If one million of you will get behind me, I'll lead you to freedom, justice and equality overnight" (*Mr. Muhammad Speaks* 1, no. 1 [May 1960], front cover [reproduced in Majied, *Teachings*, p. 309]).

[64]Muhammad, *Message*, pp. 80, 126, 132, 286-87.

[65]HEM, p. 204, in Majied, *Teachings*, p. 219. According to Elijah, the pope worships idols (pp. 286-87).

[66]Muhammad, *Message*, pp. 18, 21, 47.

[67]Ibid., p. 282. According to Elijah Muhammad, the "scribes and Pharisees" Jesus denounced were not ancient Jewish leaders but black American preachers (p. 213).

[68]HEM, p. 162, in Majied, *Teachings*, p. 204.

[69]Muhammad, *Message*, p. 111.

[70]HEM, pp. 152-53, in Majied, *Teachings*, p. 208.

[71]Muhammad, *Message*, pp. 188-90. Elijah Muhammad's assumed name may also be significant for his followers; the messenger who would prepare God's way (Mal 3:1) would be called Muhammad (Qur'an 48.29) and Elijah (Mal 4:5).

[72]Ibid., pp. 10-11, 16-17, 20. Because Jesus did not know the hour of the second coming (Mt 24:36), Elijah concludes that Jesus could not have been referring to himself (pp. 10-11); but historic Christianity affirms that Jesus laid aside absolute omniscience in becoming fully human (see Phil 2:6-11).

[73]Ibid., pp. 12-13; Majied, *Teachings*, p. 31.

[74]Muhammad, *Message*, p. 76.

[75]Ibid., p. 151; see also HEM, pp. 152-53, in Majied, *Teachings*, p. 200.

[76]Muhammad, *Message*, p. 26.

[77]Ibid., p. 32.

[78]Ibid., p. 168; see also HEM, pp. 194-95, in Majied, *Teachings*, p. 214.

[79]Muhammad, *Message*, p. 140. By contrast, some other Afrocentric writers appreciate ecstatic worship in the Spirit, including traditional expressions in black Pentecostalism, as positive links with traditional African religion (see Molefi Kete Asante, *Afrocentricity*, rev. ed. [Trenton, N.J.: Africa World Press, 1988], pp. 74-75, Robert E. Hood, *Must God Remain Greek? Afro Cultures and God-Talk* [Minneapolis: Fortress, 1990], pp. 205-7).

[80]Muhammad, *Message*, p. 89.

[81]Ibid., pp. 94, 98.

[82]Ibid., pp. 82, 97-99.

[83]Ibid., p. 82.

[84]Ibid., p. 163.

[85]Ibid., pp. 158-59. For more accurate studies on these passages, see the concise summaries from the standpoint of ancient culture in Craig Keener, *The IVP Bible Background Commentary: New Testament* (Downers Grove, Ill.: InterVarsity Press, 1993).

[86]Muhammad, *Message*, p. 108.

[87]Ibid., p. 250.

[88]Ibid., pp. 251-52.

[89]Ibid., p. 267; HEM, p. 204, in Majied, *Teachings*, p. 219; also *Muhammad Speaks* (January 15, 1965), in Majied, *Teachings*, p. 340.

[90]Muhammad, *Message*, pp. 154-55.

[91]Ibid., p. 267.

[92]Ibid., p. 269.

[93]The temple was not destroyed seventy years after Jesus' death (Muhammad, *Message*, p. 286) but about forty years after, in 70 C.E.; Moses did not live around 2000 B.C.E. (Muhammad, *Message*, p. 28), important as this appears to Elijah's schema for history, but somewhere between 1220 and 1600 B.C.E., most likely between 1300 and 1220. Elijah's claim that the tribe of Shabazz came to earth sixty-six trillion years ago (Muhammad, *Message*, pp. 31, 110) is impossible in light of modern knowledge of physics, in which the universe is at most roughly twenty billion years old and life could not yet exist during most of that period.

[94]Muhammad, *Message*, pp. 18, 290-93. At times he cites unchecked or inaccessible authorities—for example, that the world of evil expired in 1914, "as all the religious scientists agree" (p. 142).

[95]Ibid., pp. 270, 272, 276, 280.

[96]Ibid., p. 31.

[97]James D. Tabor and Eugene V. Gallagher, *Why Waco? Cults and the Battle for Religious Freedom in America* (Berkeley: University of California Press, 1995), pp. 55-56.

[98]Muhammad, *Message*, pp. 37, 56.

[99]Ibid., pp. 64-65. A friend of mine who completed his Ph.D. in a lab connected with a southern hospital has studied the records of needless hysterectomies performed deliberately on black women in the fifties. It has also been argued that Margaret Sanger, founder of Planned Parenthood, sought to promote her birth-control program especially in the black community, sometimes even using black clergy (see George Grant, *Immaculate Deception* [Chicago: North-

field, 1996] and Robert G. Marshall and Charles A. Donovan, *Blessed Are the Barren* [San Francisco: Ignatius, 1991], pp. 1-54).

[100]Muhammad, *Message,* p. 161. To his credit, Elijah Muhammad insisted on justice for all, Muslim or not (p. 163).

[101]Ibid., p. 165.

[102]See, e.g., Glenn Usry and Craig S. Keener, *Black Man's Religion* (Downers Grove, Ill.: Inter-Varsity Press, 1996), pp. 99-117.

[103]*Muhammad Speaks* (September 11, 1964), in Majied, *Teachings,* pp. 336, 338.

[104]Muhammad, *Message,* pp. 246-47.

[105]For example, Maria Stewart in 1833 in Dorothy Sterling, *We Are Your Sisters: Black Women in the Nineteenth Century* (New York: W. W. Norton, 1984), p. 157; on nineteenth-century black women's clubs and urban renewal, see Cheryl J. Sanders, *Empowerment Ethics for a Liberated People* (Minneapolis: Fortress, 1995), chap. 3, and Marcia Y. Riggs, *Awake, Arise and Act* (Cleveland, Ohio: Pilgrim, 1994).

[106]Muhammad, *Message,* pp. 277, 285.

[107]Ibid., pp. 274-75. For a Christian perspective, see West, *Race Matters,* p. 17.

[108]Ibid., p. 71.

[109]Ibid., pp. 17, 46-49. Although his interpretation of the biblical texts consistently misrepresents their original sense, one can understand his comparison of the United States with Babylon (pp. 273, 277). For overstatement, one may sample his claim that the United States (and only the United States) will soon become the lake of fire (HEM, p. 162, in Majied, *Teachings,* p. 204).

[110]First in David Wilkerson, *The Vision* (Old Tappan, N.J.: Fleming H. Revell, 1974). One need not agree with every detail to concur with the emphasis on coming judgment.

[111]Richard Abanes, *Cults, New Religious Movements and Your Family* (Wheaton, Ill.: Crossway, 1998), p. 132.

List of Contributors

Francis J. Beckwith (Ph.D., Fordham) is Associate Professor of Church-State Studies and Associate Director of the J. M. Dawson Institute of Church-State Studies at Baylor University, where he is also a Research Fellow in the Center for Religious Inquiry Across the Disciplines (CRIAD). A graduate of Fordham University (Ph.D., philosophy) and the Washington University School of Law, St. Louis (M.J.S.), his books include *To Everyone an Answer: A Case for the Christian Worldview; Law, Darwinism, and Public Education: The Establishment Clause and the Challenge of Intelligent Design;* and *The New Mormon Challenge.*

James Beverley (Ph.D., University of St. Michael's College) is a professor at Tyndale Seminary in Toronto and Associate Director of the Institute for the Study of American Religion (Santa Barbara). He has written ten ten books, including *Nelson's Illustrated Guide to Religions; Understanding Islam;* and *Holy Laughter & the Toronto Blessing.* He did his Ph.D. thesis on the inner teaching of the Unification Church.

Robert M. Bowman Jr. (M.A., Fuller Theological Seminary) is the founder and director of the Center for Biblical Apologetics. He also teaches in the Christian Apologetics program at Biola University. Formerly he served as a writer and editor for the Christian Research Institute and Watchman Fellowship. His books include *Why You Should Believe in* *the Trinity; Orthodoxy and Heresy; Jehovah's Witnesses; The Word-Faith Controversy;* and two Gold Medallion books coauthored with Kenneth D. Boa, *An Unchanging Faith in a Changing World* and *Faith Has Its Reasons.*

Ronald Enroth (Ph.D., University of Kentucky) is professor of sociology at Westmont College in Santa Barbara, California. A specialist in the sociology of religion and new religious movements, he is the author of many books, including *Churches That Abuse.*

Craig S. Keener (Ph.D., Duke University) is professor of New Testament at Eastern Seminary (Wynnewood, Pennsylvania) and an ordained minister in the National Baptist Convention. He is the author or coauthor of twelve books, including *Paul, Women & Wives; Black Man's Religion; Defending Black Faith;* and *The IVP Bible Background Commentary: New Testament.* Three of his books have won awards in *Christianity Today.*

Vishal Mangalwadi (LL.D., William Carey International University) studied philosophy at the University of Indore in Central India before spending a year studying prominent Hindu gurus in their Ashrams. Out of this came his 1977 book, *The World of the Gurus.* Since then Vishal has served the poor and untouchables in India, lectured in twenty-nine countries, and written thirteen books including *Truth and Social Reform; India—The Grand Experiment;* and *When the New Age Gets Old: Looking for a Greater Spirituality.* Currently he is revising a manuscript on the Bible as the book that created the modern world. Vishal serves as the CEO of Book of the Millennium International.

LaVonne Neff (M.A., Andrews University; M.A. [pastoral studies], Loyola University) is a writer and editor who has been an editorial director at Lion Publishing, Tyndale House and Loyola Press. Her published books include *The Gift of Faith* and *Colossians/Philemon: New Life in Christ.*

John Peck is a British philosopher, theologian and Baptist minister, and has held the post of senior lecturer at the Glasgow Bible Institute. He is cofounder of College House in Cambridge and has been its principal lecturer for twenty years. He is also cofounder and past executive of the Greenbelt Arts Festival. With Charles Strohmer he coauthored the book *Uncommon Sense: God's Wisdom for Our Complex and Changing World.*

Ron Rhodes (Th.D., Dallas Theological Seminary) is president of Reasoning from the Scriptures Ministries. He is also an adjunct professor at Dallas Theological Seminary and Southern Evangelical Seminary (Charlotte, North Carolina). His books include *The Challenge of Cults and New Religions; Reasoning from the Scriptures with Jehovah's Witnesses; The Complete Book of Bible Answers; Christ Before the Manger; Why Do Bad Things Happen If God Is God?; The Ten Things You Should Know About the Creation-Evolution Debate;* and the *Find It Quick Handy Bible Encyclopedia.*

Charles Strohmer is the author of seven books and dozens of articles. He is also the founding publisher of the magazine-journal *Opening,* in which conversations take place about the reach of biblical wisdom into all aspects of life. He speaks in both the U.S. and the U.K., is listed in the fourth edition of *Who's Who in Religion,* has worked with the BBC, and is currently writing two new books. His most recent book is *Uncommon Sense: God's Wisdom for Our Complex and Changing World,* a coauthored work with British philosopher and theologian John Peck.

James C. Stephens was a zealous youth leader in a Japanese Buddhist sect for fourteen years (1970-1984); he helped convert over fifty-four individuals. He is also a graduate of Nichiren Shoshu Study Academy. In 1981, after an accident in the midst of a spiritual pilgrimage in Asia, James began to have serious doubts about his Buddhist faith. In 1984, after a painful three-year quest for answers that led him through yoga, EST, actualizations, astrology and various New Age experiences, he and his Jewish-Buddhist wife, Elizabeth, turned to Jesus because of witnessing the exemplary lives of several Christian professionals and by reading *Beyond Buddhism* by J. Isamu Yamamoto, *More Than a Carpenter* by Josh McDowell and the Bible. In 1988, they founded Sonrise Center for Buddhist Studies as a learning organization dedicated to providing resources, accurate information and training for Christians working crossculturally in Buddhist and Asian pluralistic contexts. For further information, you may visit their website at <www.sonrisecenter.org>.

Glenn Usry is senior pastor at Christian Outreach Church in Statesville, North Carolina. He is the coauthor of *Defending Black Faith* and *Black Man's Religion*.